1885
Chemnitzer Velociped-Depot
Winklhofer & Jaenicke

1896
Wanderer Fahrradwerke AG
vorm. Winklhofer & Jaenicke,
Schönau/Chemnitz

1908
Wanderer Werke AG
vorm. Winklhofer & Jaenicke,
Schönau/Chemnitz

Takeover of
Wanderer's car
division by
Auto Union AG

Wanderer Werke AG remained in
business, with the emphasis on bicycle,
light motorcycle, tool, typewriter and
calculating machine production

1873
Mechanische Werkstätte zur
Herstellung von Strickma-
schinen Christian Schmidt,
Riedlingen

1884
Neckarsulmer Strick-
maschinenfabrik AG

1897
Neckarsulmer
Fahrradwerke AG

1913
Neckarsulmer
Fahrzeugwerke AG

1926
NSU Vereinigte Fahrzeug-
werke AG, Neckarsulm

1932
NSU D-Rad vereinigte
Fahrzeugwerke AG,
Neckarsulm

1938
NSU Werke AG,
Neckarsulm

Four Rings
The Audi Story

Edition Audi Tradition

Contents

The early years

01

01 August Horch (1868 – 1951), pioneering automobile engineer and founder of the Horch and Audi brands
02 Horch two-cylinder car (at rear), seen at the first German professional drivers' training school in Aschaffenburg

Horch – where the legend began

As the nineteenth century drew to a close, signs of technical progress emerged in a continuous flow from laboratories and academics' studies, from workshops and universities, and began to influence daily life. Methods of work in factories changed, domestic life at home too – and progress also meant greater mobility on the roads, by rail or by water. All of society was caught up in these changes, of which the development of the motor vehicle was one.

From the very outset, the motor car had something special to offer its users: a means of multiplying their effective mobility. What could have been more in accord with the pioneering spirit that was to be sensed everywhere? The railway had given people a foretaste of what mobility could mean, and the bicycle too had started out on its all-conquering journey before the end of the 19th century. The freedom that mobility offered developed into a personal desire, and every year tens of thousands of people joined those who were prepared to spend their money to satisfy it. Early traffic surveys tell us that by 1899 there were more bicycles on the roads than any other form of passenger vehicle. If it were only possible to create a reliable form of motorized transport, this

02

03

04

too would add an entirely new dimension to the quality of life. This was the demand which the automobile industry was created to satisfy. Even before the end of the 19th century, more than three dozen companies were building motor cars in Germany. One of them was August Horch & Cie, established on November 14, 1899, with head offices in Cologne. Its founder was one of the pioneering engineers in the motor-vehicle field. Even as an apprentice and journeyman, Horch had demonstrated his practical skill and ingenuity when there were complex problems to be solved.

In the mid-1890s, as a graduate in engine construction, he began to take an increasing interest in the motor vehicle, and was offered a job in 1896 by Karl Benz in Mannheim, where he was soon promoted to manager of the motor vehicle construction department. He held this key position at the epicenter of the still-young automobile industry for three years, and in that time acquired an excellent picture of the motor vehicle's growing pains and development problems. With this knowledge and experience at his disposal, Horch set up his own business in 1899, initially repairing motor vehicles that were already in use and replacing Bosch trembler ignition systems by a linkage he had himself developed and patented.

Horch was soon hard at work on the design of his first automobile, which was ready to test-drive by the beginning of January 1901. Its engine was at the front, a concept for which Horch had fought in vain while working for Benz. To eliminate the drawbacks of the hammer-blow caused by a cylinder arranged horizontally along the vehicle's direction of travel, but also of the still-unsatisfactory horizontally opposed engine, Horch's new design had two cylinders with a shared combustion chamber. He referred to it as an "impact-free" engine. Remarkably for that time, the crankcase was a light-alloy casting.

03 The first Horch car with "impact-free" engine, 1901
04 Chassis of the first Horch car, showing the belt drive, the horizontal front-mounted engine and the evaporative cooling system, 1901

01 The Horch two-cylinder model with tonneau body and sunroof

02 The factory building in Reichenbach (Vogtland), where Horch cars, mostly with two-cylinder engines, were built from 1902 to 1904

03 Car manufacture in Zwickau began in 1904 with Horch four-cylinder models

04 The Horch transmission

04

02

03

Der Siegeslauf der
HORCHWAGEN
1913

Schwedisches Eisrennen am 15. Februar 1913	Oesterreichische Alpenfahrt vom 22. bis 29. Juni 1913 – 2650 km
2 Erste Preise	1 Erster Preis 2 Ehrenpreise 2 Silberne Plaketten
Schwedische Winter-Zuverlässigkeitsfahrt vom 23. bis 26. Februar 1913 – 1200 km	Jubiläumsumfahrt des A. D. A. C. vom 17. bis 19. Juli 1913
Als bester deutscher Wagen den Wander-Pokal, ferner 5 Ehrenpreise 5 Goldene Plaketten 1 Bronzene Plakette Silberne Medaille	Erster Preis und Damenpreis
	Sternfahrt des Hamburger Automobil-Klub am 1. September 1913
Schwedische Sommer-Zuverlässigkeitsfahrt vom 20. bis 27. Juni 1913 – 2050 km	Erster Preis
Erster Preis und zweiter Preis Großer Ehrenpreis Kleiner Ehrenpreis Großer Continental-preis 1 Goldene Plakette 1 Silberne Plakette	Konkurrenzfahrt des Gaues VIIa des A. D. A. C. Hamburg am 21. September 1913 Wander-Preis zum zweiten Male Erster Preis Ossag-Pokal
	Jütland-Rennen (Dänemark) am 28. September 1913 2 Erste Preise

Horch allen voran
Siegreich im Norden und Süden

A. Horch & Cie Motorwagenwerke Zwickau Sa.
FILIALEN: BERLIN / DRESDEN / HANNOVER / LEIPZIG / MÜNCHEN

Horch next sold his small company to a businessman with a moderate-sized company in Saxony, and at the beginning of 1902 moved to Reichenbach, complete with all his machines. From that time on, he was able to work systematically on putting his ideas into practice.

August Horch was one of the first engineers in Germany to adopt shaft drive to the vehicle's wheels. Another of his innovative ideas was to adopt chrome nickel steel for highly stressed gearwheels. He was also convinced of the merits of light alloys, and now used them for transmissions and differential housings as well as for crankcases. In 1904 the young engineer moved his business to Zwickau and converted it into a joint-stock company. Its output of automobiles rose relatively quickly, from 18 in 1903 to 94 in 1907, and exceeded the magic figure of 100 units a year later. Whereas only cars with twin-cylinder engines had been built in Reichenbach, the Horch factory in Zwickau produced only four-cylinder vehicles.

August Horch gave his company a clearly defined brand policy from the very outset: in all circumstances, to build only strong, good-quality cars.

He was convinced that his cars should prove their merits and obtain the necessary publicity by means of success in motor sport. The four-cylinder models from Zwickau had 22 horsepower engines initially, later 40 horsepower. To yield these power outputs, displacements of 2.6 and 5.8 liters were necessary! The cars were lavishly equipped, with technical features notable for their great strength.

In 1906, driving one of these 22 hp cars, the Zwickau resident Dr. Stöss was the outright winner of the Herkomer Run, one of the toughest motor sport events of that time.

Despite this successful progress, Horch had adversaries on his company's Board of Management and its Supervisory Board – people who objected to his tendency to run the company like an old-style patriarch. Squabbles and intrigues were rife, and Horch was reproached when his decisions proved to be incorrect. When these disputes reached their peak, Horch withdrew abruptly from his own company on June 16, 1909. Following Horch's departure, Fritz Seidel took over as Chief Designer and Heinrich Paulmann as Technical Director, and were able for a long time

05

06

to utilize the legacy left to them by the company's founder. One of their very first moves was to protect the Horch name, after its owner's sudden departure, by means of no fewer than 13 trademark registrations. By January 10, 1910 the figure had risen to 26, covering every possible combination of the name with potential technical products of some kind: Original Horch Car, Autohorch, Horch Original, Horchuk, Horchol, Horcher! Even the name "A. Horch" was protected as a final precaution, something that the actual bearer of the name had failed to do, thus ruining his chances of operating another company under his own name. Horch's fundamental development principles were

upheld by Seidel and Paulmann: strength and quality. They launched a new 28 hp car, with an engine that was later uprated to 35 and finally 40 horsepower. German automobile engineers still regarded the valve gear of Horch's engines from the early years of the company as unsurpassed, even in 1913. In the 10 hp tax category, there were only six cars with overhead inlet valves at that time: they were above the pistons in the Mercedes, Horch and Windhoff, and over the side-mounted exhaust valves in the Audi, Komnick and Nacke. Design progress was the most important precondition for cost-effective production. In engine construction, this called above all for a change to

05 The oldest surviving Horch is in Sweden, an 18 – 22 hp sedan built in 1905
06 Dr. Stöss, winner of the 1906 Herkomer Run in a Horch 18 – 22 hp

9

01

02, 03

01 A Horch truck from the World
War I period
02 Horch passenger cars were
also used by the Imperial Army
03 Horch roadster with offset
double seats, 1914

a single-piece cylinder block instead of cylinders
cast in pairs. The new designs had side valves.
Smaller cars for newcomers to motoring also
began to take shape. In 1911, for instance, 6/18
and 8/24 hp models were introduced. They possessed a number of modern design features, with
a smooth engine block and very satisfactory road
behavior. An even smaller car was to be launched
in the summer of 1914, to be known as the "Pony"
and to have a 1.3-liter, four-cylinder engine developing 14 horsepower. The Horch company also
had plans to build cars with sleeve-valve engines.
These were considered to be particularly smooth-
running, but were also more complex to manufacture and needed very careful attention to the

design of the sleeve valves. To avoid possible
problems, Horch decided not to undertake engine
development itself but to import Daimler engines
from Great Britain for these cars, with the valve
gear manufactured in accordance with the American engineer Knight's patents. Both these projects – small cars and sleeve-valve engines –
came to nothing, due to the outbreak of World
War I.
In 1914, the Horch product line consisted of four
basic types, with 30, 40, 50 and 60 hp single-
block four-cylinder engines. There were also
older models still in production and more modern
intermediate types obtained by varying the
engines' bore and stroke. Vehicles for commercial

10

04

Company chronicle

1899	August Horch & Cie established on November 14 in Cologne
1902	August Horch & Cie Motor- und Motorwagenbau established in Reichenbach on March 3
1904	August Horch Motorwagenwerke AG established in Zwickau on May 10
1918	Company name changed to Horchwerke AG Zwickau on February 16; capital 3 million marks

The first Horch took to the road in January 1901. By December 31, 1918 about 9,100 Horch vehicles had been produced. Only chassis were supplied: the bodies had to be obtained from coachbuilders. Turnover rose to 5.8 million marks by 1914 and reached 30 million marks in 1918.

In 1904, its first business year, the company employed about 100 people; in 1918 the total was 1,800.

During the company's first ten-year production period, a Horch chassis cost between 9,400 and 16,300 marks, depending on engine size.

purposes were also becoming increasingly important.

The first Horch commercial vehicle was an ambulance dating from about 1910. It is interesting to note that the company also supplied various items of machinery, for example silage choppers, on a passenger-car chassis. The 8/24 chassis was available with a wide variety of delivery van bodies, which were very popular. The 40 and 50 hp engines were suitable for light buses and small trucks; the 55 hp engine was capable of propelling a 3-tonne truck, with a trailer if necessary. Just before war broke out, a 33/80 hp car was introduced: its four-cylinder engine still had the cylinders cast in pairs and boasted an impressive displacement of eight liters.

August Horch on his experiences with cars in the early years

"Below the ring on the steering column were two handles, which were used to transfer the drive belt from the engine to the layshaft. Below the steering tiller, on the left, was a lever to vary the strength of the fuel-air mixture. Another lever was connected to a rod that led to the throttle butterfly. This rod was used to open and close the throttle and thus vary the speed of the engine. Also to the driver's left was the handbrake, which acted on the rear tires. To start the engine, the flywheel had to be turned; in those days even the starting handle was a thing of the future. The flywheel was turned until the mixture ignited; the whole task was not only exciting but strenuous too. If ignition failed to take place, the next step was to hurry round to the front of the vehicle and turn the mixture control lever. But even if one was fortunate and the mixture did ignite, one still had to rush forward to the controls and adjust the throttle lever until the engine began to run regularly. Then, with God's blessing, the journey could begin.

"One climbed on to the driver's seat and selected low gear at the lever under the steering tiller. This moved the belt from the smallest diameter of the stepped pulley slowly on to the fixed layshaft pulley. The vehicle then began to move at its lowest speed of two to three miles an hour. On reaching a speed of five miles an hour, the belt had to be shifted to the second, larger pulley, after which the vehicle could be driven up to its maximum speed of eleven miles an hour."

05, 06

04 All Horch engines had a light-alloy crankcase with the lower section rigidly mounted on the frame

05 Starting in 1910, Horch Motorwagenwerke also built commercial vehicles, initially for the medical services

06 Even before 1914, Horch trucks with a 42 hp four-cylinder engine were very popular

The birth of Audi

01 A press cartoon on the identity of Horch and Audi
02 Within the first four years, the Audi company had expanded rapidly

Scarcely a month after Horch had disassociated himself from the Horchwerke, he established a new automobile company. It was entered in the trade register on July 16, 1909 as a limited liability company (GmbH). It took Horch only 72 hours to amass the necessary capital of 200,000 marks. This action led to an immediate protest by the Horchwerke, which won its case before the Imperial Court. This verdict prohibited Horch from using his name for another automobile company. His next move was recorded in the Zwickau trade register on April 25, 1910: the new company's name was changed to Audi Automobil-Werke m.b.H. The founders had chosen well: the new brand name was a phonetic stroke of genius and, more than any other in the industry, awakened associations with the automobile.

Horch's first aim was to publicize the new name without sacrificing the company's previous identity. Work began in much the same way as Horch's original business venture: with repair and maintenance work. The reputation attached to August Horch's name stood him in good stead: work began to come in even before the trade register entry had gone through.

Right from the start, Horch was determined to give Audi a brand image in accordance with the standards prevailing in the upper section of the market. For him, this was first and foremost a question of the technical concept: he saw power, the quality of materials and long-term reliability as the most important factors affecting car design.

01

August Horch explains the origin of the Audi brand name

1909

02

"We weren't allowed to trade as August Horch, although this was my own name! We wasted no time in holding a meeting in Franz Fikentscher's apartment, and spent some time trying to think up an alternative name. We knew that we couldn't wind up the meeting without having arrived at a different name for the company. I can't begin to

1913

explain how many strange and improbable names we came up with!

"One of Franz's sons sat in a corner of the room and wrestled with his homework – at least he pretended to do so. In actual fact he was listening to our discussion with all the passion that lurks within a young man's breast. More than once he seemed to be on the brink of saying something, but choked back the words and got on with his work. Then suddenly it burst out of him like an active volcano; he turned to his father and exclaimed: 'Father – audiatur et altera pars! Wouldn't it be a good idea to call it Audi instead of Horch?' This gem of an idea had us all speechless with amazement and delight."

13

01 Heini Zeidler opened his
Munich Audi dealership in 1910
02 Preparing cars entered for the
1914 International Austrian
Alpine Run
03 In the 1920s Audi continued
to advertise its pre-war Alpine
Run successes

The first Audi left the Zwickau factory in the early summer of 1910. In those early years, August Horch's name was to be found in every advertisement and was used to maximum effect on every Audi poster as well. Horch also pursued a policy of entering his cars for motor sport events, having realized that the general public responded positively to such successes. One of the first Audi cars won the Swedish Reliability Trial in the early summer. In the following year Horch decided to enter the International Austrian Alpine Run, held in May 1911. This event was effectively the successor to the famous Prince Henry Runs, and imposed increasingly severe requirements on the entrants. In the 1911 Alpine Run, for example, only ten of the 75 starters reached the finishing line without penalty points. August Horch took the wheel of his new Audi personally, and was rewarded with first prize after negotiating 1,398 miles of exceptionally tough mountain passes and Alpine roads successfully.

A year later, in 1912, a complete Audi team was entered for the Alpine Run, which was held in June. Three Audi cars took the team prize, a triumph that they promptly repeated in 1913.

However, it was in the 1914 event that the Audi entries demonstrated their superiority over the competition most effectively. Five cars went to the starting line, driven by Horch, Graumüller, Lange, Obruba and Mühry. All of them completed the course without penalty. The leading German-language motoring periodical of the time, *Motorwagen*, commented on Audi's victory in the following terms:

"Above all, the result is a major triumph for the German Audi brand, which entered five cars and brought them all home across the finishing line without incurring a single penalty. This Audi victory came as no surprise: on previous Alpine Runs, Audi cars have always achieved the best results ..."

The cars with which Audi pulled off this triumphant success bore the unmistakable stamp of the school of design pioneered by August Horch, and to which Hermann Lange contributed greatly in those early years. Lange had joined Horch when the latter left his company and founded Audi. The engines retained a familiar feature: the overhead inlet and side exhaust valve gear.

AUDIWERKE A-G
ZWICKAU IN SACHSEN

Internationale Österreichische Alpenfahrt 1914:
Großer Alpenwanderpreis
gewonnen auf

01

02

03

01 Audi always obtained its car
bodies from outside coachbuilders.
The open tourer or "phaeton"
was the most sought-after body
style

04

05

The exceptionally wide light-alloy crankcase was another such trademark: it provided full protection underneath the car and also performed a load-bearing function. Horch's spur-gear differential was also to be found on the new cars: it enabled the final drive to the rear wheels to be enclosed within a very compact housing.

Following the same practice as the first Horch company, Audi models were identified by capital letters, starting logically in 1910 with A. By the time World War I broke out, the Type E had been reached. All of these models had four-cylinder engines; thanks to the motor sport victories gained by the Type C, it became known as the "Alpine Victor." Its 14/35 hp engine had a crankshaft of entirely new design, offset by 0.55 inches from the engine's centerline and running in red brass main bearings with three-layer white-metal shells. The exhaust valves were inclined, to shorten the gas flow paths and improve the shape of the combustion chambers.

After their first spectacular successes, Horch and Lange had aimed this third model more specifically at motor sport. Experience had shown that if the cars had a significant weakness it was the likelihood of the engine overheating. Furthermore, a sturdy design capable of covering long distances reliably was needed.

The overheating problem was avoided by providing extremely generous cooling water jacketing around the spark plugs, exhaust valves and internal exhaust ports, together with a large-area radiator. The cars were able to climb Alpine passes without their cooling systems needing the assistance of a water pump.

Securing the Alpine Trophy outright after successive wins from 1912 to 1914 was of immense importance for Audi's subsequent development. Above all, it helped to publicize the brand and consolidate its reputation within a remarkably short time. This reputation was based on the desire to be faster and better than all the others

02 The winning 1914 Alpine Run team (left to right): Muhry, Horch, Obruba, Graumüller, Lange
03 August Horch with co-driver Schlegel and Horch's wife Anneliese at the finish line of the 1914 Alpine Run
04 Hermann Lange overtaking in his Audi during the 1912 Alpine Run
05 Audi engines also had a light-alloy crankcase bolted to the chassis frame

01

02

03

01 August Hermann Lange
(1867 – 1922), Audi's first Chief
Designer
02 Erich Horn, Lange's successor
until 1925
03 Audi military ambulance,
1916

in competition, but also to build Audi models in volume that were reliable in severe conditions and entirely suitable for practical use rather than exotic one-off designs.

August Horch's hopes of being able to increase production and sales came to fruition rapidly as a result of his cars' competition successes. If 1911 is taken as the first full year of production, then the company's output of motor vehicles had precisely doubled by 1914 – the same rate of growth as was enjoyed by the rival manufacturer Horch in the same town.

Last but not least, Horch's series of motor sport victories justified his methods in a most convincing way. The design of the Type B and C cars, the Alpine Run champions, was undoubtedly a climax in his creative technical career.

The Audi company was still modest in size. In 1914 the factory in Zwickau employed 290 people, who built 225 Audi cars in that year.

The capital had mainly been contributed by two families of industrialists: Paul and Karl Leonhardt, proprietors of a paper and cardboard factory in Crossen, near Zwickau, and Franz and Paul Fikentscher, owners of Steinzeugwerke Keramische Werke AG, a Zwickau-based factory producing earthenware. Together, these families largely determined company policy: they accepted August Horch's declared intention of selling his products in the premium segment of the market. Not least in view of the constraints imposed by the war-time economy, which were already becoming evident by the fall of 1914, the founders decided to convert Audi into a joint-stock company. With effect from January 1, 1915, Audiwerke AG was established in Zwickau with a capital of one and a half million marks.

The directors were August Horch (Sales), Hermann Lange (Technical) and Werner Wilm (General Administration). This was a clear sign that Horch

04, 05

Company chronicle

1909 August Horch Automobilwerke GmbH established in Zwickau on July 16, after Horch himself had left Horchwerke AG, the company that previously bore his name

1910 After losing a legal dispute, the company changed its name on April 10 to Audi Automobil-Werke m.b.H., with head offices in Zwickau

1915 Reorganization as a joint-stock company, Audiwerke AG, in Zwickau on January 21, with a capital of 1.5 million marks

The first Audi left the factory in the early summer of 1910; by 1914, 753 had been built. Total Audi output up to December 31, 1918 was 2,130 cars. The factory only supplied the chassis: the bodies had to be ordered from selected coachbuilders.

The company employed 33 people in the 1909 business year and 543 in 1918.

The first Audi chassis, built in 1910, was listed at a price of 8,500 marks.

04 Audi Type B, 1912
05 Audi Type C Alpine Victor, 1914
06 Audi Bt truck, 1913

06

had withdrawn from the technical design area. Hermann Lange was now responsible for this, accompanied as he had in fact been since 1910 by the graduate engineer Erich Horn as Chief Designer.

In the five years of the company's existence before World War I, the three-man team of Horch, Lange and Horn had introduced no fewer than five passenger-car and two truck models – a demonstration of remarkable creativity and ambitious design policy.

01 Founders of Wanderer-Werke, Richard Adolf Jaenicke (left) and Johann Baptist Winklhofer, seen in 1885 with a Rudge pennyfarthing bicycle

02 In 1898 Wanderer began to manufacture milling machines

03 From 1904 on, Wanderer also built typewriters under the Continental brand name

01

WANDERER – WERKE

02

CONTINENTAL
Alleinverkauf
FRANZ GLASER SONNEBERG /Thür.
Fernruf No. 72

CONTINENTAL

03

1899 – 1918 The early years – Along came a Wanderer

Along came a Wanderer

On February 15, 1885 the two mechanics Johann B. Winklhofer and Richard A. Jaenicke started a bicycle repair business in the town of Chemnitz. Before long they began to build bicycles of their own, since demand at that time was consistently high, and sell them under the brand name Wanderer. From 1896 onwards the company began to trade as Wanderer Fahrradwerke AG vorm. (formerly) Winklhofer und Jaenicke.

By then, bicycles were not the only Wanderer products. The line was expanded step by step. In 1890, milling machines had already been built for use in bicycle production, and from 1898 onwards these were made by a separate division of the company.

In 1904 a further business sector was opened up: Wanderer began to make typewriters and sell them as the "Continental" brand; in 1909, adding machines were introduced to the office machinery line.

Bicycles nevertheless remained the Wanderer company's main business area, and it was therefore only logical to consider making a motorized model. The first Wanderer motorcycle appeared in 1902, with a 1.5 hp air-cooled single-cylinder engine. The complete motorcycle weighed 99.21 pounds and had a top speed of 31.07 mph – possibly rather hard on the rider, since the bike had no suspension whatsoever! The first twin-cylinder motorcycles were introduced in 1905, with three times the first model's power output and the ability to reach a top speed of 50 mph. A sprung front fork was fitted at the same time, making Wanderer one of the first German manufacturers to provide this undoubted extra safety feature.

Further improved models were built between then and 1914, with such features as rear suspension, a center stand and a second rear-wheel brake. In due course, it was even possible

04 The Chemnitzer Velociped Fabrik Winklhofer & Jaenicke occupied premises in Hartmannstrasse, Chemnitz, from 1887 to 1895

05 Wanderer's first motorcycle was launched in 1902 and had an air-cooled single-cylinder engine developing 1.5 hp

04

05

01

02

01 The 1906 Wanderermobil was the Wanderer company's first car, but remained a prototype. This unique vehicle is now owned by the Transport Museum in Dresden

02 The first Wanderer car to enter production was the 5/12 hp Type W 3 in March 1913. The tandem two-seater layout was a typical feature. The general public soon adopted the nickname "Puppchen" ("Baby Doll") for this car

to order a kick-starter as an optional extra. To branch out into car production was clearly a further logical step. Initial test work had started in 1903, and by September 1906 the first Wanderer car, powered by a 12 hp twin-cylinder engine, had been completed. A two-seater with no especially noteworthy features, its drive train and body were similar to what competitors were already offering at the time.

It remained a one-off vehicle: overall conditions for starting car production were unfavorable at that time, and Wanderer was reluctant to press ahead with a new product if its quality and market prospects had not been thoroughly tested.

In the summer of 1911, Wanderer's engineers demonstrated a second test car to the board of directors. This was a small two-seater with the passenger's seat behind the driver.
After extensive preliminary trials, a final test

run through North and South Tyrol began on August 27, 1912. Eleven days later, after covering more than 1,243 miles, the car arrived back in Chemnitz without incident, having mastered many a high mountain pass and a seemingly never-ending series of hairpin bends with ease. The 12 hp four-cylinder engine and the light, delicately styled body satisfied all their creators' hopes in terms of performance, economy and reliability. Wanderer's basic concept was thus justified. In March 1913 a new factory building was opened in Chemnitz-Schönau to build the Wanderer 5/12 hp (5 horsepower for tax purposes, 12 brake horsepower). For fifteen years this small car, referred to internally as the Type W 3, was a regular source of income for Wanderer's car division, and surely one of the best small-car designs on the German market. The affectionate nickname bestowed on it by the German public: "Puppchen" ("Baby Doll").

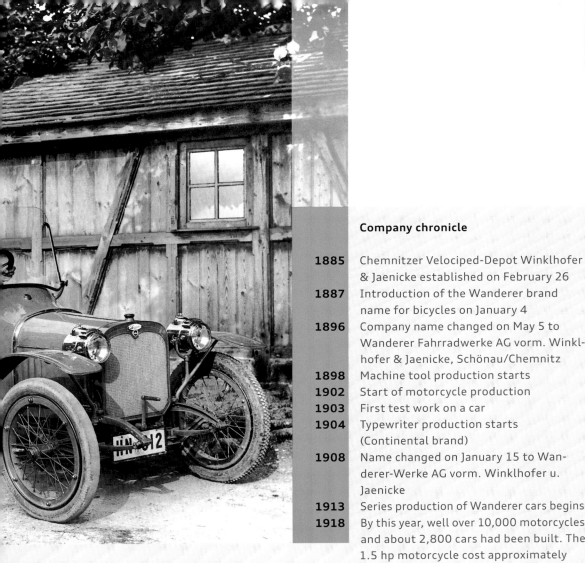

Company chronicle

1885	Chemnitzer Velociped-Depot Winklhofer & Jaenicke established on February 26
1887	Introduction of the Wanderer brand name for bicycles on January 4
1896	Company name changed on May 5 to Wanderer Fahrradwerke AG vorm. Winklhofer & Jaenicke, Schönau/Chemnitz
1898	Machine tool production starts
1902	Start of motorcycle production
1903	First test work on a car
1904	Typewriter production starts (Continental brand)
1908	Name changed on January 15 to Wanderer-Werke AG vorm. Winklhofer u. Jaenicke
1913	Series production of Wanderer cars begins
1918	By this year, well over 10,000 motorcycles and about 2,800 cars had been built. The 1.5 hp motorcycle cost approximately 750 marks, the Wanderer Puppchen car 3,800 marks

03 From the fall of 1913 onwards, customers could also buy the Wanderer Puppchen with two seats next to one another

10 commandments for the ambitious, compiled by J.B. Winklhofer, the founder of Wanderer

"1. A thorough understanding of one's own profession is a basic precondition. 2. The urge to do everything better than anyone else can. 3. Adherence to the principle that the customer must be supplied with the best possible value for money. 4. Work must always remain a constant source of pleasure. 5. The factory should always use the latest working methods and the finest equipment. 6. The bulk of the money that is earned must be devoted to the acquisition of these business improvements. 7. The right person must be allocated to the right job. 8. Live a simple, sound life, so that work can be tackled from an early hour with a clear head. 9. Be aware of the fact that not every business transaction can or must be undertaken. 10. Finally, a large amount of patience is needed when waiting for one's efforts to be crowned with success, even if the prospects sometimes look black."

03

DKW gets up steam

01

Jörgen Skafte Rasmussen was born in Denmark
in 1878 but came to Germany while still a young
man. He studied engineering in Mittweida and
Zwickau before settling in Chemnitz in 1902 and
establishing the company "Rasmussen & Ernst"
with a partner. On October 14, 1906 Rasmussen
purchased a former textile mill in Zschopau, and
transferred the company there in the following
year. The sales office remained in Chemnitz. The
trade register entry took place on April 13, 1907,
and declared the company's business purpose to
be "the manufacture of machines, metal goods
and fittings."

An indirect route to the automobile
The sales catalog for 1909 listed waste steam
recovery systems, equipment for cleaning
materials, centrifugal oil separators, mechanical
stokers, grids and firing systems for steam raising
boilers. Although this indicates a degree of
specialization in steam technology, this aspect
of the small company's activities was not to
remain dominant for long.
From 1910 onwards, accessories for motor
vehicles began to gain steadily in importance.

The company's 1912 sales catalog contained
passenger-car mudguards, motor-vehicle
lighting systems, anti-slip chains, vulcanizing
and oxyacetylene welding equipment. The
company changed its name in 1909 to Rasmussen
& Ernst, Zschopau-Chemnitz, Maschinen- und
Armaturenfabrik, Apparatebau Anstalt, then
again in 1912 to Zschopauer Maschinenfabrik
J.S. Rasmussen.

Plenty of steam – meager results
In 1916 Rasmussen began to experiment with
a steam-driven road vehicle. He recruited an
engineer and fellow Dane, Svend Aage Mathiesen,
who had acquired much experience in the design
of steam cars at the White company in the United
States until World War I broke out. The project
was extremely topical in view of the shortage of
conventional fuel from which the German Reich
suffered increasingly as the war continued.
Mathiesen first built a truck with a vertical-tube
boiler located behind the driver's seat and heated
with diesel oil. He constructed a passenger car at
the same time, in this case with a flame-tube
steam boiler under the hood at the front. Steam

02

03

04

pressure was led directly to the twin-cylinder engine, which in turn drove the rear wheels with no intermediate gears. Steam pressure and volume could be varied according to the amount of power required.

These experiments were generously subsidized by the War Ministry, but the vehicle proved to have too many technical shortcomings. It was extremely heavy, and the amount of steam needed to propel it was not always available when tackling gradients fully loaded. In addition, the amount of water that could be carried on the vehicle was consumed too rapidly, and the frequent, time-consuming task of refilling the water tank called for water columns to be set up along the route. Although this steam-driven vehicle had a theoretical operating range of 56 miles, it often came to a standstill earlier. The experiments were abandoned after the war. Should the vehicle have proved successful and entered production, Rasmussen was ready with a registered name for it: DKW, the abbreviation for "Dampfkraftwagen" ("steam-driven vehicle"). The three letters were arranged around a volcano emitting flames.

05

06

04 Rasmussen's steam-driven car took shape in this building between 1916 and 1919
05 The Zschopau steam car, seen here on a demonstration run in 1918, gave the initials of its name to the DKW brand
06 The first DKW emblem depicted an erupting volcano

Company chronicle

1902 The Rasmussen & Ernst company established in Chemnitz as a manufacturer of waste steam fittings
1907 Company moved to Zschopau on April 13, but with the sales office remaining in Chemnitz
1909 Company name changed and extended to Rasmussen & Ernst, Zschopau-Chemnitz, Maschinen- und Armaturenfabrik, Apparatebau Anstalt
1912 Company name simplified to Zschopauer Maschinenfabrik J.S. Rasmussen

01

02

05

06

09

Horch – an overview

03

04

07

08

10

01 Horch Vis-a-Vis, 1901

02 Horch 10 – 12 hp Tonneau, 1902

03 Horch 11/22 hp Phaeton with glass partition, 1906

04 Horch 31/60 hp six-cylinder car owned by the Sultan of Java, 1907

05 Horch 23/40 hp Prince Henry Run car, 1908

06 Horch 8/16 hp sports two-seater, 1911

07 Horch 10/30 hp racing car for ice racing in Sweden, 1913

08 Horch 14/40 hp swap-body sedan, 1913

09 Horch 33/80 hp truck and Horch 25/42 hp buses, 1915

10 Horch 33/55 hp artillery tractor with high-grip wheels and rope winch, 1917

01

02

05

06

07

08

Audi – an overview

03

04

01 Audi Type A 10/22 hp Phaeton, 1910
02 Audi Type B 10/28 hp sedan, 1913
03 Audi Type C 14/35 hp Phaeton, 1914
04 Audi Type C 14/35 hp Landaulet, 1913
05 Audi Type D 18/45 hp Phaeton: a civilian passenger car in use as officers' transport during the war, 1916
06 Audi Type D 18/45 hp Landaulet sedan: property of the King of Saxony, 1914
07 Audi Type G 8/22 hp Landaulet, 1920
08 Audi Bt truck, 1913
09 Audi Type C Alpine Victor 14/35 hp Phaeton (open tourer), 1913

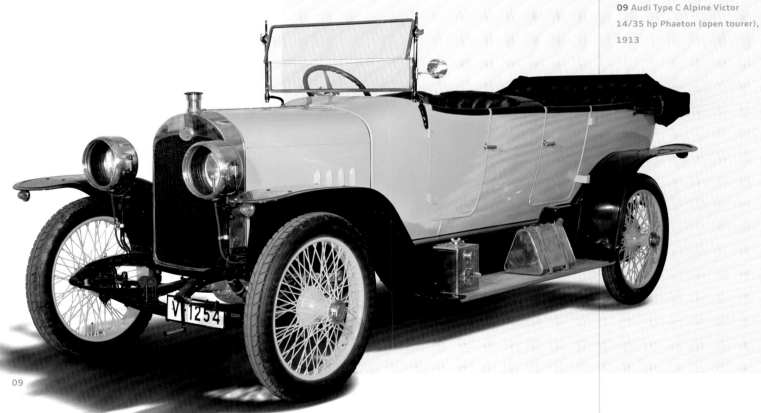

09

29

01

02

05

Wanderer – an overview

03

04

06

07

08

09

WANDERER
Lieferungswagen
WANDERER-WERKE A.G
Schönau bei Chemnitz

10

Growth between inflation and economic crisis

From workshop to assembly line

After World War I had been brought to an end by an armistice followed by the Treaty of Versailles, the automobile industry began to produce vehicles for the civilian population once again. Models dating from before the war were restored to the assembly lines almost unchanged. Then, in the early 1920s, the German currency lost its value, and although this caused export sales to boom as never before, inflation set in and by the end of 1923 the spurious boom came to an abrupt halt.

Recovery

Various attempts to introduce modern motor-vehicle engineering techniques, for instance the one-piece cylinder block, left-hand drive, four-wheel brakes and other improved technologies such as a changeover from the craftsman's workshop to volume production using conveyor-belt assembly methods, had been attempted after the war but had failed to survive the economic chaos that prevailed at that time. International competitors too were increasingly active on the German market from the mid-1920s onwards, and obliged the domestic car industry to modernize its methods. Customers demanded more powerful cars built to modern standards, which naturally increased their production costs. Motor vehicle manufacturing in fact pioneered the introduction of ultra-modern working methods. Most of the companies involved, including Horch, DKW and Wanderer, adopted conveyor-belt assembly principles between 1925 and 1929: within those few years, Germany's automobile industry doubled its output.

Growth

No single company within the German automobile industry was able to finance these developments from its own resources. The need to invest in new machinery, to finance sales (in 1928, for instance, 70 percent of all the cars sold in Germany were paid for in installments), limited market volume due to poverty among the middle classes, international competition on the domestic market – all these factors made a

03

direct commitment by the major banks essential. Motor vehicles now began to change the appearance of the streets once and for all. The total vehicle population rose from approximately 420,000 in 1924 to no fewer than 1,200,000 only four years later. In Germany, most cars were used in town, where the horse had been the most important mode of transport until World War I. In Berlin alone, 5,500 horses were needed to pull the buses! Every year, the Berlin Omnibus

01, 02

01 After the 1920s, buses, trams and an increasing number of cars dominated the street scene in our major cities
02 Street scene with pedestrians, 1927
03 Parking lot in front of the Dresden Labor Exchange, 1931

32

Company earned a hundred thousand gold marks simply from the sale of horse manure. Progress arrived in the form of the electric railway and the motor bus, which took over city traffic on behalf of the man in the street, but could not entirely satisfy the individual's desire for personal mobility. The bicycle remained the "poor man's horse," and gave him access to desirable destinations that could not be reached by rail or bus. As private motoring gathered impetus, the car became a household commodity, though until well after World War II there were still more motorcycles than cars in use.

The passenger car spread through society from the top down. Luxury travel and motor sport came first, but in the 1920s small cars appeared that were aimed at the average citizen; many new technical concepts were dreamed up and put into effect.

HORCH 8

DER DEUTSCHE ACHTZYLINDER

SCHNELL • SICHER • GERÄUSCHLOS

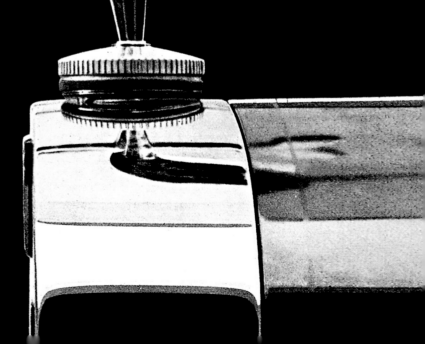

EDEL
IN DER ARBEIT

EDEL
IN DER FORM

+

HORCH-WERKE A·G
ZWICKAU-BERLIN

HAUPTVERWALTUNG
BERLIN NW7, MITTELSTR. 15

VERKAUFSSTELLEN IN
ALLEN TEILEN DEUTSCHLANDS

Horch – quality and quantity

In 1920, Dr. Moritz Straus acquired the majority of the shares in Horchwerke AG. He was already the major shareholder in the Berlin aircraft engine manufacturer Argus Flugmotorenwerken GmbH. Contacts between the two companies went back to before World War I, when Horch carried out experimental work on aircraft engines that it was planned to build under license from Argus. Although nothing came of this, the two companies remained in touch.

After the war, when the production of aircraft engines was prohibited, Dr. Straus's contacts with Horch acquired a more urgent character. He secured a majority shareholding in the Zwickau-based automobile manufacturer and commissioned the Swiss designer Arnold Zoller to work on a passenger car to be built there. It was to be a single model that would replace the variety of pre-war models that Horch was still offering for sale.

On July 1, 1922 Paul Daimler, the son of Gottlieb Daimler, became the new Argus Chief Designer in Berlin, and took over from Zoller. In a consultant's agreement he also undertook to update the design of the Horch models.

After putting the final touches to the Horch four-cylinder model that was Zoller's work, Daimler went on to design the Horch 8, which became the company's only product from January 2, 1927 onwards.

At this time Dr. Moritz Straus had planned the Horch brand's strategy in a most praiseworthy manner. For him, design and development, production and marketing were to be regarded as a single unit. He encouraged refinements to the design of the eight-cylinder engine, built up production methods geared to exceptionally high quality and, by commissioning leading coach-builders and designers, was able to ensure that the public became aware of the style and character of the car bearing the crowned H emblem.

In the second half of the 1920s, production capacity was increased from four cars a day (1925) to twelve (1928), and reached 15 a year later.

Within a very short space of time at the end of the 1920s, the Horch 8 became a symbol of the top quality of which the German automobile industry was capable. Its reputation derived from its exceptionally quiet, smooth running and its high standard of workmanship. The Zwickau-based company had amassed a unique concentration of know-how, in particular with regard to the production of large motor-vehicle engines. It included the correct treatment of the large castings that was necessary in order to prevent them from distorting during subsequent machining, the milling of valve seats and their lapping with precision hand tools, the precision balancing of all rotating parts including the dynamo pulley, and even the adjustment of the helical-cut bronze gears on the valve-gear drive shaft – using a listening tube!

Each engine ran on the test rig for an hour, including 40 minutes at full throttle. All parts subject to severe loads, for instance the main bearings, were machined with diamond cutting tools, Horch being one of the very first automobile manufacturers to adopt this method.

The funds at Dr. Straus's disposal were far from sufficient to finance the purchase of all the necessary production machinery and equipment. A financial stake in the Zwickau company was therefore acquired by the banks – the Allgemeine Deutsche Credit Anstalt (ADCA) and the Commerzbank in Berlin. These banks were members of the consortium that set up Auto Union in 1932, into which the Horchwerke were absorbed.

By 1920 Horch's post-war production was in full swing, with six cars and three trucks in the sales program. All of these were pre-war designs, including the top model with a four-cylinder engine developing 80 horsepower from a displacement of no less than 8.5 liters!

In 1923 this variegated collection of models was taken out of production, and only the 10/35 hp car designed by Zoller remained; it had entered production a year previously. This car's 35 hp

02, 03

01 Advertising the Horch 8. The radiator mascot consists of the winged arrow designed by Hadank
02 Horch 10/35 hp in front of Hagia Sophia, 1923
03 Before final acceptance, Horch engines were given a "listening test" to detect unacceptable noises

35

engine was a four-cylinder side valve unit. The chassis, which was also new, was protected by seven patents and eight registered designs. These related to the rear axle casing and also the engine, which formed a single ready-to-install unit together with the steering gear and the front bulkhead – what would today be called a modular element.

Paul Daimler's first task was to revise the design of this model. It acquired four-wheel brakes and a more conventional front-end appearance, in contrast to the previous 10/35, which had been given a fashionable pointed radiator grill. The new company emblem also appeared on it for the first time: an H surmounted by the word Horch curved to resemble a crown. This emblem

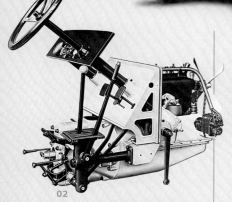

01 Horch 10/50 hp Pullman sedan with two junior drivers, 1926
02 Zoller's design for the 14/35 hp four-cylinder model consisted of a ready-to-install engine, transmission and steering module, together with other components; it was protected by numerous patents
03 Horch Type 306 roadster convertible with compartment for golf clubs, 1927
04 The Horch 8, Germany's first volume-produced straight-eight engine, 1927

05

06

was designed by Prof. Ernst Böhm, Lecturer in Practical Graphics at the Berlin College of Advanced Free and Applied Art.

The climax of Paul Daimler's period of activity for Horch, however, was most definitely his straight-eight engine.
This engine had a displacement of approximately 3 liters and a power output of 60 horsepower. The valves were operated by double overhead camshafts driven by a vertical shaft with bevel gears using the Gleason tooth contact pattern. The distributor was mounted at the top of this shaft. The bevel gear at the bottom of the vertical shaft also drove the engine's gear-type oil pump. Since the worm drive to the water pump and dynamo was also taken from the same shaft, no fewer than eight gearwheels were in mesh at this point.
Many of the car's design details were well ahead of their time. To minimize effort at the pedal, the four-wheel brakes, for instance, had vacuum servo assistance using the engine's manifold depression (the system developed by the Belgian engineer Albert Dewandre). The cooling system included a thermostat that opened the main circuit only when a temperature of 162 degrees Fahrenheit was reached, to help maintain an optimum operating temperature.

The new Horch was shown to the public for the first time at the Berlin Motor Show towards the end of 1926. The most basic version, an open tourer, cost 11,900 marks. Few of its competitors were more expensive, indeed many of them undercut this price significantly, for example the Mercedes Mannheim and the 3.3-liter Röhr. Two years later a successor, the Horch 350, was announced. Its bodywork was styled by Prof. Hadank from the same Berlin art college as Böhm, the designer of the Horch emblem.
Half a dozen of the new cars were on display at the Berlin Motor Show in December 1928, including a Pullman sedan and a Pullman convertible, an open tourer, a sedan and a sports convertible. The main attraction, however, was the four-door "sedan cabriolet," its gray paint finish harmonizing with scarlet leather upholstery and trim, and with a sand-colored soft top. Horch was also the first German manufacturer to supply its cars from that time on with safety glass windows. The front-end styling was dominated by large headlights made by the Zeiss company in Jena. They were linked by a crossbar with a central badge consisting of an 8 in a circle to draw attention to the Horch's eight-cylinder engine. The radiator, previously exposed, was now concealed behind a shutter system, painted in the same color as the body and with a chrome border. Another new departure

07

05 A Horch 8 exhibit with a hammered finish
06 The Horch as VIP transport, seen here with von Hindenburg, President of the German Reich
07 Horch 350 sedan cabriolet

37

01 02 03

04, 05

01 Paul Daimler (1869 – 1945),
designer of the Horch straight-
eight engine

02 Fritz Fiedler (1899 – 1972),
responsible for the design of the
Horch V 8 engine and the twelve-
cylinder types

03 Beauty in competition –
Countess Günderode with her
Type 400 Horch convertible

was the mascot on the radiator cap: a winged
arrow, designed by O.H.D. Hadank.
A further two years later, Horch introduced a
special version of its eight-cylinder model, with
the rather anonymous model code 375. Its body
was again styled by Prof. Hadank, and Paul
Daimler had subjected the mechanical elements
to his usual careful scrutiny. An innovation was
the sharply cranked frame where it passed over
the rear axle, and repositioned springs to permit
a wider track and more satisfactory spring
locations. The rear springs were 4.76 feet long,
with 18 chrome vanadium steel leaves. This Horch
was the first to have hydraulic shock absorbers.
The mascot on the radiator cap changed once
again, and now consisted of a winged globe, also
the work of Ernst Böhm.
This car was the culmination of Paul Daimler's
creative efforts. Initial difficulties with the eight-
cylinder engine had long since been overcome,
and it now ran with impressive smoothness. The
chassis and body were fully its equal, and set
new standards within the German automobile
industry, with unsurpassed quality of workmanship and an air of restrained luxury. When Paul
Daimler retired in 1929, more than 7,000 Horch
eight-cylinder cars had been built, a figure of
which other German companies could only dream.

Daimler's successor Fritz Fiedler, who came from
the Stoewer company in Stettin, revised the
sales line-up. The straight-eight engine, in future
with a single overhead camshaft only, was offered
in three sizes: 4 liters with an output of 80 hp,
4.5 liters with 90 hp and 5 liters with 100 horsepower. Each was available in a short- or long-
wheelbase chassis. The manufacturer was able
to supply eight different body styles, though
Horch customers were welcome to purchase a
chassis only and have their preferred body built
on it by coachbuilders such as Gläser or Erdmann
& Rossi.

06

04 Lifestyle and the Horch car
05 The globe designed by Prof.
Böhm as a Horch radiator mascot
06 The Horch 375 was the first
car to have safety glass as
standard equipment, 1929
07 Horch 375 Pullman convertible
with coachwork by Gläser

07

01 Six-liter, 120 hp V12 engine, 1932

02 German tennis ace Gottfried von Cramm's wife with her 12-cylinder convertible, which had white-walled tires

03 A full set of instruments in the Horch 12

04 The 12-cylinder convertible (Type 670) styled by Hermann Ahrens had an aura of harmony and prestige

01

02, 03

04

At the 1931 Paris Motor Show it was once again Horch that created the major sensation. Its stand featured a yellow-painted convertible with a brown soft top and green kid leather upholstery, flanked on one side by a Type 500 in steel blue with a gray soft top and on the other by a Type 470 sedan cabriolet with gray paintwork, a lighter gray soft top and blue leather upholstery. The hood of the main attraction, the yellow sports convertible, was open to reveal the Horch company's latest and most dramatic development: a 6-liter V12 engine! Fiedler had spared no effort or expense to achieve the highest levels of refinement. To safeguard against vibration problems from the crankshaft, despite its seven main bearings, he had given it twelve balance weights and a front-end vibration damper.

For this impressively quiet car, only the ZF company's "Aphon" transmission was considered good enough. This was incidentally one of the first in Germany to have a low-noise second gear as well as the higher ratios.

The new flagship of the Horch fleet was available as the two or four-door Type 670 convertible and as the Type 600, a Pullman sedan or convertible. A striking feature of the Horch 670 was its three-piece windshield, the center section of which could be opened outwards. The fascia, with its fine wood trim, included a map reading lamp and various warning and indicator lamps. The luxurious interior specification included fully reclining front seats as standard equipment.

The new model reached the market early in 1932, and cost between 24,000 and 26,000 Reichsmarks (RM), depending on the version ordered. The luxury car market in Germany was more vigorously contested than in almost any other country, with up to 17 eight-cylinder cars in 47 versions contending for the wealthy customer's business. Horch's success in the face of such competition was all the more impressive: in the over 4.2-liter class, the Zwickau company's share of the market in 1932 was 44 percent.

05 Crown princess Cecilie von Hohenzollern and her Horch 500 B in the courtyard of Cecilienhof Palace
06 Horch cars regularly won concours d'élégance
07 A Type 500 Horch sedan with steel body by Ambi Budd

05

06

07

This 1934 leaflet shows the 12-cylinder Pullman convertible, with the Type 780 eight-cylinder sports convertible at the top

6-LITER-PULLMAN-CABRIOLET MODELL 600

RADSTAND 3750 mm

01

01 Despite the central propeller-
shaft tunnel, the Pullman convertible had plenty of space at the
rear; there are two folding seats
on the left

02

03

Company chronicle

From 1920 until liquidation took place on June 29, 1932, Horchwerke AG belonged to Argus-Flugmotorenwerke of Berlin. During this period the Horch Board of Directors had its headquarters at Mittelstrasse 15 in Berlin. The company's capital was 5 million Reichsmarks.

About 15,000 Horch cars were produced between 1922 and 1932, including from 1927 onwards about 12,000 with eight-cylinder engines. These figures represent an average annual output of 1,300 cars. Between 1925 and 1930, the company's annual turnover averaged 23 million Reichsmarks. The workforce fluctuated between 2,200 and 2,400 employees.

In 1932 Horch achieved a market share of more than 44 percent in the engine-size class above 4.2 liters in Germany.

The 10/50 hp tourer cost 12,876 Reichsmarks in 1926. The eight-cylinder cars were often more expensive than their competitors. 11,900 Reichsmarks were charged in 1927 for the 303 tourer, and 14,000 Reichsmarks for the same version of the 350. The twelve-cylinder Pullman sedan was listed at 24,500 Reichsmarks.

Just-in-time production at Horch in 1928

"When calculating the time needed for deliveries of raw materials, the starting point must be when the finished car leaves the assembly line. Working backwards from this point, a precise 'manufacturing timetable' has to be compiled, showing every work stage and the time needed to complete it. Specially appointed 'progress chasers' must supervise this timetable in the central office and ensure that it is complied with. The engine and rear axle must leave the 'listening rooms' (the final stage in their production cycle) and reach the chassis assembly line at precisely the moment when their installation is due to take place. Each engine and rear axle should only be completed in sufficient time to reach the designated installation point when needed. The body should have been fully painted just before it is installed on the completed chassis: the process should then continue until the car has been thoroughly inspected under powerful spotlights and leaves the factory."

P. Friedmann in the magazine Deutsche Motor-Zeitschrift, *1928, No. 6*

Ernest Friedländer: Auto Test Book, 1931

"The car has exceptionally flowing lines. Although it has clearly been styled with more of an eye to current fashion than the standard products from Daimler-Benz, it is superior to them in elegance and sublime expression. Horch today gives precedence to formal matters, with even questions of design rendered subservient to this overriding principle. Not surprisingly, the results of this concept are of a delicacy scarcely to be surpassed. Despite their size, the current large Horch convertibles and sedans are among the most inspired, dramatic creations that automobile technology has to offer."

02 Horch 750 B
03 The Horch Type 780 was exhibited for the first time in 1932, in fish scale silver

Audiwerke A. G.
Zwickau - Sa.

01

Audi – noblesse oblige

Like many of its local competitors, Audiwerke AG emerged from the war years with considerable profits at its disposal, and reverted to the production of civilian motor vehicles. These included light trucks, an attractive market segment in the immediate post-war years when there was a shortage of transport capacity.

For the future, Audi's owners agreed on a two-model policy consisting of a four-cylinder and a six-cylinder car.

Inflation caused Audi no problems at first, and as paper money rapidly lost its value it was even possible to take on more workers.

Audi had remained a company of moderate size, but one dedicated to the development and manufacture of high-quality cars. Although the financial situation was difficult from 1925 onwards, efforts were made to adhere to this product policy. When they failed, the owners took the advice of the State Bank of Saxony and sold their shares to the man who controlled the DKW empire, J. S. Rasmussen. He had previously been to America and purchased production equipment for six- and eight-cylinder engines. After having this shipped to the town of Scharfenstein in Germany's Erzgebirge mountains, he began the search for manufacturers prepared to install his engines in their cars. In 1931 Rasmussen made the decision to

assemble his front-wheel-drive DKW small cars at the Audi factory in Zwickau.

Following the death of Hermann Lange in 1922, graduate engineer Erich Horn took over as Chief Designer. He drafted out the first Audi six-cylinder model (1923). His place was taken in 1926 by Heinrich Schuh, who had been Factory Director since 1920. Schuh not only developed the first Audi eight-cylinder model (1927) but was also responsible for reorganizing the company's entire production routine.

Before World War I, the Audi logo had consisted only of the name. In 1919 Lucian Bernhard, one of Germany's leading typeface designers, was commissioned to develop an Audi typeface. The result was registered on April 27, 1920, and has characterised the Audi wordmark ever since then. In 1922, company management announced a competition for a new product emblem to complement the wordmark as a means of identifying the brand.

150 entries were received, and the Board of Directors chose a submission from Professor Arno Drescher consisting of a figure 1 placed in front of a segment of a globe. Audi registered the new trademark in June 1923, and it appeared on the radiator grills of all Audi cars until production ceased in 1940.

01 Lucian Bernhard's wordmark and the radiator mascot created by Drescher/Gilbert gave Audi unmistakable signets
02 Returning from a successful Batschari Run in 1925
03 Audi took part in the test trials with streamlined bodywork organized by Paul Jaray in 1923

02, 03

04

From a 1919 Audi owner's handbook

"When driving in city traffic, always select the gear ratio that matches your road speed. Never attempt to control the car's speed by slipping the clutch … the leather clutch facing needs to be treated with special care. If it becomes dry and hard, a squeaking noise will be heard when the clutch is engaged. The leather must then be washed thoroughly with gasoline or petroleum spirit and

coated with liver, fish or castor oil or the finest quality Vaseline. This will render it supple again, so that it conforms smoothly to the shape of the flywheel cone. To ensure that the leather facing absorbs the oil effectively, you are advised to leave the clutch disengaged overnight by wedging a piece of wood between the pedal and the transmission."

04 The Audi had a body made entirely from light alloy by Gläser in Dresden

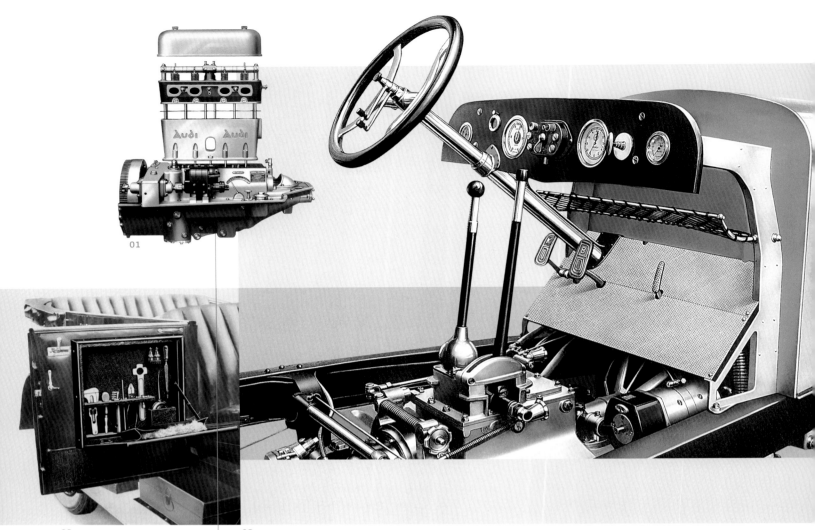

01

02

03

01 Audi Type K four-cylinder
engine with light-alloy cylinder
block and crankcase, 1921
02 A practical tool compartment
03 An Audi dashboard with
speedometer, clock and – an
interesting item – the net for
carrying small items safely

The products
The first new post-war Audi, developed by Hermann Lange, was clearly a direct successor to
the triumphant "Alpine Run" model. It was given
the designation K and had an engine with the
same bore and stroke, though Lange discarded
the cylinders cast in pairs in favor of an aluminum block with a cast iron head. The overhead
camshaft was driven by helical-cut gears. Engine
lubrication was taken care of by no fewer than
three oil pumps. The cooling system retained
the traditional thermosiphon principle, with
no water pump, but was aided effectively by a
four-bladed fan that could be driven at various
speeds.
A notable feature of this car, which was exhibited
at the 1921 Berlin Motor Show, was the steering
layout. It was the first series-production German
passenger car to have left-hand drive. After
thorough testing, including evaluation of Ameri-

can experience and reports submitted by the
Berlin traffic police, Audi came to a quick decision,
which it expressed in concise form:
*"We have now given up the previous practice of
installing the steering wheel on the right-hand
side of the car, having come to accept the
advantages of left-hand drive for the right-hand
rule of the road."*
Audi's competitors were left well behind: in 1922
about 90 percent of all new passenger cars in
Germany had right-hand drive, and even in 1923
the figure was still about 75 percent.

The Type K cars were elegant and sporty: as
usual in many sports cars of that time, the
steering wheel could be hinged out of the way
to make it easier for the driver to enter. Among
the standard instruments was a revolution
counter. The Audi K's fuel tank held a remarkable

05

AUDI 18/70 PS. SECHSZYLINDER-PULLMANN-LIMOUSINE, REISEWAGEN

AUDI 18/70 PS. SECHSZYLINDER-TOURENWAGEN

06

33 gallons, including 4 gallons in reserve. An engine-driven tire inflating pump was another unusual feature.

At the 1923 Berlin Motor Show a successor to this model was launched. Developed by Erich Horn, this was the prototype of Audi's first six-cylinder car. The crankshaft ran in eight white-metal bearings and had very large balance weights. Later, a torsional vibration damper was attached, with Audi once again able to claim a place among the few pioneering manufacturers who understood the need for such a device and appreciated its practical benefits.

The valves were again operated from a single overhead camshaft, driven by a vertical shaft and gears from the crankshaft. Cast iron cylinder liners were inserted into the light alloy engine block. The engine, which developed 70 horsepower, was supplied with intake air through circular holes in the frame on the carburetor side, and then through a filter wetted with oil. This was located in the lower part of the crankcase. The intake air was pre-heated by the exhaust system and reached the carburetor with most of the turbulence eliminated. Here too Audi played a pioneering role in automotive technology.

This six-cylinder car was the first model from Audi to be equipped with hydraulic brakes; these were designed in-house, and were among the first hydraulic brake systems to appear on a German motor vehicle.

04

From the introduction to the Audi K owner's handbook, 1924

"To own such a noble vehicle is to have one's good taste and culture legitimized in no uncertain way – just as an upper-class Englishman might regard membership of a select club as evidence of his character as a gentleman. To possess an Audi motor car, therefore, is to respect the laws of 'noblesse oblige' ..."

04 Audi Type K 14/50 hp, 1924
05, 06 Audi Type M, 18/70 hp
07 Chassis of Audi Type M,
18/70 hp

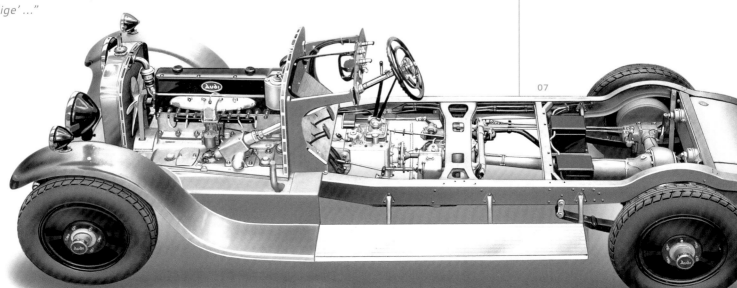

07

01

02

01 The Audi Imperator with a convertible body by Josef Neuss, Berlin

02 The Audi Imperator was the first Audi with an eight-cylinder engine, 1927

03 Audi commissioned this poster from Offelsmeyer to introduce its first eight-cylinder model in 1927

In 1927 the first Audi with an eight-cylinder engine was announced. It was given the model letter R within the Audi alphabet. It was a 19/100 hp model, and the number of cylinders and fiscal horsepower rating were therefore combined as the Type 819. The engine's actual power output was 100 horsepower, giving the new car a top speed of 68 mph. Only the crank-case was of light alloy; a cast iron cylinder block was now used. For the first time in the history of Audi, the transmission had only three forward ratios.

Heinrich Schuh had greatly simplified the design and eliminated a number of overly elaborate details. Although the new car was larger than before and created a distinctly luxurious

impression, it was actually much cheaper to build "under the skin." Based on the same production volume as for the M model, the R was 47 percent cheaper to manufacture. The new model was named the "Imperator."

After Rasmussen took control of Audi in 1928, the Zwickau-based company was required to install the ex-Rickenbacker engines that he was building in Scharfenstein, using the plant and equipment he had purchased in the United States. The eight-cylinder engine was used for the next Audi model, the "Zwickau," and also developed 100 horsepower. A year later a related model, the "Dresden" appeared, with a six-cylinder Rickenbacker engine developing 75 horsepower.

01, 02

03

04

01 The Audi Dresden, with 75 hp
six-cylinder engine
02 The Audi Zwickau with the
Rickenbacker eight-cylinder engine
03 The coat of arms of the town
of Zwickau, for which the Audi
Type SS was named, was displayed
on the radiator grill
04 The Audi Zwickau, with 100 hp
straight-eight engine

Rasmussen, who at that time was anxious to make better use of the capacity of his DKW factory in Berlin-Spandau, but also to boost sales of Audi models, now planned to introduce the smallest Audi in the company's history. He took the DKW he was building in Spandau and installed a 1,000 cc four-stroke engine purchased from Peugeot, with a rated output of 30 horse-power. The car was given the "1" badge on its radiator and sold as the Audi Type P.

By the fall of 1930, however, Rasmussen had created an entirely new Audi model line. Accompanied by Heinrich Schuh, he appeared one day in the Audi design office and instructed the

surprised staff to develop a small car with a DKW motorcycle engine, swing-axle suspension, front-wheel drive and a wooden body. For this he graciously allowed them a period of six weeks. In fact the two designers confronted with this task not only kept within Rasmussen's deadline but produced a model of which more than a quarter of a million were to be sold in the years to come, making it Germany's most popular small car – though as a DKW rather than as an Audi. Rasmussen was concentrating at that time on gaining public acceptance for front-wheel drive in the midsize car category. He felt that what was such a success in the DKW "driving machine" ought to work equally well in a larger car.

52

05

05 The Audiwerke AG factory site in the early 1930s
06 A coat of many colors! A DKW from Spandau with a Peugeot engine from France was badged as an Audi and sold as the Audi Type P

Company chronicle

1928	J. S. Rasmussen acquired a majority shareholding in Audiwerke AG on August 20 and 21
1929	Rasmussen purchased the remaining shares. The share capital was 2,600,000 Reichsmarks
1932	On June 29 the company was liquidated and integrated into Auto Union AG

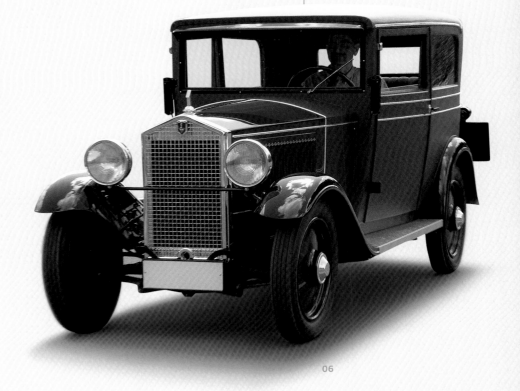

06

Approximately 2,500 Audi cars were built between 1921 and 1932, equivalent to an average annual output of about 200. The company's share of the German market in its sales category was marginal, at about 3.7 percent.

The number of employees decreased, for example from 370 in 1925 to only 169 in 1930. The prices charged for Audi cars were geared to the levels prevailing in the large luxury class. The six-cylinder Type M was offered at 22,300 Reichsmarks in 1925; a Maybach with the same specification could be had for 25,000 Reichsmarks. Thanks to design changes and more efficient construction methods, the eight-cylinder Audi "Imperator" had come down in price to only 16,575 Reichsmarks in 1927; the Type S with an eight-cylinder Rickenbacker engine was actually listed at only 12,950 Reichsmarks.

02

Wanderer – from tradition to innovation

In the 1920s, the Wanderer-Werke in Chemnitz counted among Germany's leading vehicle manufacturers in the widest sense of the term. Wanderer bicycles, but also the company's motorcycles, were increasingly popular. During World War I, Wanderer had supplied almost half of the motorcycles needed by the German Army. Even the small Wanderer "Puppchen" two-seater car, having overcome initial doubts and convinced the military authorities of its merits, was widely used within the Imperial Army.

Wanderer models began to secure more and more of the midsize car market in the 1920s, competing successfully against all the leading German makes. The Wanderer-Werke were regarded as a company firmly rooted in tradition, with a conservative approach to design and a loyal group of customers who were not interested in epoch-making innovations. The Wanderer name became a watchword for quality and reliability.

Starting in the mid-1920s, all Wanderer's production areas were thoroughly streamlined. The process was linked to a change of location: starting with the machine-tool manufacturing division, a move was made from the company's headquarters in Schönau to new production buildings in Siegmar. In the spring of 1927 the automobile manufacturing division also moved to these new premises, where 25 cars a day were built initially, using modern assembly-line methods.

In September 1928 Baron Klaus Detlof von Oertzen became a member of the Wanderer Board of Directors. His task was to add sparkle to the conservative brand image and modernize the company's sales and marketing activities. It was he who established the highly important link with Ferdinand Porsche, which was to prove of such importance for the future. Thanks to his initiative, Porsche's recently established design office was awarded a development contract for several new projects. An early highlight in this most fruitful relationship was an agreement for Porsche to develop a racing car for Wanderer.

The products

Immediately after World War I a twin-cylinder, 616 cc motorcycle developing 10 hp was introduced. It was a thoroughly modern design, with the transmission in unit with the engine, a kick starter and chain drive, and remained in the sales line-up until 1924. In that year it was followed by the legendary Wanderer Type 708 twin, which had four valves per cylinder. There was also a smaller version of this model powered by a 200 cc horizontal single-cylinder engine, again with a four-valve cylinder head. However, the last of the large Wanderer motorcycles, with a 500 cc single-cylinder engine, a pressed-steel frame and shaft drive, incurred a number of teething troubles and was not a sales success. Midway through 1929,

01 This Wanderer-Werke AG advertisement appeared in the fall of 1922
02 A new Wanderer factory was built in Chemnitz-Siegmar and opened in the spring of 1927
03 Wanderer's "Puppchen" was very popular in the Imperial Army during World War I
04 Motorcycles from Wanderer were also used by the German Army in large numbers. This is a 4 hp twin-cylinder model dating from 1914
05 Baron Klaus Detlof von Oertzen (1894 – 1991) joined the Board of Directors of Wanderer-Werke AG in September 1928

03

04

05

55

01

Wanderer decided to withdraw from motorcycle production. The new 500 cc shaft drive model was taken on by the Janeček company in Prague. This was the origin of the Jawa (Janeček-Wanderer) brand. The designs for the other models were sold to NSU.

The automobile division initially kept the still-popular "Puppchen" (the 5/15 hp Type W 3) in its line-up, adding a three-seater version in 1917. In 1921 this small car underwent an extensive technical redesign. The engine was given a detachable cylinder head with overhead valves and a slight increase in swept volume to 1.3 liters. Carefully designed cantilever leaf-spring rear suspension replaced the three-quarter elliptic leaf spring system used until then. The revised model, known as the Type W 8, reached the market in May 1921. The "Puppchen" was developed further with a four-seater body in the fall of 1924, and had its power output increased to 20 hp a year later. It was not until 1927 that this highly successful Wanderer design was replaced by a more powerful model.

Since the end of 1920, Wanderer had in fact manufactured just such a more powerful model with four seats, in parallel with the "Puppchen."

This was the 6/18 hp Wanderer Type W 6 (sold from February 1924 onwards with a 6/24 hp engine as the Type W 9), but it was initially built only in small numbers.

In the mid-1920s a preference for larger, more powerful cars became increasingly evident. It had its origins in the United States. Wanderer therefore resolved to offer only an improved version of its large four-seater from 1927 onwards. The Wanderer type codes had in the meantime reached W 10. The 1.5-liter, four-cylinder engine's output was increased to 30 horsepower. At the same time the car was given all the latest features of modern automotive engineering practice: left-hand drive, a central floor-mounted gear lever, a multiple dry plate clutch, a transmission in unit with the engine and four-wheel brakes. This Wanderer 6/30 underwent several later design revisions and remained in the line-up until 1932.

In the fall of 1928 the Wanderer-Werke introduced the Type W 11, a 10/50 hp six-cylinder model that succeeded in polishing up the rather outmoded image of the company's products. Bodies were supplied by leading companies, including Reutter in Stuttgart, Neuss in Berlin, Gläser in Dresden and Zschau in Leipzig.

02

03   04

01 Wanderer sold its products all over the world, like this 1.5 hp motorcycle in Prague in the mid-1920s

02 Wanderer 8/40 hp Type W 10/II, 1928

03 A family outing in the Wanderer 5/15 hp Type W 8, 1922

04 The first Wanderer 10/50 hp six-cylinder Type W 11 appeared in 1928. This is the phaeton (open tourer) version

05 Sporty looks: the 1931 Wanderer W 11 roadster convertible

06 Wanderer Werke discovered women as a target group at a very early stage; the car in this picture is a 1929 Wanderer W 11 six-cylinder sedan

01 As early as 1914, Wanderer's small cars performed excellently in the International Austrian Alpine Run

02 The victorious Wanderer team at the Wanderer factory in Siegmar, after returning from the 1931 International Alpine Run

03 For competition purposes (here the 1931 Alpine Run) the Wanderer W 11 was given a special roadster body

In October 1929 the world economic crisis meant a rough awakening for the technical and commercial staff in Siegmar and Schönau. Attack, it was decided, was the best form of defense. One of the leading designers of his day was hired: Ferdinand Porsche. For the Saxony-based company he drafted out a new generation of six-cylinder OHV engines with a light alloy cylinder block and wet cylinders; the 1.7-liter version developed 35 hp, the 2-liter version 40 horsepower. These engines were installed in the largely unchanged W 10 chassis. The new models were the Type W 15 (7/35 hp) and the Type W 17 (8/40 hp).

Wanderer cars in motor sport

The Wanderer brand had always been well known in motor sport events. Even in the 1914 Alpine Run the company's small cars had proved so remarkably lively that after the war private enthusiasts began to prepare them for competition in the 5 tax-horsepower class. Privately owned Wanderer cars were particularly successful in hillclimbs and short-distance races. They were especially popular in Italy, following a number of wins on local circuits by Wanderer driver Cercigiani, often at average speeds not far below 56 mph. In view of the brand's popularity on the Italian market, the company entered two 1.5-liter Wanderer sports cars for the 1922 Targa Florio in Sicily. Although both retired from the race, this motor sport commitment was so popular that the management in Schönau built a small batch of "Type Targa Florio" two-seaters for private customers.

When Klaus Detlof von Oertzen joined the Board of Directors of Wanderer-Werke in September 1928 with the task of refurbishing the company's sales and marketing activities, he was convinced that motor sport would have a key role to play. From 1929 onwards, Wanderer cars were frequently entered for long-distance races and reliability trials. Wanderer teams achieved major successes in the International Alpine Runs, for instance an overall team victory in 1931 and the Alpine and Glacier trophy in the following year.

01

02   03

04

Company chronicle

1921 Construction work starts on a new Wanderer factory in Siegmar, near Chemnitz

1925 Wanderer's machine tool production moves from Schönau to the new factory in Siegmar

1927 In the spring, the new Wanderer car factory starts production

1929 In July, Wanderer gives up motorcycle production

1930 The Wanderer car body construction department is closed in March 1930, after which all bodies are obtained from outside coachbuilders

1932 The contract dated June 29, 1932, sells the Wanderer automobile division to the newly established Auto Union AG, effective retroactively from January 1. At the same time, the automobile factory in Siegmar is leased to Auto Union AG for ten years

In the early years, production seldom exceeded 500 vehicles annually.
In the 1920s, it rose from an initial 1,500 to 3,500 cars annually.
In 1932 Wanderer's share of new registrations in the 1.2 to 2.1-liter engine-size category was just over 10 percent.
The prices charged reflected Wanderer's perceived status in the midsize automobile class. As an open tourer, the W 8 was listed at 7,300 Reichsmarks in 1925. In 1928, the W 10 with the same body sold for 6,000 Reichsmarks. In 1931 the four-door W 10/IV sedan cost only 4,850 Reichsmarks.

Wanderer director von Oertzen on the commercial and technical developments with which he was associated

"I visited Mercedes in Sindelfingen and said to them: 'Come on, people, you make such good car bodies, why don't you make a few for us?' And in due course we had an agreement. Thyssen never forgot how I summoned up all my courage and gave them an order on the spot for a thousand bodies. Sindelfingen didn't mind all that much. I never had any internal problems about this at Wanderer. I was too well established, and the Supervisory Board was on my side. In 1929 and 1930 we didn't build any bodies of our own. They all came from the Rhineland, except for the convertibles from Gläser in Dresden and the sedans from Reutter in Stuttgart. I persuaded Ferdinand Porsche to develop the engines – six-cylinder units with either 1.7 or 2 liters' capacity. Wanderer used them first, then the Auto Union. Porsche sent his son-in-law Dr. Piëch to me in Chemnitz and we signed two contracts."

Source: tape-recorded archives

CABRIOLET vierfenstrig

LIMOUSINE

PHAETON

ROADSTER-CABRIOLET

05

04 Touching up the paintwork of a 1927 Wanderer Type W 10/I 6/30 hp tourer

05 Colored illustrations of various body styles for the six-cylinder Wanderer W 11, from a 1931 brochure

DKW – forging the Auto Union

Toward the end of World War I the founder of DKW, Rasmussen, encountered Hugo Ruppe in Zschopau. Ruppe had already gained a reputation as a designer of small air-cooled two and four-stroke engines in particular. Before the end of 1918 he had designed a ported 25 cc two-stroke engine for Rasmussen, which the latter exhibited at the 1919 Leipzig Spring Fair as a toy and instructional engine. In order to retain the DKW initials that had been applied to his steam-powered vehicle experiments, Rasmussen named this small engine "Des Knaben Wunsch" (literally: "The Boy's Wish").

In parallel with this toy engine, Hugo Ruppe developed a larger-capacity 118 cc engine with an output of 1 horsepower, which Rasmussen intended to sell as an auxiliary bicycle engine. This was exhibited at the Leipzig Autumn Fair, and was such an overwhelming success that plans were immediately made for it to go into production. Once again, the DKW initials were re-interpreted, this time as "Das kleine Wunder" ("The Small Miracle").

From that time on, Rasmussen had a clear picture of the direction his company should take: motorcycle and engine construction. His company was accordingly renamed "Zschopauer Motorenwerke J.S. Rasmussen" in 1921. In the period that

01

02

03, 04

05

followed, Rasmussen bought up a considerable number of metalworking companies in the German Erzgebirge region, and used them to supply components to the DKW factory in Zschopau. "Everything from a single source" was clearly his policy.

DKW's motorcycle production flourished. The company's advertising contained such encouraging claims as "DKW – the Small Miracle: goes up hills like the others come down!" By 1928, DKW was the largest motorcycle manufacturer in the world – an incredible success after only eight years. The key to this success was company management that was extremely well-informed on technical matters, combined with plenty of commercial talent. Above all, it was to Rasmussen's credit that he found the right people to put his ambitions into practice. Hugo Ruppe from Leipzig introduced him to the two-stroke engine; Friedrich Münz from Stuttgart offered him the "dynastarter," a unique combination of dynamo and starter motor that has a firm place in automotive history. Dr. Herbert Venediger was the first person in the company to subject the two-stroke engine to systematic analysis, whereupon he immediately discovered the work of Schnürle and recognized its immense importance for small-engine design in particular. Hermann Weber

was Chief Motorcycle Designer in Zschopau: his work was among the best on the market at that time.

One name above all deserves special mention: The Austrian, Dr. Carl Hahn, who was Rasmussen's personal assistant and combined an awareness of technical matters and commercial acumen with a dynamic approach rich in ideas. The DKW brand owed a considerable proportion of its image to his dedicated work. Hahn never forgot that success depended on far more than technical skills, and that organisation and management had to work together at the same high level. DKW built up a widespread network of factory-authorized dealers. They attended annual conferences and enrolled their mechanics for systematic training courses. This encouraged loyalty and maintained communication on both technical and commercial levels.

New paths were explored in marketing and sales as well. DKW was a pioneer of credit purchase for motorcycles; starting in 1924 a DKW could be bought for weekly installments of 10 Reichsmarks. Witty, intelligent advertising strategies also helped to make the DKW name widely known. At the end of the 1920s, the Zschopauer Motorenwerke possessed one of the German motor vehicle

01 The small two-stroke toy engine developed about 0.1 hp
02 Motorcycle production at the DKW factory in Zschopau, 1924
03 Dr. Carl Hahn (1894 – 1961) joined the Zschopau company in 1922 and built up a modern marketing and sales system
04 The factory operated a DKW publicity bus in the 1920s to support DKW dealers' advertising campaigns
05 DKW advertising artwork for the auxiliary bicycle engine, 1922

01

02

03

04

industry's most advanced sales organizations. An increasingly important source of funds for Rasmussen's expansion policy was the State Bank of Saxony. It had held 25 percent of DKW's shares since 1929 – easily its largest commitment in the State of Saxony at that time. There was clearly much to be said for amalgamating the remaining Saxon automobile companies, which were suffering badly from the world economic crisis. The Horchwerke, also borrowers on a considerable scale from the State Bank, were an obvious candidate, and the Dresdner Bank was prepared to offer the automobile division of the Wanderer Werke for sale if such a project could be organized. Audi had already been bought by the Rasmussen Group, but there were no plans to include commercial vehicles in the scheme. The concept of an "Auto Union," a conglomerate of automobile manufacturers in Saxony, took shape in Rasmussen's mind, with support from the Director of the State Bank, Dr. Herbert Müller.

Motorcycles

In view of the success of Ruppe's designs, Rasmussen decided to pin his faith entirely on the two-stroke engine. This had distinct disadvantages such as its loud, staccato exhaust note, its high fuel consumption, its poor braking effect and its tendency to oil up its spark plugs. Against this, compared to the four-stroke engine, the two-stroke principle produced higher power from a unit of equivalent size, considerably lower weight, the unrivalled simplicity of its petroil lubrication, the need for far fewer parts and the benefit of lower manufacturing costs.

Ruppe and Rasmussen regarded the advantages as decisive. The auxiliary engine for bicycles that they developed from the original miniature engine, the "Small Miracle" as it was called, was an indication of the path they intended to take. Sold initially as a 1 horsepower unit and later with 1.75 hp, the engine had forced-air fan cooling, a system of brilliant simplicity with the airflow produced by blades on the rotor of the flywheel magneto and guided round the cylinder by a sheet-metal jacket.

By November 1922 about 30,000 of these DKW engines were in use, and about 70 other motorized bicycle and lightweight motorcycle manufacturers were buying them for installation in their own products.

In due course a dispute arose between Rasmussen and Ruppe, which led to the latter leaving the company in 1921. His successor as Chief Engineer in Zschopau was the young Hermann Weber. Weber's handwriting, so to speak, can be seen on all the remaining DKW models that appeared up to the outbreak of World War II. Without him, it is difficult to imagine that DKW's technical development could have made such progress during those years.

Weber was also successful as a motor sport and racing rider for DKW. His first design for the company was the "Reichsfahrt" model, weighing 88 pounds and capable of reaching 25 mph. It was DKW's major step forward from the motorized bicycle to the genuine motorcycle.

The Lomos "chair bike" was developed at the same time. An ambitious design, especially in the suspension area, the final version had a cast

62

Auf einem 6PS Modell
da geht es mit der Liebe schnell.

Da steht schon eine Kleine
Im goldnen Sonnenscheine.
So süß wie eine Dattel,
Schielt nach dem leeren Sattel.

01 The 20,000th DKW auxiliary bicycle engine was produced on June 17, 1922

02 DKW built auxiliary engines for bicycles between 1919 and 1923. Rasmussen also offered customers bicycles with a reinforced frame, for installation of these engines

03 DKW introduced the Golem chair bike in 1921; it was a forerunner of the motor scooter

04 The Golem was followed by the Lomos chair bike, built in Zschopau between 1922 and 1925. A special feature of this model was its extremely light magnesium frame

05 A 1925 postcard showing the DKW Type ZM light motorcycle

05

Vom Gehalt abgeknappst

Ein preisgekröntes Bild aus dem letztjährigen DKW-Damen-Preisausschreiben (Frl. Marie Weinhold — Aachen)

Neues DKW-Preisausschreiben

für die besten Bilder von Damen auf ihrem DKW-Motorrad
Einzusenden bis zum 30. September 1927
Preise: Gesamthöhe RM 5000,— / 1. Preis RM 1500,— in bar
Nähere Bedingungen auf Anfrage

DKW-Einzylindermodell 206 ccm, Kassapreis RM **750**,— ab Werk,
Ratenzahlung wöchentlich RM **10**,—, Anzahlung RM **240**,—
Auf Wunsch führerschein- und steuerfrei RM **740**,—

DKW-Zweizylindermodell 500 ccm, Kassapreis RM **1275**,— ab Werk,
Wochenraten RM **17,50**, Anzahlung RM **365**,—
15 Monate Kredit!
Verlangen Sie die neuen Ratenbedingungen von der

ZSCHOPAUER MOTORENWERKE
J. S. RASMUSSEN A.-G.   ZSCHOPAU 31/SA.

magnesium frame and a rear swinging arm with coil-spring suspension strut. The back of the sheet-steel seat was formed by the fuel tank. The years that followed were also notable for a series of advanced ideas from DKW's engineers. One of the first was the E 206, which soon became a sales hit. Sold at 750 Reichsmarks, this motorcycle was on average between 100 and 200 Reichsmarks cheaper than similar products from competitors.

In 1928 all motorcycles with engines of up to 200 cc were exempted from road tax, and could be ridden without a driver's license. This opened up new prospects for the Zschopau company. The cylinder bore of this top-selling motorcycle was reduced by by 0.04 inches in order to bring its swept volume down from 206 to 198 cc. At the same time the cast iron piston was replaced by an aluminum one. For bikes already delivered – about 35,000 in all – conversion kits were made available without delay. The resulting E 200 made DKW the first, and for some months the only, manufacturer to offer a model in this new engine-size category. Demand was correspondingly high: in 1928, output rose from 5,000 to more than 65,000 motorcycles, with 375 motorcycles and 500 engines leaving the factory every day. No fewer than 450 complete motorcycles were produced on one occasion. It was announced not without pride that DKW had become the world's largest motorcycle manufacturer. Between 60 and 65 percent of all German motorcycles were either DKWs or were powered by a DKW engine;

03

records show that more than 60 German motor-cycle manufacturers installed these engines. Starting in 1929, a bolted pressed-steel frame was introduced step by step for all models larger than 200 cc, and achieved a worthwhile reduction in manufacturing costs.

At the same time, a transition to the modern saddle tank took place, and the motorcycle began to acquire a quite different, modern appearance. The unit-construction engine and transmission too was typical of the DKW motorcycle's styling and technical specification for more than ten years.

In 1931, Rasmussen happened upon a dissertation written by Dr. Herbert Venediger on "Improving the power output and economy of two-stroke carburetor engines for vehicles." In it, the author analyzed the reverse-flow scavenging principle put forward by Schnürle. Rasmussen was imme-diately aware of the promise that more intensive research into the two-stroke motorcycle engine had to offer. He hired Dr. Venediger to manage the testing department in Zschopau and instruc-ted him to look closely into the Schnürle principle, which had already been patented in 1924. The impressive advantages of this system were soon revealed: reduced thermal loads on the engine, so that the cooling fan or radiator could be dispensed with; improved fuel consumption, higher power output and the ability to use pistons with a flat crown which was clearly more efficient than the existing type with a high baffle and poor weight distribution, which was needed to

deflect the incoming mixture. On behalf of his Zschopau factory, Rasmussen wasted no time in acquiring the sole rights to the Schnürle patent for spark-ignition engines from the owner, Klöck-ner-Humboldt-Deutz AG, where Schnürle had been employed. In this way he once again paved the way for a technical breakthrough in two-stroke engine design; thanks to the ingeniously formulated and defined patent application, only DKW engines were able to benefit from this development at first. Competitors had no choice but to pay a considerable sum of money to DKW for a licence. It was not until 1950 that the patents governing this two-stroke principle expired.

Cars

In parallel with motorcycle development, Ras-mussen soon began to implement his plan to build cars with two-stroke engines. Shortly after the end of the war he examined a midget car built in Berlin by one Dr. Ing. Rudolf Slaby; it was driven by an electric motor located under the seat. Rasmussen got in touch with the designer at once, and with him set up the Slaby-Beringer Automobilgesellschaft mbH in Berlin-Charlotten-burg, in which he had a one-third stake. By June 1924, precisely 2,005 of these small electric cars had been built.

At the Berlin Motor Show held in the fall of 1923, the same vehicle was exhibited with a 170 cc, 2.5 hp single-cylinder DKW engine.

In 1924, Rasmussen took over the company com-

01 The introduction of payment by weekly installments of 10 Reichsmarks made the DKW E 206 one of Germany's top-selling motorcycles
02 A view of the frame construc-tion shop at DKW's Zschopau factory, 1927/28
03 The Slaby-Beringer electric car of 1921. Dr. Rudolf Slaby is at the steering tiller with Hermann Beringer behind him

01

01 The first car built by Zschopauer Motorenwerke was the
DKW P 15, introduced in 1928

pletely, but kept Slaby on as Director of what was now the Berlin DKW factory. It moved to Spandau in 1927, after which it developed electric vehicles jointly with AEG; these were used as taxicabs or delivery vans in city traffic. The load-bearing bodyshell was made of plywood covered with copper sheet. The electrical equipment was designed by Dr. Klingenberg. The vehicles were sold under the DEW brand name, in order to establish a link with DKW. In 1926/27, some 500 of them were allegedly in use in Berlin.

The first DKW small car with a two-stroke engine went on show at the Leipzig Spring Fair in 1928; its 600 cc engine developed 15 horsepower. The Slaby load-bearing construction principle was used, with a wooden frame paneled in plywood. The customary steel girder frame used in other motor vehicles was dispensed with. The body was covered with imitation leather to protect it in poor weather. The rear wheels were driven, and the front and rear axles both had transverse leaf spring suspension.

Although the two-stroke engine and the load-bearing wooden body with its imitation leather surface were unusual features in motor-vehicle construction, the subsequent success of these DKW cars, with sales in the hundreds of thousands, proved that their designers were by and large on the right track. By 1932, about 10,000 DKW cars with rear-wheel drive (including the 4 = 8 four-cylinder models) had been built in Spandau, an average annual output of 2,500.

New drive train

At this time the designers Gehle and Paffrath offered to sell Rasmussen an engine they had designed. It was a V4 two-stroke with the two cylinder blocks at an included angle of 90 degrees, each with a double-acting charge pump that filled one cylinder on the upward and one on the downward stroke.

The first of these cars, with an engine of just under 800 cc and an output of 22 horsepower, was delivered early in 1930. It was advertised

ZSCHOPAUER M

VERTRETER:

02

ambitiously as the "4 = 8," the aim being to suggest "four cylinders with the same effect as eight" to the general public accustomed to four-stroke engines. In this way Rasmussen acknowledged the trend in the late 1920s, when the German automobile industry was endeavoring to launch larger, more powerful six and eight-cylinder models in order to withstand competition, in particular from the United States.

DKW

ORENWERKE J. S. RASMUSSEN A.-G.
ZSCHOPAU

℗ Presse: Dr. Selle-Eysler A.-G. Berlin SW 29

02 A Zschopauer Motorenwerke advertising poster of 1928, showing a DKW P 15 and an E 200 motorcycle

03 A V4 two-stroke engine with charge pumps, from the 1930 DKW 4 = 8; it developed 22 hp from a displacement of 800 cc

04 The Type V 800 DKW 4 = 8, seen here with a two-seat convertible body, was introduced in 1930 and had a load-bearing wooden body

03

01 Various versions of the DKW
Front F 1 illustrated in a 1931
brochure

Viersitziges Cabriolet
Viersitzige Innensteuer-Limousine
Zweisitziges Cabriolet (2 Hilfs-Sitze)
Zweisitziger Roadster

01

02 Although compact in its dimensions, the DKW Front was a full-scale passenger car
03 The DKW Front's wooden body was supplied from the DKW coachbuilding factory in Spandau to the Audi factory in Zwickau, where final assembly took place
04 The DKW F1 was introduced at the IAA in Berlin in February 1931

04, 05

05 A DKW F 1 roadster with a steel body from the Schneider & Korb company
06 Diagram of the DKW front-wheel drive

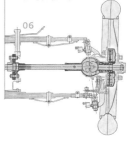

06

The large DKW with its V4 charge-pump engine was subjected to regular development in the years that followed. From 1932 onwards it was known as the DKW "Sonderklasse" (literally: "Special Class"). The customer was asked to pay 3,495 Reichsmarks for the car – a large sum in the prevailing conditions, but still reasonable value compared with what competitors had to offer. Rasmussen systematically developed his small-car program as well. After acquiring the Audi factory in Zwickau in 1928, he was searching for a worthwhile product to make use of the production capacity there.

In view of dwindling purchasing power as a result of the world economic crisis, Rasmussen was considering the manufacture of a small car with front-wheel drive. Some preliminary development work had been in progress in Zwickau since mid-1928, but there had been frequent delays in the development department there.

In September 1930 Rasmussen and Audi factory director Heinrich Schuh paid a surprise visit to the Audi design office. The company was clearly severely affected by the crisis. The yard was full of unsold cars, and of the 24 designers employed in better times, only two remained: Oskar Arlt and Walter Haustein.

Rasmussen called for a complete small car with front-wheel drive to be developed – and for the task to be completed within six weeks! Arlt and Haustein achieved what most people would have regarded as impossible: a prototype ready for its first road trials was finished in only 36 working days. Once again, Rasmussen reacted promptly: development work was to be over by January 1931, cars ready for sale were to go on display in February at the Berlin Motor Show.

Even these deadlines were complied with. The small DKW "Front" was one of the stars of the Berlin show. At 1,685 Reichsmarks, it was the lowest-priced car on the German market. Production of this front-wheel-drive DKW began in February 1931 at the Audi factory in Zwickau. This model also had a wooden body covered with imitation leather, but in contrast to the rear-wheel-drive DKW models, the front-wheel-drive principle called for the use of a subframe made from U-section girders.

This project from the Audi design office was not so much a new development as a highly ingenious combination of familiar, well-proven components. It not only set the Zwickau plant on the road to a new and extremely active future, but also stimulated the development and introduction of front-wheel drive cars for the first time on a worthwhile scale. Before the establishment of Auto Union, fewer than 5,000 DKWs with front-wheel drive had been produced, but after 1932 the proportion of new registrations accounted for by DKW Front cars reached significant levels.

01 Ove Rasmussen with a DKW
Front prototype at the Eibsee race
meeting early in February 1931
02 Between 1931 and 1933 the
DKW F 1 single-seater enjoyed
repeated successes in the small-
car racing category, for example
at the Eibsee ice racing meeting
in 1932
03 DKW attached great importance to its sporty image from
the very start, as this 1925 poster
by Ludwig Hohlwein demonstrates
04 The Eifel race on the Nürburgring circuit in June 1931 was the
first outing for the DKW F 1 single
seater

**Businesses established or bought by
the Rasmussen Group**

1919	Rota Magnet Apparatebau GmbH, Zschopau (flywheel magnetos)
1922	Metallwerke Zöblitz (fittings)
1923	Metallwerke Frankenberg, later Franken-berger Motorenwerke-Framo (motorcycle saddles, carburetors, three-wheel delivery vans from 1926 on); moved to Hainichen in 1934
1924	Takeover of the Slaby-Beringer company, Berlin (production of electric cars); from 1928 on, DKW's Spandau factory (cars and bodies)
1926	Takeover of the Scharfenstein factory formerly owned by Moll Werke (manu-facture of engines, cooling systems, pressed-steel components)
1927	Aluminiumgiesserei Annaberg (an aluminum foundry)
1927	Takeover of the Nestler & Breitfeld company of Erla in the Erzgebirge moun-tains (iron foundry, drop forging at the branch premises in Wittigsthal)
1928	Takeover of Audiwerke AG, Zwickau
1928	Takeover of the Schüttoff Werke, Chemnitz (motorcycles)
1930	Luma Werke, Stuttgart (dynastarters)

Company chronicle

1916	Experiments with steam-driven vehicles (until 1920)
1919	25 cc toy two-stroke engine known as "Des Knaben Wunsch" ("The Boy's Wish"); first auxiliary bicycle engine "Das kleine Wunder" ("The Small Miracle") introduced
1921	Company renamed Zschopauer Motorenwerke J.S. Rasmussen
1922	DKW trademark registered for engines and motorcycles
1923	Zschopauer Motorenwerke J.S. Rasmussen AG established on December 22
1924	Introduction of installment payment scheme for motorcycles
1928	World's largest motorcycle manu-facturer; start of DKW car production
1932	On June 29, the company amalga-mated with Horchwerke AG, Audi-werke AG and the Automobile Division of Wanderer Werke AG to form Auto Union AG, with head offices in Chemnitz

Motor sport

Even the company's first auxiliary bicycle engines, the "racing" versions of which were capable of reaching 40 mph, were entered for sporting events. DKW's first victory in this category was on September 20, 1920 in The Hague. Successful participation in the ADAC club's "Reichsfahrt" in the fall of 1921 attracted much attention. This victory led to the name of the first DKW motorcycle: the "Reichsfahrt" model. These first successes were achieved by private entrants, but in 1925 DKW formed a racing de-partment which began to build special versions of the company's products for use in competition. The fast DKW racing two-strokes soon acquired water cooling and a charge pump to boost the fuel-air mixture flow. The first 175 cc bikes were followed in 1928 by a 250 cc single-cylinder version with an output of 18 hp and a top speed of 81 mph. In the same year the twin-cylinder PRe 500 appeared: it developed 26 hp initially, later boosted to 32 hp. These engines were ex-tremely successful: DKW's advertising was able

02

to point to no fewer than 1,000 racing successes in only two years.

On the automobile scene, private DKW owners mainly took part in reliability trials in the early days. Their cars were in standard trim, as the following newspaper clipping from 1928 implies: "Miss Hildegard Kallweit of Danzig entered her DKW for the ADAC Overnight Rally from Danzig to Königsberg and back (249 miles) on the very day she took delivery of it, and won a silver trophy and a plaque."

The DKW factory in Spandau also established a racing department in 1920; Gerhard Macher, an extremely well-known Dixi/BMW competition driver, was appointed its manager. The sports cars were powered by the charge-pump twin-cylinder engine; among the successful drivers were Simons, Oestreicher, Macher and Bauhofer. In April 1930, at the Montlhéry racing circuit near Paris, racing driver Friedrich Carl Meyer took twelve international class records in a car developed by the aerodynamics expert Koenig-Fachsenfeld. The DKW was driven for 24 hours at an average speed of 56.9 mph! In 1931 the new DKW Front was entered for races with a single-seat body, and achieved considerable success, particularly in hillclimbs.

04

01

03

04

07

08

Horch – an overview

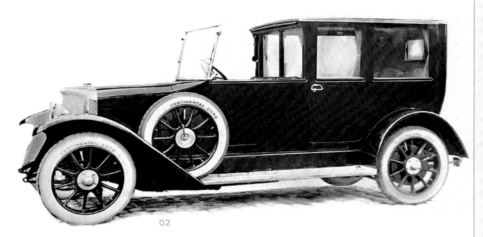

02

05

06

09

10

01

02

05

06

11

Audi – an overview

03

04

07

08

09

10

01 Audi Type C 14/35 hp Phaeton, 1925
02 Audi Type C 14/35 hp boat-tailed Phaeton, 1924
03 Audi Type E 22/50 hp sedan, 1923
04 Audi Type K 14/50 hp, 1924
05 Audi Type R Imperator, 19/100 hp, 1927
06 Audi Type SS Zwickau, 19/100 hp with Rickenbacker engine, 1929
07 Audi Type T Dresden 75 hp convertible, 1932
08 Audi Type P 5/30 hp, 1931
09, 10 Buses for service in Denmark, 1923/24
11 Audi Type M, 18/70 hp, 1924

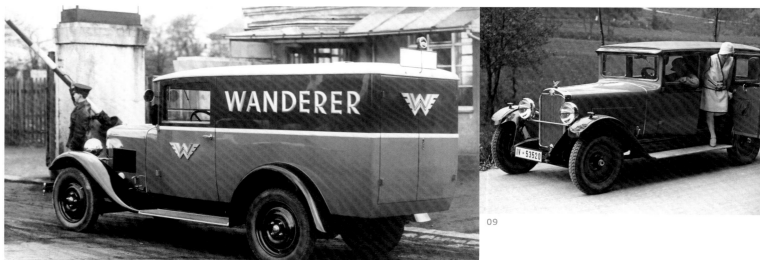

Wanderer – an overview

02

03

06

07

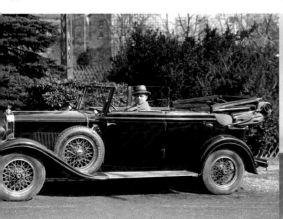

10

11

01 Wanderer W 6 6/18 hp, the first four-seater Wanderer, 1921

02 The Type W 6, the first series-production Wanderer sedan, 1923

03 Wanderer W 8 5/15 hp two-seater, 1921

04 Wanderer W 8 5/20 hp four-seater, 1925

05 Wanderer W 9 6/24 hp open tourer (phaeton), 1925

06 Wanderer W 10/I 6/30 hp, 1926

07 Wanderer W 10/IV 6/30 hp sedan, 1930

08 Wanderer W 10/IV 6/30 hp delivery van, 1930

09 Wanderer W 11 10/50 hp sedan, 1929

10 Wanderer W 11 10/50 hp four-door sedan cabriolet, 1931

11 Wanderer W 14 12/65 hp sports convertible, 1931

01

02

05

08

09

78

DKW – an overview

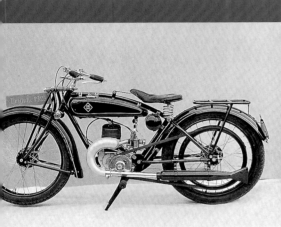

03

04

06

07

10

01 DKW auxiliary engine for motorized bicycles, 1919 – 1923
02 DKW Reichsfahrt model, 1922
03 DKW E 206, a best-seller from Zschopau, 1925
04 DKW Golem with horizontal single-cylinder two-stroke engine, 1921
05 DKW Luxus 200, nicknamed the "Blood Blister," 1929
06 DKW Super Sport 500, 1929
07 DKW P 15 convertible, 1928
08 DKW 4 = 8 (V 1000), 1931
09 DKW F 1 roadster, 1931
10 DKW F 1 convertible, 1931

The sign of the Four Rings

Auto Union AG, Chemnitz

01 The four-ring emblem was born when the Auto Union was formed. It symbolizes the inseparable unity of the four brands: Audi, DKW, Horch and Wanderer

02 The former Presto factory was converted to serve as Auto Union's administrative offices at the Group's headquarters in Chemnitz

03 The Wanderer assembly line in Siegmar near Chemnitz

04 The celebrated Mundorff poster, 1937

The company was established on the initiative of the State Bank of Saxony, which held the majority of the shares from the start (culminating in a 97% holding). On June 29, 1932, Audiwerke AG, Horchwerke AG and Zschopauer Motorenwerke J.S. Rasmussen AG joined forces to create Auto Union. At the same time a purchase and leasing agreement was concluded with the Wanderer company for the takeover of its car division. The new Board of Management consisted of Dr. Richard Bruhn, Jörgen Skafte Rasmussen and Klaus Detlof von Oertzen. Dr. Carl Hahn was appointed Deputy Director.

The founding companies retained their familiar brand designations. Auto Union AG of Chemnitz immediately became Germany's second-largest motor-vehicle manufacturing group. Its own emblem, with four intersecting rings, was mainly intended to symbolize the inseparable character of the new undertaking. In view of the varied product ranges that the individual companies were selling at the time, it took about three years for the desired concentration process to take effect and for a clear Auto Union profile to emerge. This can be seen in the model brochures dating

01

02

03

ILLUSTRIRTE ZEITUNG

NUMMER 4824 · Die älteste illustrierte deutsche Wochenschrift · 26. AUGUST 1937

V. MUNDORFF

Motorcycles

01 DKW motorcycles were made and sold in all engine-size categories from 100 to 500 cc

01

Small cars

02 DKW small front-wheel-drive cars dominated the small-car market up to 1-liter engine size

02

Midsize cars

03 Audi sold midsize cars with front-wheel drive until 1938
04 Wanderer cars represented Auto Union in the midsize class

03

04

Luxury market segment

05 Horch cars were the luxury-class market leaders in Germany

05

1932 – 1945 The sign of the Four Rings – Auto Union AG, Chemnitz

clearly based on the member companies' traditions, but was not averse to fundamental changes either. The primary emphasis, however, was on cost-cutting, above all by standardizing chassis frames, the four, six and eight-cylinder engines and the transmissions. Improving the vehicles' economy was another priority; in this context special attention was devoted to improved aerodynamics, in particular by adopting the principles patented by Paul Jaray and by conducting wind-tunnel tests. These principles reached series-production maturity on the DKW F 9 and the Horch 930 S. By 1935 all technical development was being coordinated by the new Central Design Office (ZKB) and Central Testing Department (ZVA) in Chemnitz, including work on the Audi 920, the DKW F 9, the Wanderer Types W 23 and W 24 and the Horch 930 S. Two-stroke engine research also went ahead enthusiastically there, with special emphasis on scavenging air blowers and injection pumps and nozzles. The search continued for a better form of scavenging than the Schnürle system. By 1939, two-valve two-strokes and engines with tubular-sleeve and rotary slide valves were under development. Auto Union AG of Chemnitz remained in existence for 16 years. Six of these were war years, and the liquidation process took another three, leaving only seven years – less than half of the company's lifetime – for it to demonstrate its powers of innovation and growth.

This was the period in which motoring progressed by leaps and bounds in Germany. Demand rose

from 1935 onwards: the cars' bodies became more standardized and various mechanical assemblies were shared between the models. This marked the end of decentralized model strategies. Auto Union's technical policy was

06 Since the Audi factory in Zwickau was entirely devoted to building DKW small cars, the Audi models were built at the Horch factory not far away

07 A DKW on the test rig at Auto Union's central test department, which was located on the Kauffahrtei in Chemnitz

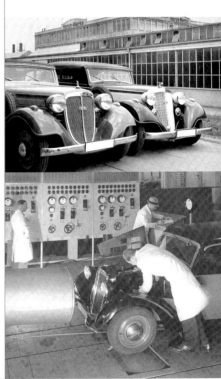

06, 07

08 One of Auto Union's earliest plans was to organize a central development and test department to serve all the group's brands. The building was handed over in 1936

08

01 The DKW F9, with three-cylinder two-stroke engine and a sheet-metal body developed with the aid of wind-tunnel tests, was intended to go into production in 1940 in response to the sales threat posed by the "KdF Car" (later the Volkswagen Beetle)
02 Since 1935 the Auto Union's central body development and design office in Chemnitz had drafted out the bodies for all the group companies' new models
03 The first drawings were followed by a one-fifth scale clay model

01

02

03

1932 – 1945 The sign of the Four Rings – Auto Union AG, Chemnitz

steeply, so that thorough preparations for long-term production were called for instead of many companies' prevailing "build to order" policy. New development and testing methods were also needed. The DKW F 8, launched in 1939, was one of the first cars in Germany for which not only a pre-production run as we would understand it today, but also a genuine pilot production batch of cars were authorized.

In 1936 the Central Development and Design Office run by Oskar Siebler and Werner Strobel began work on the DKW F 9 – not only as the latest front-wheel-drive model but also as

Auto Union's response to the challenge implied by announcements of the "Volkswagen," the forthcoming "people's car." The Saxon automobile group was the first and indeed the only German manufacturer to have a solution to the demands of mass motorization on hand. In 1940 it intended to offer the F 9 for sale with a 30 hp, three-cylinder two-stroke engine, front-wheel drive and a wind-tunnel tested body. A new engine factory took shape on the Chemnitzer Kauffahrtei, and there were plans to reduce the car's asking price to 1,200 Reichsmarks within five years.

04 A cavalcade including vehicles from all four Auto Union brands took part in the opening ceremony for the Frankfurt – Heidelberg highway in 1935

04

01

02

The Auto Union's Central Testing Department (ZVA) in Chemnitz was organized as three divisions: technical, scientific-technical and road testing. In connection with its development and testing work on the last pre-war DKW models, particularly those that reached production readiness with a plastic body developed jointly with the IG Farben company, it is interesting to note that Auto Union was the first German automobile manufacturer, in 1938, to draw up a well-founded, empirically based crash testing program with thoroughly modern criteria: even side-on impacts and sideways roll-over accidents were simulated. The sheer inventiveness of the Saxon automotive engineers is best documented by the granting of more than 3,000 patents at home and abroad. The company reaped the deserved rewards: in 1938 every fourth car newly registered in Germany was an Auto Union product, and every fifth had been built in Zwickau. Furthermore, every third motorcycle registered for the first time in Germany was a DKW.

03

04, 05

Company chronicle

1932 Backdated to November 1, 1931, Auto Union AG of Chemnitz was formed by amalgamating Zschopauer Motoren-werke J.S. Rasmussen AG (DKW), Horch-werke AG, Zwickau and Audiwerke AG, Zwickau, and by a lease and purchase agreement for the Wanderer Werke of Siegmar near Chemnitz.
Share capital: 14.5 million Reichsmarks

1943 Share capital on May 31: 20.3 million Reichsmarks

1943 Share capital on October 31: 30 million Reichsmarks

More or less overnight, Auto Union had become Germany's second-largest motor-vehicle manufac-turer. It expanded a further four times over in the following six years. Its consolidated turnover went up from 65 to 276 million Reichsmarks, and the workforce grew from 8,000 to more than 23,000. Annual motorcycle output rose from below 12,000 units to more than 59,000 and car output from just over 17,000 units to more than 67,000. Compared with the year in which Auto Union was established, the output of Horch cars had more than doubled by 1938; five times more Wanderer cars were being built and DKW's sales had gone up more than tenfold.

Auto Union's share of new motorcycle registrations in Germany was in the region of 35 percent in 1938; its share of new car registrations was 23.4 percent, and it accounted for 27 percent of German motor-vehicle exports.

Auto Union also became one of the major suppliers of vehicles to public authorities and the armed forces. By 1937/38, this market had reached a volume greater than the civilian sales of Audi, Horch and Wanderer taken together.

Orders 124 and 126 issued by the Soviet Military Administration in Germany (SMAD) on October 30 and 31, 1945, declared Auto Union AG of Chemnitz to be expropriated by the occupying powers; in 1948 its name was expunged from the trade register.

01, 02 In 1938, Auto Union was the first German automobile manufacturer to implement a modern crash testing program, including roll-over and side-on impacts
03 DKW final assembly using modern production engineering methods in Zwickau, 1937
04 In April 1933 Auto Union displayed its complete program at an exhibition in Mannheim
05 Variety in unity was demons-trated by the Auto Union product range at the Berlin Motor Show in 1939

Audi's new dynamism

01

01 Auto Union aimed to appeal
to customers interested in technically more challenging midsize
cars with its Audi Front
02 Although they had advanced
technical features under the skin,
Audi cars were of largely conventional appearance
03 This most attractive Audi
Front Roadster was an eye-catcher
at the 1935 Motor Show

Even before the new company group was established, Audi's design office had drawn up plans
for a new model. It was to have front-wheel drive
and a six-cylinder engine. The most suitable
source of power was considered to be the new
40 hp Wanderer engine designed by Ferdinand
Porsche. Its low weight of 287 pounds was
another point in its favor.

To keep the complete car as light as possible, a
box-section chassis frame was used, which in turn
encouraged the designers to adopt independent
suspension at the front and rear.

Auto Union exhibited this new Audi Front model
at the 1933 International Car and Motorcycle
Show in Berlin. Together with Stoewer and Bren-
nabor, the brand thus paved the way for front-
wheel drive to become accepted in the medium-
size car class.

Audi customers at that time were primarily
interested in comfort, convenience and ample
space rather than sheer performance. By the
mid-1930s a change had set in: dynamism and
sporting character gained in importance: the

car should be powerful, but not too large. In
accordance with company policy, the new Audi
was again to feature extremely progressive
design elements. Jaray's streamlined body out-
lines were considered, together with pulsating-
action automatic transmission. The car was to be
aimed at a specific buyer group with greater
awareness of automobile engineering developments – one that would appreciate the technical
merits of a car designed for sporty day-to-day
driving, and one that possessed the necessary
financial resources to adopt this approach.

In view of all this, the designers had to find more
power from somewhere. The Wanderer engines
had now been uprated to 55 hp and could not be
developed any further. The front-wheel-drive
shaft joints, too, were rated for a maximum
operating life of 18,641 miles. Since a top speed
of well over 75 mph was targeted, the only option
was to revert to conventional rear-wheel drive.
The new Audi 920 was the work of Auto Union's
Central Development and Design Department in
Chemnitz; since early 1934, Audi had had no

02

03

04

05

06

design office of its own. Instead of being able to adopt unusual technical features, and also because of the industry's permanent shortage of raw materials and the resulting delays in development schedules, there was no alternative but to be content with a modified standard body and various other well-proven design elements. The new six-cylinder OHC engine had a power output of 75 hp, enough to give the car a top speed of more than 81 mph.

04 Although the Audi 920's dashboard was made of sheet metal, its wood-grain finish and rectangular instrument dials were in keeping with the latest trends (1938)

05 All convertible bodies for the Audi 920 came from Gläser in Dresden

06 The Audi 920 sedan possessed various features characteristic of Auto Union's upper midsize cars. It was introduced at the end of 1938

der neue Au

3,2 Liter · 75 PS · 130 km Spitzengeschwindigkeit · 118 km Autobahn-Dauer

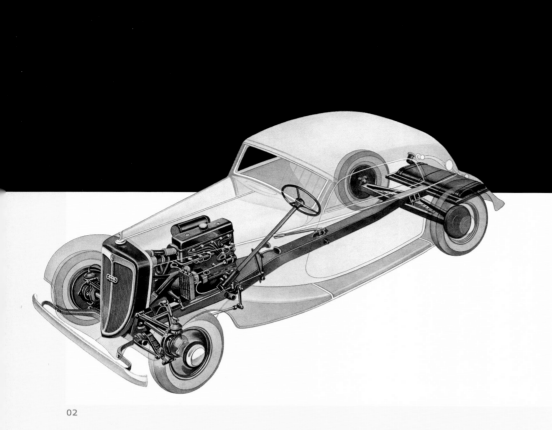

02

03

01

01 A deluxe version of the front-wheel-drive Audi 225 was the last version of this model to appear before series production ceased in 1938

02 Front-wheel drive, a box-section backbone frame and swing

axles were state-of-the-art features of the Audi concept in 1932

03 – 05 The Type 920 was a new departure for the Audi brand, combining ultra-modern technology, elegant styling and sublime pleasure of living

3,2 Liter · 75 PS · 130 km Endgeschwindigkeit · 118 km Autobahn-Dauerleistung

04

Auɒi

3,2 Liter · 75 PS · 130 km Endgeschwindigkeit · 118 km Autobahn-Dauerleistung

DKW – Auto Union's eco

DKW
AUTO UNION
Die neue RT 125

35 ccm - 5 - PS - Zweitaktmotor mit Umkehrspülung (Patent Dr. Schnürle), Batteriezündung, starke Gleichstrom - Lichtanlage mit 35/45 Watt Leistung, elektrisches Horn, Dreigang-Blockgetriebe mit Fußschaltung und Ganganzeiger, großdimensionierter gezeichneter Rohrrahmen für 185 kg Belastung, Gummifederung. Kraftstoffverbrauch: 2,25 Liter auf 100 km

Motorcycles

The years of economic crisis in 1929 and after led to DKW in Zschopau developing a very large range of motorcycle models. One of the aims was to make the most effective use of parts in stock, the other was not to miss even the smallest market opportunity in the engine-size categories between 175 and 600 cc. Major importance was attached at the same time to the ongoing technical development of the two-stroke engine, based to a large extent on adoption of the Schnürle loop scavenging principle. The first DKW motorcycle to be so equipped was the "Block 350,"

06

c foundation

introduced in 1932. The advantages included replacement of the raised-center piston by one with a flat crown, better temperature control, improved mass compensation, higher running speeds and increased power output. For many years, DKW motorcycles and DKW front-wheel-drive cars benefited from these advantages to an extent that should not be underestimated.

When Auto Union was established, the DKW motorcycle program was streamlined to a large extent. The much-praised SB series appeared in 1933/34, with engine sizes between 200 and 500 cc; some of these models were equipped with an electric starter (the "dyna-starter"). At the end of 1934 the RT 100 was added to the lower end of the range; it was sold at a list price of only 345 Reichsmarks. The RT 100 was DKW's most successful model: no fewer than 72,000 were built.

In 1937 DKW produced 55,470 motorcycles, of which 11,500 were exported, making it once again the world's largest motorcycle manufacturer.

In 1938, Germany accounted for approximately two-thirds of world motorcycle production: 200,000 units, about one-third of them DKWs. This was the year in which the NZ series began to succeed the SB models. There were three types, with 250, 350 and 500 cc engines. The largest model was the first DKW motorcycle to have rear suspension as standard equipment.

In 1939, twenty years after engines had first been produced in Zschopau, the RT 125 was introduced – the culmination of a long period of development, it set entirely new standards for a popular motorcycle. In a straightforward, practical and entirely logical manner, it embodied more than two decades of dedication to the Zschopau factory's fundamental concepts of simplicity, practicality, reliability, economy, long life and performance, all achieved at minimum expense and upkeep cost. This was the declared objective, and by and large it was attained. When the millionth DKW engine left the assembly line in March 1940, it was used – how could it have been otherwise – to power an RT 125.

During the war, the DKW factory in Zschopau was the only Auto Union location that was permitted to keep its established motorcycle models in production until the spring of 1945. Both the RT 125 and the NZ 350 were built in considerable numbers for the German Army. All the other Auto Union factories were obliged to switch at a much earlier date to making products for the war effort: trucks, tracked vehicles and aircraft components under license.

By 1945, Zschopau had turned out some 660,000 motorcycles.

07

01 For many people, the motorcycle was a new key to individual mobility. The picture shows a DKW NZ 250 with a Stoye sidecar, 1938
02 DKW SB 500 with sidecar, 1935
03 Summer delight with the DKW NZ 350, 1939
04 The RT 125 was a highly practical lightweight motorcycle, but it only reached the market in 1940 and therefore found scarcely any civilian buyers
05 The twin-cylinder DKW NZ 500 in use by the German Post Office in 1939
06 The Block 350 of 1932 was the first DKW motorcycle to use the Schnürle loop scavenging principle that revolutionized the two-stroke engine
07 A poster advertising DKW NZ models, 1939

01 DKW service van based on the
DKW Schwebeklasse, 1935
02 The "floating axle" principle,
with the characteristic high-
mounted transverse leaf springs
03 A special version of the DKW
Schwebeklasse folding-roof sedan,
1935

01

02

03

04

05

DKW passenger cars

Development of four-cylinder models went ahead in accordance with the strategy laid down by Rasmussen. For the new model year in 1933, a replacement for the "Sonderklasse" known as the 1001 was launched, to be joined later by a cheaper version, the 1002. As well as the four-seater folding-roof sedan, a four-door sedan was offered for the first time.

The "Schwebeklasse" ("Floating Class") followed in 1934, with a more powerful engine and an entirely new body. Its name was derived from the new suspension layout, with wheel location on the axis of the center of gravity, thus greatly reducing pitch and roll when cornering. This form of suspension called for a rigid axle with high-mounted transverse leaf spring. The "Schwebe-achse" ("floating axle") was protected as a trademark by Auto Union.

The same rear suspension principle was also used on DKW's front-wheel-drive cars from 1935 onwards, and in 1937 became a standard feature on Wanderer models as well.

Technical problems on the V4 charge-pump two-stroke engine proved difficult to solve. Although the design concept was convincing enough, production units incurred all kinds of unforeseen problems in the hands of the customers. Rectifying these shortcomings had an adverse effect on the brand image. Poor fuel consumption and a tendency for the pistons to seize were regularly complained of. During the next two years, extensive after-sales service campaigns were necessary before the defects could be largely eliminated.

The next model, introduced in February 1937, was the "Sonderklasse 37," an entirely new design. The body was of pressed steel rather than the load-bearing wooden body covered in imitation leather which DKW had used until then. The appearance of the "Sonderklasse" revealed its resemblance to the Wanderer W 24, which was also introduced in 1937. Both cars now had a full chassis frame, with the previous rigid front axle replaced by a low-mounted transverse spring combined with upper wishbones and with the

04 Introduction of the DKW Sonderklasse in the spring of 1937 meant a departure from the wooden body previously used for the large DKW
05 Highway rest area with DKW Sonderklasse, 1938

03

01, 02

96

shock absorbers pivoted on the wishbone axes. At the rear, the "floating" axle layout, which had proved highly successful, was retained, as was the four-speed transmission and the freewheel that was a typical DKW feature. The power unit was still the V4 charge-pump engine, though of revised design. Unfortunately not much could be done to minimize the sheer complexity involved in manufacturing and machining parts for the charge-pump engine, though the final version was certainly competitive. The medium-term plan, nonetheless, was to replace it by the three-cylinder engine which Carl Hahn had suggested as long ago as the fall of 1935, and which was due to appear in 1940: it developed the same power and was technically very much more straightforward.

About 25,000 large DKW models with the four-cylinder charge-pump engine were built, exclu-

sively at the DKW factory in Spandau, between 1932 and the end of production in 1940.

"Reichsklasse" and "Meisterklasse"

After 1932, DKW's front-wheel-drive cars, from Type F 2 to Type F 9, underwent further improvement. The loop scavenging principle (Schnürle license) adopted at the end of 1932 distinctly improved the engine's power delivery. In the spring of 1933 the DKW front-wheel-drive car program was divided into "Reichsklasse" (600 cc, 18 hp) and "Meisterklasse" (700 cc, 20 hp) models. With a specific power output of 30 hp per liter, the small DKW occupied a leading position among German cars of that time, and soon began to sell in quantity.

The F 5 model, which appeared in 1935, was given a box-section backbone frame with the "floating" rear suspension layout, the patented system

04

05

01

02

DKW

AUTO UNION

wirtschaftlich · fahrsicher · formschön

03

01 Preparing for a journey in the
DKW F 5 Front-Luxus convertible
(left) and the F 5 Meisterklasse
folding-roof sedan, 1935
02 A contemporary color photo
of the DKW F 5 Roadster, 1935
03 The DKW de luxe convertible's
attractive styling often earned it
the description "baby Horch."
This 1938 poster shows the four-
seater F 7 Front-Luxus convertible

that had already demonstrated its advantages
on the four-cylinder cars. At the same time, two
attractive cars were added to the DKW front-
wheel-drive programme, and billed as "Front-
Luxus" models in the upper section of the DKW
price list. One was an extremely elegant two-seat
full convertible, the other a sports roadster.
Both had a pressed-steel body and high-quality
interior trim in genuine leather. In 1936 a four-
seat convertible joined this range of deluxe front-
wheel-drive models.

With certain modifications only, notably the
introduction of a completely new type of frame
for the F 8, the basic design with its twin-cylinder,

two-stroke engine in unit with the front-wheel-
drive transmission was retained until the end.
Export-only Type F 7 and F 8 models were an
unusual feature. They included a four-door sedan
and in particular the "Meister Super" with a
pressed-steel body specially intended for tropical
regions; certain elements were the same as for
the "Sonderklasse" body of 1937.

At that time the DKW front-wheel drive cars
were among the small cars built in the highest
volume anywhere in the world, and also the
leading pioneers of front-wheel drive for passenger
cars. They were extremely popular in other
countries too, and were in fact built in Switzerland, Denmark and Australia, but also exported
in considerable numbers to European countries
and to South America, South Africa and India.
One of the most interesting research projects
was the development of plastic bodywork, with
the various elements molded at high pressure
from phenolic resin reinforced with paper. A
series of prototypes was built and their behavior
tested in a variety of ways including crash and
rollover tests from 1938 onwards. The outbreak of hostilities put an end to this research
program, but it was revived after the war both by
the new Auto Union in West Germany and at the
former factory in Saxony. The best-known result
of this work first appeared in 1958: the IFA
Trabant.

98

Company chronicle

Another project to which great importance was attached in both East and West Germany in the post-war years was the development of a front-wheel-drive DKW with a three-cylinder, two-stroke engine and a streamlined body. This car was given the next available type designation, namely F 9. Its body, based on Jaray's patents, was developed by wind-tunnel testing. Series production of this model was planned for 1940, but the outbreak of war meant that only ten prototypes were built.

About 260,000 DKW Front cars were built at the Zwickau factory between 1931 and 1942, by an average workforce of 1,350. In addition, nearly 8,000 DKW Front models were assembled at the Spandau factory.
DKW's share of new registrations reached approximately 19 percent in 1938, so that effectively every fifth new car in Germany was a DKW.
The lowest-priced DKW was the two-seater F 7 and F 8 folding-top sedan with 18 hp, engine, which sold at 1,650 Reichsmarks. The "Front-Luxus" four-seater convertible with pressed-steel body cost 3,400 Reichsmarks.

04 The Baur coachbuilding company in Stuttgart built the body for this 1939 DKW F 8 Front-Luxus convertible
05 A weekend trip in the DKW F 8 Meisterklasse folding-top sedan, 1939
06 Only a few prototypes of the DKW F 9 with stream-lined body were built between 1939 and 1942. This model formed the basis for post-war DKW passenger cars

D·KW RT-3 PS

V. MUNDORFF

DKW
SB 300
SB 350

Kolt BWM

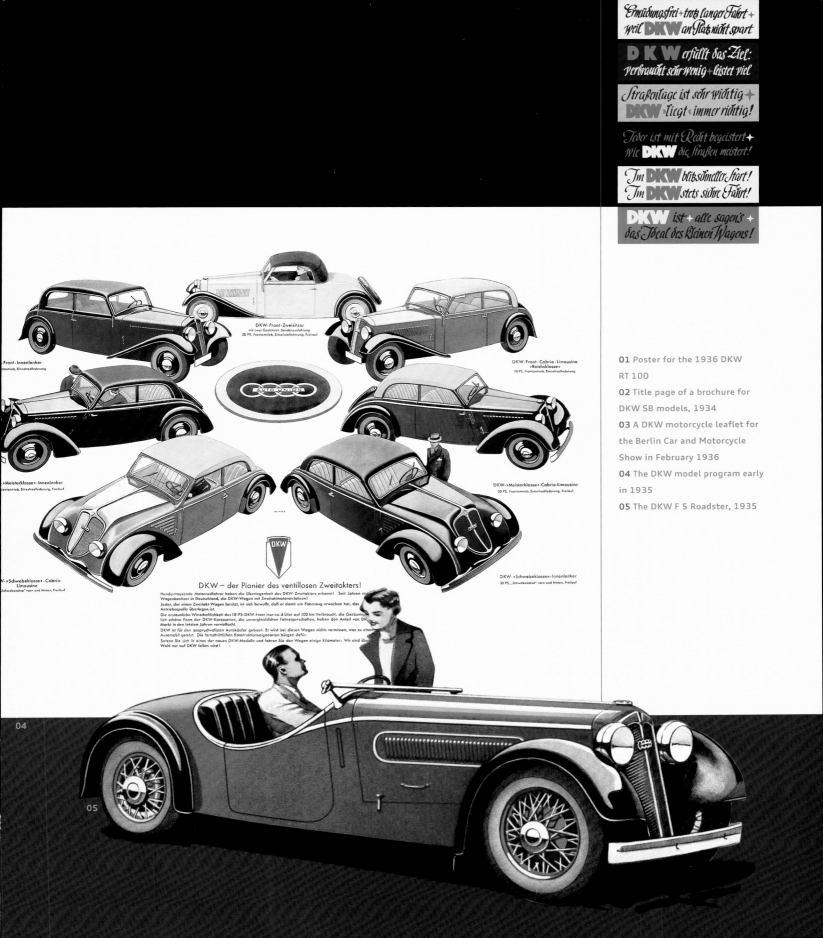

DKW-Front-Zweisitzer
mit zwei Gastsitzen Sonderausführung
20 PS, Frontantrieb, Einzelradfederung, Freilauf

DKW-Front-Cabrio-Limousine
›Reichsklasse‹
18 PS, Frontantrieb, Einzelradfederung

‹Front-Innenlenker
antrieb, Einzelradfederung

AUTO UNION

›Meisterklasse‹-Innenlenker
antantrieb, Einzelradfederung, Freilauf

DKW-›Meisterklasse‹-Cabrio-Limousine
20 PS, Frontantrieb, Einzelradfederung, Freilauf

V-›Schwebeklasse‹-Cabrio-
Limousine
Schwebeachse" vorn und hinten, Freilauf

DKW-›Schwebeklasse‹-Innenlenker
30 PS, "Schwebeachse" vorn und hinten, Freilauf

DKW

DKW — der Pionier des ventillosen Zweitakters!

Hunderttausende Motorradfahrer haben die Überlegenheit des DKW-Zweitakters erkannt! Seit Jahren st
Wagenbesitzer in Deutschland, die DKW-Wagen mit Zweitaktmotoren fahren!
Jeder, der einen Zweitakt-Wagen besitzt, ist sich bewußt, daß er damit ein Fahrzeug erworben hat, das
Antriebsquelle überlegen ist.
Die erstaunliche Wirtschaftlichkeit des 18-PS-DKW-Front (nur ca. 6 Liter auf 100 km Verbrauch), die Geräumig
lich schöne Form der DKW-Karosserien, die unvergleichlichen Fahreigenschaften, haben den Anteil von DK
Markt in den letzten Jahren vervielfacht.
DKW ist für den anspruchsvollsten Autokäufer gebaut: Er wird bei diesen Wagen nichts vermissen, was zu einem
Automobil gehört. Die fortschrittlichen Konstruktionseigenarten bürgen dafür.
Setzen Sie sich in eines der neuen DKW-Modelle und fahren Sie den Wagen einige Kilometer: Wir sind übe
Wahl nur auf DKW fallen wird !

04

05

Ermüdungsfrei + trotz langer Fahrt +
weil DKW an Platz nicht spart

DKW erfüllt das Ziel:
verbraucht sehr wenig + leistet viel

Straßenlage ist sehr wichtig +
DKW liegt immer richtig!

Jeder ist mit Recht begeistert +
wie DKW die Straßen meistert!

Im DKW blitzschneller Start!
Im DKW stets sichre Fahrt!

DKW ist + alle sagen's +
das Ideal des kleinen Wagens!

01 Poster for the 1936 DKW
RT 100
02 Title page of a brochure for
DKW SB models, 1934
03 A DKW motorcycle leaflet for
the Berlin Car and Motorcycle
Show in February 1936
04 The DKW model program early
in 1935
05 The DKW F 5 Roadster, 1935

Horch – setting the tone in the luxury car class

The first new product from Horch after the creation of Auto Union was the 3-liter V8 engine developed by Fritz Fiedler. From 1933 onwards it was used in the forthcoming "small" Horch. By virtue of its number of cylinders and displacement, it was known as the 830. In a similar way, the "large" Horch was known as the 850 because of its 5-liter straight-eight engine.

Beauty on the move
One of Horch's finest-looking production cars was exhibited at the 1935 Berlin Motor Show: a two-door, four- to five-seater sports convertible with a two-window body and admittedly monumental but nonetheless stylish lines. With the luggage rack extended, it was almost 20 feet long; over its boldly curved running boards, it was 5.9 feet wide. The attraction went below the splendid outer skin as well: the chassis was an entirely new development. The front swing-axle suspension featured two transverse leaf springs and wishbones. At the rear there were double universal-joint halfshafts and a De Dion axle tube. As a result this large car's roadholding was outstanding. The smaller Horch models had already acquired this independent front suspension, and shortly afterwards were given the new rear axle layout as well.

In addition to these running-gear improvements, the manufacturer's main concern was to increase power output. The opulent luxury equipment of these bodies took a severe toll in terms of weight, but more powerful engines were still some way from production readiness. It was not impossible to boost the output of the existing units: the 5-liter engine was accordingly given a camshaft with more aggressive valve timing and a higher compression ratio, which boosted its output to 120 horsepower. Similar measures applied to the smaller V-engine proved even more satisfactory: its initial power output of 62 hp went up to 70 and later to 82 hp in 1937, and by 1938/39, a figure of 92 hp had been reached – an increase of almost 50 percent in power output from the

same basic design. The car's performance now gave no grounds for complaint. On November 25, 1938, testers from the *Allgemeine Automobil Zeitung*, one of Germany's most reputable car magazines, drove the Horch 930 V with the 92 hp 3.8-liter engine on the highway from Munich to Berlin in 3 hours, 53 minutes, an average speed of 85 mph! Like most Horch cars from that year on, the car was equipped with the company's "motorway gear" transmission, a planetary gear train with synchromesh attached to the main transmission, and containing a direct-drive ratio and a higher ratio which reduced the engine speed when the car was in use on one of Germany's new high-speed main roads. The effect was the same as with the overdrives or high top gears frequently offered in later years.

01

01 The large Horch had a characteristic front-end appearance, with large radiator grill and headlights, marker lights, fog lights and powerful horns

04

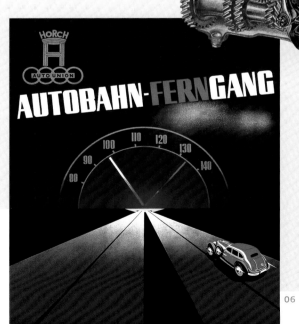

02 The Pullman sedan on the long-wheelbase V 8 chassis was popular with those seeking a distinguished business conveyance
03 About 2,000 of these four-door "sedan cabriolets" on the long-wheelbase V 8 chassis were sold
04 The Horch Type 853 sports convertible is regarded now as one of the most attractive cars of the 1930s. It was introduced early in 1935 and more than a thousand were sold by 1939

05

HORCH
AUTO UNION
AUTOBAHN-FERNGANG

100   110   120
90   130
80   140

05, 06 In 1938 Horch began to supply the ZF "motorway gearbox" as an optional extra. It lowered the engine speed and kept fuel consumption low at high speeds

06

Höchstgeschwindigkeit jetzt Dauergeschwindigkeit durch verringerte Motordrehzahlen! Bei 130-140 km wird der Motor nicht mehr beansprucht, als bisher bei 90-100 km

03

04

05

Horch's car designers had an abundance of far-reaching ideas and innovations up their sleeves, so to speak, for forthcoming models. One of the most dramatic examples was the streamlined body for the 930 S, developed in the wind tunnel in accordance with Paul Jaray's patents. It was displayed at the 1939 Motor Show. The body had no B-post, and for the first time there was a full-width bench seat at the front instead of the usual separate seats. The body's aerodynamic drag coefficient (c_d) was 0.43, far lower than any rival model. Such developments by Auto Union were evidence that it had identified future trends in automotive technology more clearly and effectively than other manufacturers.
The demand for Horch cars had already risen rapidly, and by the summer of 1939 customers were obliged to wait up to nine months for delivery.
August Horch had declared many years before that he intended, come what may, to build only large, powerful and above all good cars. In this respect, nothing had changed at the company that bore his name. In the 1920s and 1930s, the Horch company employed only the very finest designers. Zoller, Daimler and Fiedler created and shaped the Horch power-unit culture, the refinement of which has remained a byword to this very day.

01 Sports convertibles and special roadsters were always the highlights in the Horch program, even though they were only built in small numbers. This applied to the 930 V ...
02 ... and also to the Type 855, both dating from 1938
03 Convertibles on a long-wheelbase chassis were a challenge to the stability of the body, for instance this 851 Pullman
04 The final innovation from Horch: the ultra-modern model exhibited in 1939 combined a great tradition and far-sighted progress
05 The Horch 930 S seen at the 1939 Berlin Motor Show had a pillarless streamlined body developed in the wind tunnel and a high standard of interior equipment and trim

01 – 03 With its long wheelbase of more than 12.14 feet, the large Horch models, especially the Pullman types, provided extremely generous interior space
04 Driver's area of the Horch 8
05 The 25,000th Horch eight-cylinder car left the factory in Zwickau on July 25, 1937

04

Company chronicle

05

06 A Horch 951 convertible with body by Erdmann & Rossi, Berlin
07 At 22,500 Reichsmarks the 951 Pullman convertible was the most expensive standard Horch model ever produced. At the time, this money would have bought a house for the family

Apart from the V12 units, Horch built only eight-cylinder engines from 1927 onwards – almost 70,000 of them by the time production ceased. None of its German rivals succeeded in matching this figure. The Horch 8 symbolized the quality expected of a top product from the German automotive industry. Its reputation was based on quietness and high-quality workmanship: for the production of these large engines, the Zwickau engineers could call upon a concentration of skills and know-how unique in Germany. The crowned H emblem was effectively synonymous with the contemporary concept of the elegant, distinguished car. The Horch name stood for the finest manufacturing precision and for restrained substance combined with elegance and an exceptionally high standard of luxury travel. As the annual registration figures confirm, Horch gained an increasingly firm grip on the luxury car class (engine size above 4 liters). In 1938, about 55 percent of the large cars registered in Germany had the crowned H adorning their radiator grill. Even in the class below, that is to say with engines between 3 and 4 liters' displacement, Horch maintained a very strong sales position.

About 15,000 Horch 8 cars had been built by Auto Union AG by the time production for civilian purposes ceased in the spring of 1940. The 25,000th Horch 8, counting from the start of production in 1927, had already left the production line in Zwickau in July 1937. From 1934/35 to 1942 about 45,000 special-purpose military vehicles were also built.
The Horch workforce amounted to more than 3,000 wage-earning and salaried employees. In Germany's 1938 new-car registration statistics, the Horch brand accounted for a 21.7 percent share of the market in the 3 to 4-liter class, with 55 percent of the class with 4-liter engines or larger.
The "small" V8 Horch cost 8,500 Reichsmarks as a sedan and 9,700 Reichsmarks as a convertible. The "large" Horch, with straight-eight engine was sold for 17,500 Reichsmarks as a Pullman sedan and for 15,250 as the Type 853 sports convertible. The open Type 951 six-seater, at 23,550 Reichsmarks, was the most expensive Horch in the company's standard program.

06

07

01

02

1932 – 1945 The sign of the Four Rings – Horch – setting the tone in the luxury car class

01 The Horch 930 V was launched in 1937. At 122.05 inches, the V 8 chassis had a short wheelbase, which made the car lighter and faster than the previous model
02 The 830 Bl four-door convertible was only available on a long-wheelbase chassis

Wanderer – quality and advanced engineering in the midsize class

01

01 In 1931 Ferdinand Porsche designed a new family of six-cylinder OHV engines for Wanderer. They first reached the market in the fall of 1932 in the Types W 15 and W 17

02 Wanderer W 21 sedan (right) and W 22 convertible, 1933

03 Wanderer W 24 convertible with four-cylinder engine, 1937

04 Wanderer W 21 delivery van, 1934

Wanderer cars went through their most radical modernization process shortly before the Auto Union era began, when the 1.7 and 2.0-liter six-cylinder OHV engines designed by Ferdinand Porsche were introduced. These engines were the dowry, so to speak, that the bride brought into the Auto Union marriage.

At the Berlin Motor Show in February 1933, the new Wanderer W 21 and W 22 models that were to be the cornerstones of the company's program for some years were launched. The Porsche six-cylinder engine was installed in a new chassis with swing-axle independent rear suspension as a special feature; independent front suspension had to wait until 1936. The cars' appearance was changed to such an extent by more modern body-work that not only loyal, conservative customers but also less conservative, upwardly mobile buyers found it attractive. All these innovations were completed in a very short time and gave the Wanderer model program a sound basis for approximately the next five years.

In 1936, however, a new Wanderer body, the W 51 Special, was exhibited at the Berlin Motor Show; it was of importance not only to the brand itself but also to the entire Auto Union group. This was the first time that a body concept valid for all Auto Union's upper midsize cars had become available – a sign that the four brands, although still on sale separately, had formed a single overall concept for the group and its products. A year later the unification process was taken a stage further with an entirely new Wanderer model line. This was indeed new: the side-valve engines, the chassis and the bodies had not been seen before. For the first time the task of standardization and the use of shared components and assemblies had been adopted effectively. This Wanderer enjoyed greater sales success than at any time in the manufacturer's previous history.

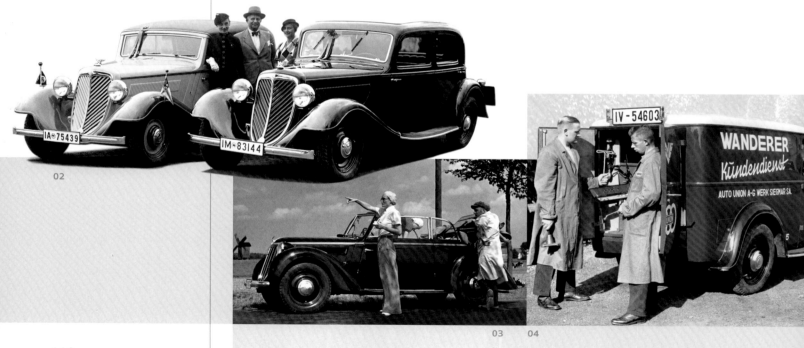

02

03 04

WANDERER
SPEZIAL W 51 CABRIOLET

05 Auto Union referred to the
new Wanderer radiator from 1936
on as "Reshaping the Outline."
The picture shows the front end
of the W 25 K sports car
06 Victor Mundorff's poster
advertising the Wanderer W 51
in 1936

01

02

01 The Wanderer Type W 23 six-
cylinder convertible, 1939
02 The distinguished Wanderer
Type W 26 Pullman sedan, 1937
03 The Wanderer W 25 K sports
car was announced in 1936. This
was the title page of the brochure

*From his report on technical
progress to the Auto Union's
Supervisory Board on May 3, 1939,
with reference to the new Auto
Union transmission under development for Wanderer cars*

Automatic shift ...

*"A transmission should be developed with three
regular ratios incorporating synchromesh and a
fourth gear acting as an automatic overdrive,
which would cut in by itself at a speed still to be
determined. Assuming that the car's top speed
will be about 75 mph, it would be best for this
overdrive ratio to engage at 50 mph. However, to
permit rapid passing, the third gear should be
re-engaged if the driver depresses the accelerator
pedal fully, say at 56 mph. After this, the overdrive ratio would not be engaged again until the
car had reached 62 mph. This would avoid any
risk of the engine over-revving in any circumstances and would make operation at speeds
above 50 mph considerably more economical."*

William Werner, Auto Union AG's Technical Director

The W 23 designation for the six-cylinder model
(2.7 liters, 62 hp), with W 24 for the four-cylinder
version (1.8 liters, 42 hp) continued the customary
Wanderer naming system. The W 25 K, on the
other hand, was not only an extremely attractive
sports car but also rather special in another way:
it was powered by a supercharged version of
Porsche's six-cylinder engine and also had the
new standard chassis with independent suspension at the front and the group's "floating" axle
layout at the rear.
Only the large Wanderer Pullman sedan, known
from 1937 on as the W 26 and powered by the
new 2.7-liter side-valve six-cylinder engine, was
still equipped with swing-axle rear suspension.
This was unavoidable because the rear seats had
to be located above the rear axle in a car with this
body style, which left insufficient space for the
"floating" rear axle's high-mounted transverse
leaf spring.

03

V. MUNDORFF

The W 26 was the last model number to be allocated by this brand. A Pullman sedan with double universal-joint rear axle was originally planned for production as the W 28, but the plan was abandoned as it was felt that the design was too similar to Horch's models. Wanderer cars under development for the period after 1940 were to appear with simplified model names, as the W 4 (four-cylinder) and W 6 (six-cylinder). Here too, versions with a streamlined body similar to the DKW F 9 were envisaged, but as in other cases too, the project was halted by the outbreak of war.

At the end of 1942 the last of the Wanderer Type W 23 cars were delivered. After the war there were plans both in Ingolstadt and in Chemnitz to restart production of the Wanderer W 24 in order to have a midsize car in the program, but the extremely difficult conditions that

Company chronicle

74,000 Wanderer cars were built between 1932 and 1942. Their share of total German new-car registrations was approximately 5 percent, but in the class between two and three liters they often exceeded 40 percent (for instance in 1937).
The average workforce at the Auto Union factory in Chemnitz-Siegmar, where the cars were built, was 3,220.
Wanderer cars were sold at prices between 3,875 and 6,950 Reichsmarks.

prevailed in the reconstruction phase after 1945 prevented any such projects from being undertaken.

04 In addition to the roadster, the Wanderer W 25 K was sold as a sports convertible

04

Motor sport – races, victories and records

01

01 The Auto Union mid-engined Grand Prix racing car
02 In its final development stage the 16-cylinder engine designed by Porsche developed 520 hp
03 With their superior technology, Auto Union and Mercedes-Benz dominated Grand Prix racing in the 1930s
04 Motor sport had immense public appeal, with spectators flocking to the racing circuits by the hundred thousand

The four brands that formed the Auto Union differed in their motor sport traditions. Audi's golden age had been before World War I, with successes for the Audi team in the 1912, 1913 and 1914 International Austrian Alpine Run. In these three events, eleven first prizes and the coveted trophy itself had been won.

With its motorcycles, DKW undoubtedly qualifies as the most successful brand in motor sport. A racing department was formed in 1927 at the Zschopau factory, with August Prüssing as its manager. Two years later, the company's advertising was able to claim no fewer than a thousand race victories. Many great names were associated with DKW at that time: Walfried Winkler, Arthur Geiss, Ewald Kluge and others.

Like Audi, Horch's greatest motor sport successes were gained before World War I. In 1906 it won the Herkomer Run and followed this up with numerous victories in reliability trials in Scandinavia and Russia. After only moderate success on the Avus circuit in 1922 and 1923, the company maintained a lower motor sport profile. In 1929, however, Prince zu Schaumburg-Lippe caused a sensation by competing in the Monte Carlo Rally in an almost standard Horch 350 Pullman limousine reaching the finishing line as the only German driver within the time limit and securing a creditable nineteenth place overall. Not long after this, Horch cars began to record one success after another in a different

kind of competition, the newly fashionable gymkhanas and "concours d'élégance" where good looks and high quality were the criteria. Horch models were entered for these competitions in large numbers, and frequently swept the board.

Wanderer joined the motor sport scene in 1922, by entering for the Targa Florio, but this brave attempt to reach for the stars remained a one-off occurrence. It was not until the end of the decade that cars bearing the winged "W" emblem began to notch up victories in arduous long-distance events such as the Alpine Run and Ten Thousand Kilometer Run in 1931. Although the brand was never especially prominent on the motor sport scene, it did make a specific contribution to the Auto Union's subsequent glory: it was the Wanderer company that commissioned Porsche to design a racing car, an order placed with him by Managing Director Klee during the Paris Motor Show in the fall of 1931.

After establishment of Auto Union, a department was opened on March 7, 1933, in Zwickau to build racing cars. The existing motorcycle racing department continued to operate from Zschopau, and in 1934 a new factory motor sport department was organized in Chemnitz with August Momberger as its manager, to coordinate the Group's entire off-road, reliability trial and long-distance racing activities.

02

03   04

114

06

The public's attention was naturally focused on the new racing cars bearing the four-ring badge. For the first time, the sixteen-cylinder engine was installed behind the driver; it initially developed 295 hp, and was shown to the world on March 6, 1934, precisely 365 days after work had started on it. Hans Stuck took the brand-new car round the Avus circuit on that date, and immediately began to notch up world records. During the next racing season, Stuck won the German, Swiss and Czechoslovakian Grand Prix races. He was also successful in the major hill-climbs and was runner-up in the Italian Grand Prix and at the Eifel race. With this new car he took the German road racing champion's and hillclimb champion's titles.

05 For hillclimbs, Auto Union used short-chassis versions of its racing cars, as seen here in 1939 on the Grossglockner Pass

06 Even after its very first season the Auto Union racing car developed by Ferdinand Porsche could look back on an impressive list of successes

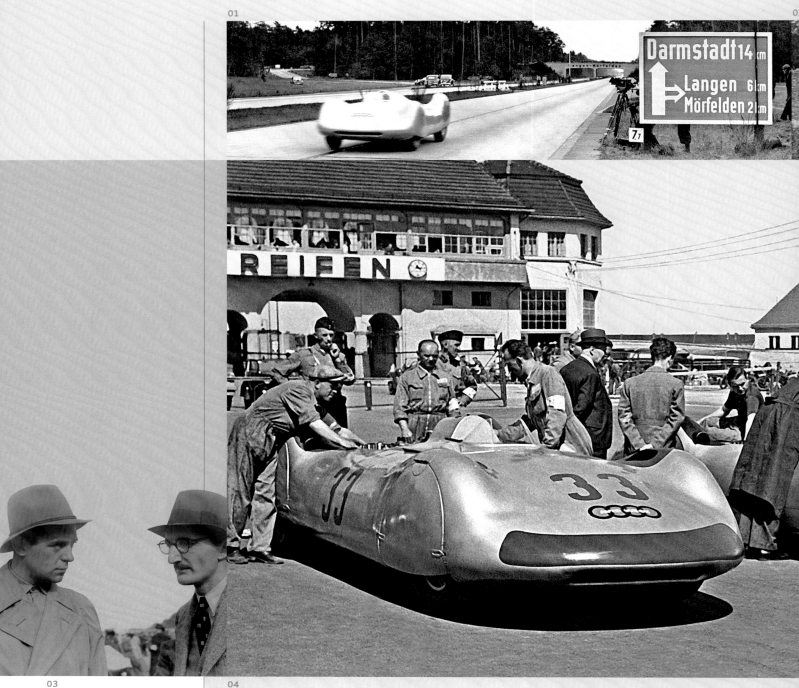

04

01 During speed record attempts held in October 1937 on the highway between Frankfurt and Darmstadt, Bernd Rosemeyer in the Auto Union Type C reached more than 249 mph for the first time on a public highway

116

The other founding members of the Auto Union racing team were Prince Leiningen and August Momberger, with the star Italian driver Achille Varzi joining a year later. Bernd Rosemeyer began to make a name for himself within the team from 1935 onwards. Other drivers who joined the team were Ernst von Delius, Rudolf Hasse and H. P. Müller, and in 1937 another top-class Italian driver, Luigi Fagioli, was seen behind the wheel of the sixteen-cylinder Auto Union racing car. By the end of 1937, it had been entered for 54 races

1932 – 1945 The sign of the Four Rings – Motor sport – races, victories and records

possible for speed-record attempts. It is interesting to note that the corresponding engine speed only rose from 4,500 to 5,000 revolutions per minute, yet the peak torque went up from 54 mkg at 2,700 rpm to 87 mkg at 2,500 rpm. The power-to-weight ratio improved from 6.17 to 3.31 lb/hp, in other words by almost half! For the new three-liter formula that was applicable from 1938 on, Auto Union unveiled the Type D, developed by test engineer Eberan-Eberhorst after Ferdinand Porsche had ceased to be involved. The new car had a supercharged V12 engine with three camshafts; its initial power output, in accordance with the requirement specification, was 420 hp. By the end of 1939 the engine was delivering almost 485 hp from an unchanged swept volume of three liters – nearly as much as an engine twice the size had developed only a few years earlier. Following Bernd Rosemeyer's fatal accident during a record-breaking run on January 28, 1938, his place as the team's top driver was taken by the Italian Tazio Nuvolari, supported by Hans Stuck, Rudolf Hasse, H.P. Müller and, for one season, the Swiss driver Christian Kautz. In 1939 the legendary racing motorcyclist "Schorsch" Meier also joined the team. Although victories were not as frequent as under the previous 1,653-pound formula, the Zwickau engineers, mechanics and drivers nonetheless scored many an impressive triumph.

Auto Union's total financial outlay on Grand Prix racing amounted to just under 15 million Reichsmarks. Since 1935, the racing department had maintained a large store of components and assemblies – engines, clutches, superchargers and complete frames – from which cars were built up. As a result the actual cars were never the same from one race meeting to the next. After World War II the Soviet occupying powers in East Germany took possession of the remaining Auto Union racing cars and shipped them back to the Soviet Union as reparations, where they were made available to the indigenous automobile industry for testing purposes.

and won 32 of them. In the same period, it also set 15 new world records and 23 class records.

Ferdinand Porsche's original design for the racing car was steadily improved from one season to the next. The successive development stages were identified by capital letters: A for 1934, B for 1935, C for 1936 and 1937. In that time the engine's displacement went up from 4.3 to more than 6 liters and the maximum power output to 520 hp, though a figure as high as 560 hp was

02 What proved to be the last appearance of the Auto Union racing cars was on September 3, 1939: while the Belgrade Grand Prix was being run, the guns were already firing in Poland – World War II had broken out
03 Bernd Rosemeyer and racing engineer Robert von Eberan-Eberhorst
04 The streamlined racing cars enjoyed their first triumph at the 1937 Avus race meeting, driven by Fagioli (No. 33) and Rosemeyer

06

05 For the 1938 Swiss Grand Prix, Auto Union brought a veritable armada of 3-liter (Type D) cars
06 Bernd Rosemeyer after his greatest success: winning the 1937 Vanderbilt Cup in the United States

01

DKW dominated the scene in motorcycle road
racing. The twin-piston engines with charge
pump first developed in the early 1930s proved
capable of delivering considerably increased
power outputs. DKW's URE 250 racing bikes were
developing 22 hp at 4,200 rpm in 1933, but in
their final development stage in 1937 the power
output had been boosted to 25 hp at 4,700 rpm,
and the potential top speed was 99 mph.
The ULD that appeared in 1937 was both the
climax and conclusion of development work on
the successful twin-piston racing engines. The
new rotary disk valve increased the 250 cc engine's
power output by 15 percent, initially to 28.5 hp
at 6,000 revolutions per minute, but in the final
version to 30 hp at 6,500 rpm. During record
attempts in 1937, a top speed of precisely
114 mph was reached.
At the end of 1934 the Zschopau-based engineer
Küchen was instructed to develop a DKW road
racing bike that could be sold to private entrants.
The target price was 1,550 Reichsmarks, and the
motorcycle was to be capable of a top speed of
93 mph. At that time, this DKW was the only
racing motorcycle that could be bought "over the
counter."

In the 250 cc class, DKW motorcycles seemed to
have a season ticket to victories and championship
titles year after year, until the outbreak of war.
In 1936 DKW riders were the champions in four
of the six racing classes: 250 cc (Kluge), 500 cc
(H.P. Müller) and both sidecar classes (Braun/
Badsching and Kahrmann/Eder). In the following
season, Ewald Kluge on the new ULD became the
first German to win the Tourist Trophy, the road
race that had been held on the Isle of Man since
1907. Sidecar racing ceased in 1938, and DKW
concentrated on its solo bikes and riders. With
every success: in the 350 cc (Fleischmann) and
250 cc (Kluge) classes, the company carried off
the German and European championship trophies.
The factory's motor sport department concentrated for the most part on off-road events and
reliability trials. Notable among these were the
annual Alpine Run and the international Liege –
Rome – Liege long-distance rally. In some cases,
Auto Union developed entirely new cars for these
events. The special chassis of the model developed
in 1938 for off-road competition was adapted
from a DKW off-road vehicle, but powered by a
Wanderer engine reduced in size to 1.5 liters. It
proved far superior to all its rivals.

03

02

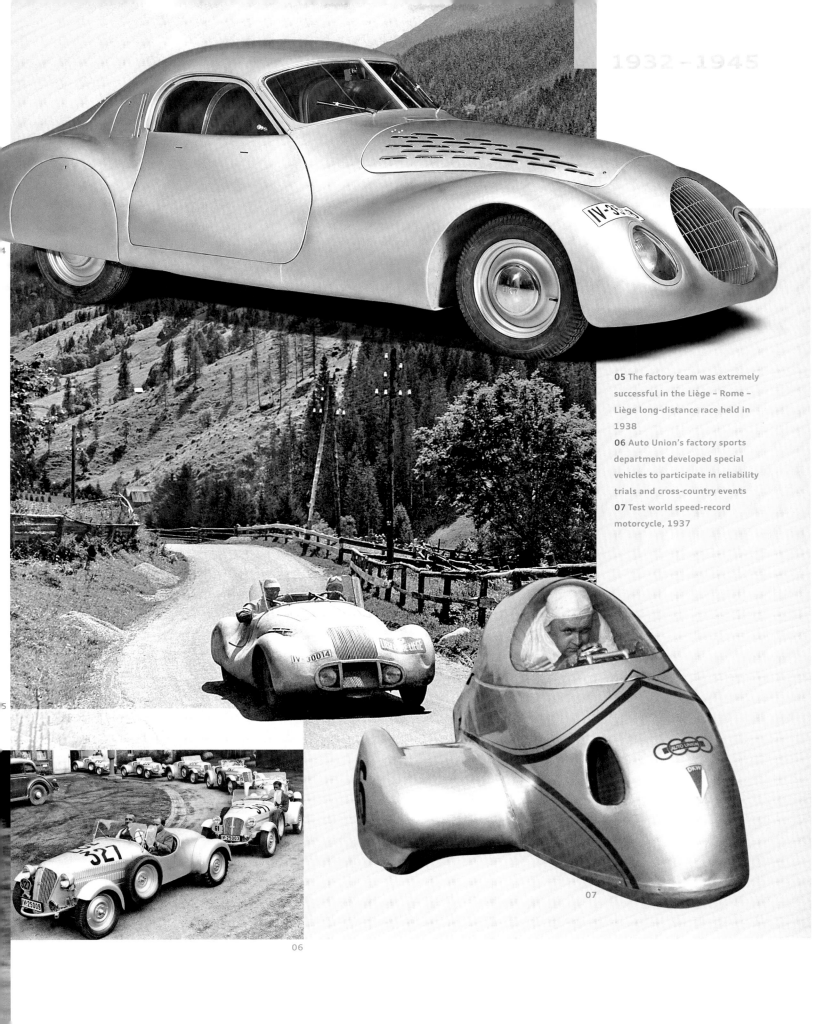

05 The factory team was extremely successful in the Liège – Rome – Liège long-distance race held in 1938

06 Auto Union's factory sports department developed special vehicles to participate in reliability trials and cross-country events

07 Test world speed-record motorcycle, 1937

06

07

01

02

05

06

08

09

120

Audi – an overview

03

04

07

01

02

05

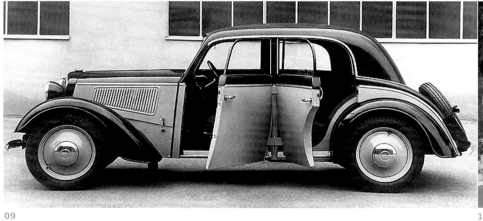

06

09

10

122

DKW – an overview

03

04

07

08

11

01 DKW F 5 Front-Luxus
convertible, 1936
02 DKW Sonderklasse 1001,
1933
03 DKW Schwebeklasse, 1935
04 DKW Sonderklasse with steel
body, 1937
05 DKW F 2 Meisterklasse 701,
1933
06 DKW F 4 Meisterklasse, 1934
07 DKW F 5 delivery van, 1935
08 DKW F 7 Reichsklasse Special,
1937
09 DKW F 7 Meisterklasse Export
four-door sedan, 1938
10 DKW F 8 Meisterklasse folding-
top sedan, 1939
11 DKW F 9 sedan, 1940

01

02

05

06

08

09

Horch – an overview

03

04

07

10

01 Horch 500 B Pullman sedan, 1933

02 Horch 780 sports convertible, 1933

03 Horch 830 BL Pullman sedan, 1938

04 Horch 850 Pullman convertible, 1937

05 Horch 853 A sports convertible, 1938

06 Horch 855 special roadster, 1938

07 Horch 930 V convertible, 1937

08 Horch 950 A Pullman sedan, 1939

09 Horch 930 S, 1939

10 Horch 930 V roadster, 1938

01

02

04

05

08, 09

126

Wanderer – an overview

03

06

07

10

11

01 Wanderer W 17 sedan, 1932

02 Wanderer W 21 sedan, 1933

03 Wanderer W 22 convertible, 1934

04 Wanderer W 240 sedan, 1935

05 Wanderer W 250 convertible, 1935

06 Wanderer W 51 sedan, 1936

07 Wanderer W 52 convertible, 1937

08 Wanderer W 25 K roadster, 1936

09 Wanderer W 26 Pullman sedan, 1937

10 Wanderer W 23 convertible, 1939

11 Wanderer W 24 two-door sedan, 1937

01

02

04

05

08

09

128

Motor sport – an overview

03

06

07

01 Auto Union Type A racing car, 1934
02 Auto Union Type B racing car, 1935
03 Auto Union Type C racing car, 1936
04 Auto Union Type D racing car, 1938
05 Auto Union Type C racing car, Avus version with streamlined body as used for speed-record attempts, Berne 1937
06 Auto Union Type C racing car; last record attempt by Bernd Rosemeyer, 1938
07 Auto Union Type D racing car with streamlined body, 1938
08 Kahrmann and Eder with their DKW ULD 700 sidecar outfit, Budapest 1937
09 DKW ULD 250 ridden to victory by Ewald Kluge on the Sachsenring circuit in 1937
10 DKW SS 250 with charge-pump engine during the 1935 Six Day Trial, with riders Walfried Winkler, Arthur Geiss and Ewald Kluge
11 Speed-record attempt with a streamlined 175 cc DKW ridden by Walfried Winkler, 1937

10, 11

From mountains of rubble to the economic miracle

A new era dawns

"Give me ten years, and you will not recognize Germany again!"

Hitler's prophecy had fulfilled itself in the most gruesome manner possible by 1945. At the end of a merciless war, the world mourned the deaths of fifty million people. Germany was one vast heap of rubble, its cities destroyed, its industry buried in the ruins and its population in dire straits. Six million of them had failed to survive Hitler's policies of genocide.

When at long last the gun smoke and dust began to clear, and mental desperation gave way to more sober considerations of how to survive, life began to stir again in the ruins. Machinery was dug out and cleaned, wheels began to turn on the roads and railways and an occasional factory chimney emitted a plume of smoke. Regardless of what was inscribed on the company's nameplate, its remaining employees set to and produced what people needed: grist mills and handcarts, hoes and cooking pots. The motor-vehicle industry was no exception, though its initial task proved to be repairing an assortment of vehicles in order to keep them mobile. The occupying powers encouraged this task: wrecked cars were collected and repaired as a means of getting local administrations moving again, and even a few private customers brought their cars in to be patched up. At two places in Germany, new cars were being built before the end of 1945: at VW in Wolfsburg and at BMW in Eisenach. Mercedes-Benz, Opel and Ford restarted production too in the years that followed.

But much of what had formerly been an automotive industry had ceased to exist. Its machines and equipment had been dismantled and taken away. The Kadett assembly line from Opel in Rüsselsheim, the engine production plant at BMW in Munich suffered this fate. Farther to the east, however, in East Germany or what was now the Soviet Military Zone, complete factories were requisitioned. Horch and Audi in Zwickau, DKW in Zschopau and Wanderer in Chemnitz: they were all stripped bare, down to the last electric light switch, door and window frame. Where once the assembly lines had hummed with activity, there was nothing but bare walls and floors. The automotive industry in Saxony alone had to deliver 28,000 machine tools as reparations.

This scorched-earth policy was effectively a death-blow for Auto Union. To make matters worse, the occupying powers had the company's name erased in 1948 from the trade register in Chemnitz. This was surely the end for Auto Union.

However, many of its former senior executives had already found each other again in South Germany and were negotiating with the banks for loans and with local authorities for potential factory sites, so that Auto Union could be resuscitated somewhere in the zones occupied by the Western powers. After a year, these efforts bore fruit, and in 1949 Auto Union celebrated its recall to life in the Bavarian town of Ingolstadt. In the same year, the first new vehicles began to leave what were still temporary production buildings.

Many former employees followed the "Four Rings" from Saxony to Bavaria, inspired by the notion that Auto Union could shine forth once more in

01

02

03, 04

its original glory. But at the group's previous headquarters in Chemnitz, later to be renamed Karl-Marx-Stadt, but also in Zwickau and Zschopau, something of the original company floundered along as an industrial management undertaking, the "Industrieverwaltung Fahrzeugbau" (IFA). Ninety percent of the IFA's research and development staff consisted of former Auto Union employees. This is where the basic technical and design principles for the German Democratic Republic's automotive industry were formulated, developed and in due course took to the road.

The hardships of the immediate post-war period were gradually overcome. Many scars healed, many memories either faded or were suppressed. What remained was the sadness of people forced apart by a divided Germany, despite all hopes that this might be of short duration. Mobility was the dream in both German states, severely limited in one area, almost boundless in the other. West of the River Elbe, the car population rose with almost unbelievable speed, in the East, a waiting period of ten years or more for a new car soon became commonplace. Condemned to persist with the two-stroke engine and to suffer a series of interminable shortages, the automobile industry in what had formerly been Saxony found itself increasingly incapable of complying with international standards.

131

An end and a new beginning – the Four Rings in Bavaria

The company

The Board of Management of Auto Union AG and its remaining senior executives held a final meeting in Chemnitz on May 6, 1945. A day later Dr. Bruhn, Dr. Hahn and Dr. Werner left their place of work and traveled westwards, having agreed with the newly constituted works council on those, Dr. Hanns Schüler being one, who should represent the Board.

On July 12, 1945, Germany was officially split into four occupied zones. Any attempt to re-enter the town of Chemnitz required a special permit, and would have been a risk and possibly fatal under-

taking for the Auto Union's executives following their successful flight to the West. As it became known that all the Auto Union's plants in Chemnitz, Zwickau and Zschopau were being dismantled, it was obvious that the future was totally uncertain. Bruhn and Hahn, together with a group of former colleagues, met at the company's Munich branch to discuss the next moves that could help to get Auto Union back on its feet. Karl Schittenhelm, the former Service Manager, was there, and also Erhard Burghalter, formerly Director of the subsidiary in Stettin and Oswald Heckel, Auto Union's General Agent in Sofia.

01

02

03

Ingolstadt, a former garrison town north of Munich directly on the highway to Nuremberg with many empty military buildings, offered excellent prospects for a large parts store to be established and preparations made for restarting vehicle production. The State Bank of Bavaria agreed to make a loan on the basis of Dr. Bruhn's and Dr. Hahn's personal standing. On December 19, 1945, a company named "Central Depot for Auto Union Spare Parts Ingolstadt GmbH" was established, with head offices at Schrannenstrasse 3 in Ingolstadt, and with the principal objective of supplying urgently needed spare parts for Auto Union vehicles still on the road. In these buildings, formerly occupied by the Army provisions office and an Army bakery, the first tentative steps were taken towards rebuilding Auto Union – a stony path plastered with many doubts and uncertainties.

By the end of 1946 the Ingolstadt spare parts depot was the largest in Germany, with a turnover of more than three million marks. During the year, more and more former Auto Union workers from East Germany found their way to Ingolstadt. The news that a "new Auto Union" was taking shape there had spread like wildfire.

Following the currency reform of June 1948 and the liquidation of the parent company in Chemnitz, which took place in August of that year, it was clearly necessary to clarify the legal and property situation in the interest of maintaining the com-

pany's status, especially in dealings with the banks. As a means of ensuring continuity once and for all, it was decided to set up an independent company having no links with the previous one. On September 3, 1949, again with its head offices at Schrannenstrasse 3 in Ingolstadt, Auto Union GmbH was established as a production company with equity of 3 million Deutschmarks (DM). Dr. Bruhn was appointed General Manager, with Dr. Carl Hahn as his deputy.

Among other executives of the former Auto Union AG who were still arriving in Ingolstadt were the Horch Factory Manager Fritz Zerbst, Development Engineer Kurt Schwenk, Testing Department Manager Werner Geite, the former Commercial Director of the Horch company Paul Günther and its former Sales Manager Ludwig Hensel. Together with Dr. Hanns Schüler, who moved to Ingolstadt in 1947, these additional arrivals were able to strengthen the Auto Union management team. As a gesture of gratitude and loyalty to one of the original company founders and a pioneering engineer, August Horch was invited to join the Supervisory Board of Auto Union GmbH. Its Chairman was Friedrich Carl von Oppenheim, one of the new company's principal partners alongside Ernst Göhner from Switzerland.

The Auto Union had now been successfully transplanted to its new home. This was the beginning of an often capricious but always fascinating success story.

01 Auto Union's new home in Ingolstadt from the fall of 1945 onwards was the former Military Provisions Establishment. A central depot for Auto Union spare parts was operated from these premises at first, before being joined by the newly established Auto Union GmbH in September 1949

02 In May 1950, the new DKW car models were shown to the press in Ingolstadt. Among those at the presentation were (from left to right): Dr. Richard Bruhn, W. A. Ostwald (the doyen of German motoring journalists), Dr. August Horch, one of the partner-companies' founders, and Dr. Carl Hahn

03 The first official post-war Auto Union advertising motif, dating from March 1949

133

AUTO UNION

Die DKW KOLONNE kommt

01 Employees of Auto Union ride and drive DKW motorcycles and cars in a cavalcade through West Germany in 1950/51. Their message: "DKW is back!"

02

01

03

04

Initial success – and those who helped

Fritz Zerbst and Kurt Schwenk had begun to plan the Auto Union's very first post-war product in 1948, while occupying premises at the central parts depot. It was to be a DKW delivery van, since this was considered the most suitable conveyance to help tackle post-war transport problems. The new DKW rapid delivery van was shown to the public for the first time at the Hanover Spring Fair in 1949; it had a two-stroke engine and front-wheel drive, and broke new ground with its forward-control cab – the first of its kind in this vehicle category. The company's dealers were delighted, placed their orders – and paid their first deposits.

In a sense, the new Auto Union's most valuable initial capital was immaterial in character, namely a feeling of loyalty among the workforce, which was even prepared to earn very little and work unpaid overtime as the company struggled through its first difficult period.

Equally important was the existing dealership, which waited patiently for the first products from the new Auto Union although other brands were long since back on the market. Later, Dr. Hahn was to comment:

"We had our loyal dealers everywhere in the new Federal Republic of Germany [...] more than 90 percent of the former DKW dealers waited for us, often making considerable financial sacrifices to do so."

And finally, to quote Dr. Hahn's words again, there were *"the customers, the community of DKW two-stroke owners and enthusiasts, who waited eagerly for everything we could supply and never lost their faith in our products."*

Brand traditions and the simple structure of the product were bound to lead to the new Auto Union being primarily identified with the previous DKW brand. Production commenced in Ingolstadt before the end of 1949, and by the end of the year 504 Type F 89 L rapid delivery vans and 500 Type DKW RT 125 W motorcycles had left the

factory. The "W" stood for "West," to set the new Ingolstadt product clearly apart from motorcycles of the same type being built in Zschopau.

It was clearly Auto Union's ambition to build passenger cars again, and it was equally obvious that in the prevailing circumstances this would only be possible with the DKW brand. A practicable solution was to start production of the F 9, development and testing of which had continued until 1944. Drawings were acquired by various means and missing parts were made again. One of the few wartime prototypes was rebuilt to act as a guinea pig.

In Derendorf, a suburb of Düsseldorf, a site that formerly belonged to the Rheinmetall company was rented with a view to starting production of DKW passenger cars, there being no suitable premises for car production in Ingolstadt. The first workers for a pre-production run were recruited in April 1950, and the first cars left the provisional assembly line, incredibly, by August. 1,538 units were built in the first year.

Although Auto Union was able to benefit to a considerable extent from European Reconstruction Fund (ERP or "Marshall Plan") and other special loans, it still suffered from a chronic shortage of capital. But help suddenly appeared from an unexpected source: ever since the 1930s there had been close links with the Zürich-based Swiss businessman Ernst Göhner in Zürich. He had imported DKW cars for a time and later installed his own wooden bodies on the two-stroke engined chassis. Göhner's company Holzkarosserie AG, or Holka AG for short, had built no fewer than 1,647 DKW Front cars between 1935 and 1945.

In the post-war years, Ernst Göhner's business affairs flourished. As a means of expressing his gratitude for the help he had received from Auto Union AG in Chemnitz, Göhner contributed the princely sum of two and a half million Deutsch-marks to the new company's equity. This made him, together with Bankhaus Oppenheim, one of the two main partners in the company with the four-ring emblem.

05

02 In Ingolstadt, DKW twin-cylinder engines were built in very primitive conditions in the former arsenal
03 Since no suitable premises were available, part of the delivery van assembly work had to be carried out in the open air
04 In 1950, the first post-war Auto Union models were shown to the public: the DKW F 89 L rapid delivery van and the DKW RT 125 W motorcycle
05 DKW Type F 89 Meisterklasse passenger cars were built at the Auto Union factory in Düsseldorf

Endlich!

AUTO UNION

DIE NEUE DKW RT 125 W

01 Germany was a nation of motorcyclists, which made it all the more important for the Auto Union to have a sturdy bike ready for sale as soon as possible
02 "It pays to wait!" – with this slogan, Auto Union did its best to encourage customers and dealers to be patient. The great day finally came in November 1949, when the first Type RT 125 W motorcycles were delivered

Under a new star

From the moment the new Auto Union GmbH went into business, it was managed by staff that had worked in Chemnitz, Zwickau and Zschopau. They knew each other well, and the hard times they had all gone through made them champions in the art of improvisation. But before long the reconstruction period was over, and Germany's "economic miracle" began. Fundamental decisions for the future were needed. Dr. Bruhn, still the company's General Manager, had proved capable of working miracles with very little money at his disposal. But entrepreneurial vision and willingness to take risks were not his strong points, with the result that important decisions were postponed time and again.

As early as 1954 the industrialist Friedrich Flick acquired a financial stake in the Ingolstadt and Düsseldorf motor-vehicle manufacturing operation, having been obliged by an international court verdict to dispose of his traditional coal and steel interests. His initial commitment was concealed by making purchases through various companies in Flick's vast business empire. As increases in equity were decided on, Flick's holding in Auto Union rose considerably.

His growing influence on the fortunes of Auto Union led to increasingly forceful demands for its structure and management to be reorganised. This could only mean the departure of the existing members of management. On October 15, 1956, Dr. Werner Henze took the place of Richard Bruhn. Henze's first contact with the motor-vehicle industry had been when he joined Famo Fahrzeug- und Motorenwerke of Breslau before the war. He soon succeeded in altering the direction that Auto Union's development was taking, but it was clear that equity was still not high enough to provide the necessary security. This was a permanent sore point that obliged Flick to make a fundamental decision. Fresh short-term capital had to be found, but in the medium to long term cooperation with a strong partner was unavoidable. At the end of 1957, the Ford Motor Company expressed interest in a takeover of Auto Union, and initial talks were held.

Before any such deal could be negotiated, however, Flick in his capacity as a major Daimler-Benz shareholder (38 percent), contacted Deutsche Bank spokesman Hermann Josef Abs and offered the Stuttgart company an opportunity to purchase Auto Union. After hesitating for only a short time, the Daimler-Benz Board of Management resolved on March 6, 1958, to take up this offer, and the sale was concluded by April 26 of that year. In addition to Flick's shares, Mercedes-Benz acquired those held by Ernst Göhner and Friedrich Carl von Oppenheim.

In this way, Auto Union became a subsidiary of Daimler-Benz. Daimler's board spokesman Dr. Könecke, commented as follows on the transaction:

"We've married a nice girl from a good, old-established family!"

It seems only fair to recall, however, that following Volkswagen, Opel, Daimler-Benz and Ford, Auto Union was at that time the fifth-largest German automobile manufacturer in terms of production volume – well ahead of Lloyd, Borgward, NSU and BMW.

The products – motorcycles back on the road

As well as the rapid delivery van, the first post-war DKW motorcycle also went into production in Ingolstadt in 1949: the RT 125 W (W = West). At the new Bavarian plant, the motorcycle first developed at the end of the 1930s in Zschopau by Chief Engineer Hermann Weber was relaunched in slightly modified form. Straightforward in design, light in weight, sturdy and extremely economical in its concept, it was precisely the means of transport needed in the years of hardship following World War II. Series production started in

03 Assembling motorcycles at the Ingolstadt factory, 1951
04 A former granary in Ingolstadt, later used by the German Army, housed Auto Union's first DKW motorcycle production line

04

03

01 The DKW RT 200 S with
swinging-fork rear suspension
was built in 1955 and 1956
02 DKW's VS models with
swinging-fork suspension at
front and rear reached the market
in October 1956
03 The RT 350 S had a twin-
cylinder engine and was the
largest DKW motorcycle in the
post-war period
04 "Just ride, don't shift" was
Auto Union's slogan for its DKW
Hobby scooter, which had an
Uher automatic transmission
05 The DKW Hummel, the first
moped with a three-speed transmission, was introduced in the
summer of 1956

November 1949 in a former granary building. This entry-level model, giving access as it did to the mobility that was part of the "economic miracle," was subjected to steady further development. At the end of 1950 the RT 125 acquired telescopic-fork front suspension, and in May 1952 the RT 125/2 was introduced with a more powerful engine. Rear suspension became standard equipment in 1954. When the last RT 125 was produced in Ingolstadt in August 1957, the proud total of 134,000 had left the assembly lines.

Starting in 1951, the motorcycle sales program was expanded. The first new model to appear was the RT 200, followed a year later by the RT 250 with a 250 cc engine. The RT 175 introduced in January 1954 enabled the Auto Union to enter the 175 cc class, which was extremely popular at that time. Before long the RT 175 was Germany's top-selling motorcycle.

A new motorcycle manufacturing building with modern production facilities was opened in Ingolstadt in the spring of 1954, to satisfy the increasing demand for motorcycles.

In parallel with the more modern production methods, the motorcycle range itself was regularly improved. Typical innovations, applied to all models except the RT 125, included a four-speed transmission, full drive chain enclosure and a streamlined carburetor housing.

In March 1955 the RT 350 was introduced, the first (and only) post-war DKW twin-cylinder model. A notable feature was its swinging-fork rear suspension. The same technical innovation appeared in the fall of 1955 on all other DKW bikes except for the RT 125, and was identified by adding an "S" (shock mounted frame) to the model name. Cylinder barrels with "porcupine" fins enabled the engines to withstand higher thermal loads.

In October 1956 the VS models with swinging-fork instead of the previous telescopic-fork front suspension were introduced, with the exception of the RT 125 and RT 350. This modern suspension system kept DKW motorcycles abreast of current design trends.

Ingolstadt was rather slow in investigating the possibility of developing a motor scooter. Design work was started on a model with a powerful engine (up to 200 cc) but it proved to be too expensive. It was decided instead to exploit evidently unsatisfied demand at the lower end of the performance scale. Ingolstadt therefore developed a two-seat motor scooter with a 3 hp, 75 cc engine. It was remarkable for being the first such vehicle to have automatic transmission, which gave rise to the advertising slogan "Just ride, don't shift." The scooter, which was named "Hobby," was demonstrated to the press on October 1, 1954, and soon became a favorite among women riders in particular. 45,303 had been built when production ceased in 1957.

The DKW Hummel ("Bumblebee") moped was introduced at the lower end of the Auto Union motorcycle range in June 1956. It was the first moped with a three-speed transmission, and with its swinging link front and swinging fork rear suspension, with rubber spring struts at the rear, it was distinctly more comfortable to ride than most of its competitors. 117,617 of these mopeds had been built by 1958.

DKW
Hummel
DAS MOPED
MIT
DREIGANG-
GETRIEBE
DM 598.—

04, 05

01

01 An advertisement placed by
the Karl Baur company in 1950
02 For the DKW F 10 interim
model, the Auto Union used bodies
built by Baur in Stuttgart
03 Production of the DKW rapid
delivery van at the Auto Union
factory in Ingolstadt

Including the motor scooters and mopeds, Ingolstadt built a total of 518,735 motorcycles from 1949 onwards. The most successful model was the RT 125, of which 133,945 were built.
All Auto Union's efforts to revitalize motorcycle construction by means of modern developments proved to be in vain, when motorcycle sales dropped alarmingly in the mid-1950s. In 1957 the Auto Union factory in Ingolstadt produced only 10,372 DKW motorcycles (125 cc and above), a production volume for which two months would have sufficed in 1954. It was only a matter of time before the decision was made to abandon motorcycle production altogether. On October 1, 1958, Victoria Werke AG of Nuremberg acquired the production and selling rights to all DKW motorcycles. This marked the end of a long tradition that had begun in 1919 with the first auxiliary bicycle motor from Zschopau.

Cars from Ingolstadt and Düsseldorf

If one disregards the versions of the pre-war front-wheel-drive DKW F 8 built in Zwickau, now in the German Democratic Republic, from 1949 onwards, the first post-war DKW passenger cars in fact came from Stuttgart. The Baur coach-building company, which had cooperated closely with Auto Union in earlier years, developed two

pressed-steel bodies, a sedan and a convertible, for the F 8. At a time when new cars were in any case rare, these bodies were intended to replace the pre-war wooden bodies that were suffering badly from the effects of the weather.
In January 1950 the only recently established Auto Union GmbH began to supply modified F 8 chassis – unlike the pre-war version, with hydraulic brakes and telescopic front shock absorbers – to the Stuttgart company, where the new body was installed. The resulting vehicles were sold as the DKW F 10. This was a solution born of desperation, adopted to keep both dealers and customers content until the company could set up its own production line. Nearly 200 Type F 10 cars had been built by the summer of 1950, when Auto Union was able to start up its own passenger-car production line in Düsseldorf.
This had been preceded in July 1949 by the start of F 89 L rapid delivery van production in Ingolstadt. This compact vehicle had front-wheel drive and was powered by the twin-cylinder two-stroke engine of which ten thousand or more had given satisfactory service before the war. The F 89 L was the first post-war German delivery van to feature a modern forward-control cab. The idea was widely copied and soon appeared on all light commercial vehicles.

02

03

04, 05

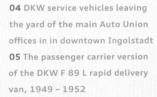

07

04 DKW service vehicles leaving the yard of the main Auto Union offices in in downtown Ingolstadt
05 The passenger carrier version of the DKW F 89 L rapid delivery van, 1949 – 1952
06 Assembling DKW rapid delivery van chassis at the Ingolstadt factory, 1952
07 Inside the F 89 L passenger carrier, showing the folding bench seat

06

141

01

A year later, in August 1950, the first passenger car was built at the new Düsseldorf factory. As in former times, it was called the DKW "Meisterklasse." The internal code was F 89 P, to signify a combination of the F 8's two-cylinder engine with the F 9's modern streamlined body. The new "Meisterklasse" was available as a sedan, a four-seater convertible (with body by Karmann) and a two-seater convertible or coupé (body by Hebmüller). In 1951 a station wagon known as the "Universal" was added to the range; its chassis was lengthened by 3.94 inches.

In 1953 the DKW acquired the three-cylinder two-stroke originally intended for it, and became DKW 3 = 6 "Sonderklasse." It was first exhibited at the Frankfurt Motor Show in March 1953.

02, 03

04

01 The body of the 1951 DKW
F 89 S Universal had a visible
wooden structure

02 DKW F 89 Meisterklasse
convertibles (left with two seats,
right with four seats) on St.
Peter's Square in Rome, 1952

03 The DKW cavalcade presenting
new models in Berlin, 1951

04 The new DKW 3 = 6, the Type
F 91 Sonderklasse, was introduced
in May 1953. Particularly striking
features included retractable side
windows and the panoramic rear
window on the de luxe coupé.
This model was finally given the
three-cylinder two-stroke engine
planned for introduction back in
1939

05 The DKW 3 = 6 model program
in 1953

06 A camping holiday in the DKW
F 91 S Universal. This drawing is
from a leaflet issued in 1954

05

The 3 = 6 name put across an important publicity
message: since a three-cylinder two-stroke
engine has twice the number of working strokes,
its power flow was therefore equivalent to a six-
cylinder four-stroke. The engine for the new car,
which was referred to internally as the DKW F 91,
had a displacement of 900 cc and developed 34 hp.

06

Sommerfreuden mit dem neuen **DKW**

AUTO UNION GM

01

01 Bodies for the four-seater
F 89 Meisterklasse convertible
came from the Karmann company
in Osnabrück
02 Drawing of the F 91 Sonderklasse sedan from a 1955 leaflet
03 In the fall of 1955, the
successor to the F 91, the large
DKW 3 = 6 or Type F 93, was
exhibited at the Frankfurt Motor
Show

02

01

02

03

04

The "large DKW 3 = 6" followed in the fall of 1955, with the power output boosted to 38 hp and a body wider by 3.94 inches. The F 93 type reference applied to all two-door sedans and coupés, but the four-door cars and the "Universal," built on the 3.94 inch longer chassis, were referred to as the F 94. In 1957 the power output of the "large 3 = 6" was increased to 40 hp. This model range, which remained in the programme until July 1959, restored the Auto Union's fortunes. About 159,000 cars of this type were built at the Düsseldorf Auto Union factory.

01 The large DKW 3 = 6 Type F 93 as a de luxe coupé in 1957. The two-tone paint finish was a typical feature of these models
02 The F 93 de luxe coupé, here with a sliding roof
03 In 1956, the first model year, the large DKW 3 = 6 model had a radiator grill with striking cross-ribs
04 When a four-door version of the large DKW 3 = 6 appeared, it had a lengthened chassis and was renamed the F 94

147

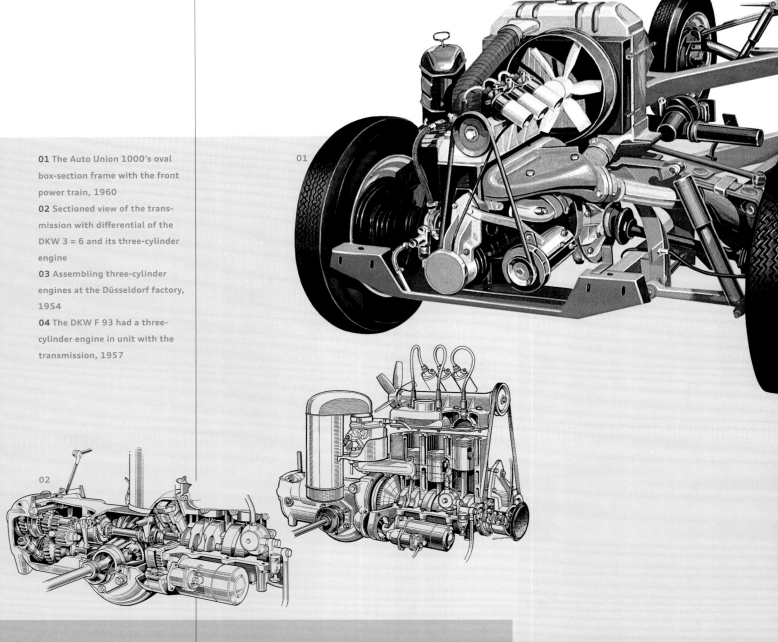

01 The Auto Union 1000's oval box-section frame with the front power train, 1960

02 Sectioned view of the transmission with differential of the DKW 3 = 6 and its three-cylinder engine

03 Assembling three-cylinder engines at the Düsseldorf factory, 1954

04 The DKW F 93 had a three-cylinder engine in unit with the transmission, 1957

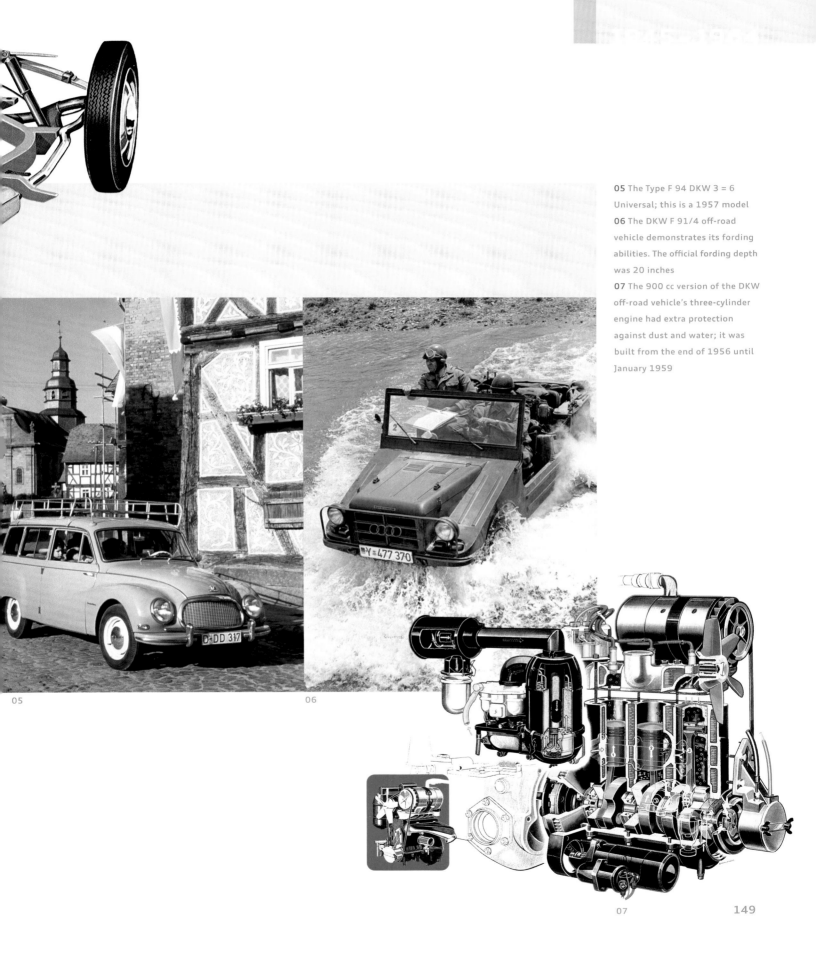

05 The Type F 94 DKW 3 = 6 Universal; this is a 1957 model
06 The DKW F 91/4 off-road vehicle demonstrates its fording abilities. The official fording depth was 20 inches
07 The 900 cc version of the DKW off-road vehicle's three-cylinder engine had extra protection against dust and water; it was built from the end of 1956 until January 1959

05

06

01

02

DER **DKW** - GELÄNDEWAGEN
mit Allradantrieb

03

Ingolstadt unveiled a rather special type of vehicle in the fall of 1953. It was the first test prototype of an off-road multipurpose vehicle, built in response to a development tender invited by the government for a standard off-road vehicle to equip the German army that was in the process of being built up again at that time. Auto Union was able to fend off competition from Porsche and Borgward/Goliath and secure the development contract with its DKW M (multi-purpose) vehicle, which had all-wheel drive and the well-proven three-cylinder two-stroke engine. The testing engineers and government officials were convinced by its performance, and after further extensive trials deliveries of the DKW M off-road vehicle to the new German Army began in November 1956. In 1962 it acquired the acronym "Munga," standing for its official German designation (multipurpose universal off-road vehicle with all-wheel drive), and been known by this short but effective name ever since. When the German Army order expired in December 1968, 46,750 DKW M and Munga vehicles had been built in Ingolstadt, together with a further 7,550 assembled under license by the Brazilian

Vemag company in São Paulo and known as the Candango.

Although Auto Union enjoyed mostly welcome market demand in the 1950s, and sold its cars and motorcycles in correspondingly large numbers, Ingolstadt and Düsseldorf were nonetheless well aware that the brand's success was based on pre-war development work. By 1949 the engineering staff knew that a successor to the existing models was needed. They decided on a small car of simple construction as the most suitable solution. Kurt Schwenk, the main contributor to the development of the F 89 L, produced a draft design for a follow-up model, which was given the code name FX. As before, the car was to have front-wheel drive and a two-stroke engine, but the craze for small cars at that time led to the mistaken decision that an engine of smaller size would be sufficient. In 1952, in parallel with this, work began on developing a "multi-passenger scooter," to sell at the same price as a motorcycle and sidecar. For no very evident reason, an additional design office run by Karl Jenschke was set up, leading to unnecessary internal competition.

150

04

This was the situation in 1953, when Dr. Bruhn invited the former Head of Testing of the Auto Union's Racing Department, Professor Eberan-Eberhorst, to come to Ingolstadt, hoping that his acknowledged authority and skills would put an end to this unsatisfactory process of groping around in the dark. He was asked in addition to other work to develop a plastic body for the small car.

The technical result was a glass fiber-reinforced polyester body. Several prototypes for the STM, as the plastic-bodied car was referred to internally, were produced, either as a three-seater with a centrally mounted steering wheel, or as a conventional four-seater. They were subjected to prolonged testing and reached a level of maturity almost suitable for volume production. However, economically viable production would have necessitated giant presses costing about 35 million Deutschmarks, a sum that Auto Union would have had difficulty in raising in view of its chronic shortage of capital.

The position was exacerbated by the management's increasing inability to reach decisions. Neither the FX nor the STM went into production, so that the time and money devoted to their development was wasted.

The company's partners started to rebel. A game of musical chairs began at top management level. In May 1956 William Werner, Technical Director of the pre-war Auto Union AG in Chemnitz, joined the company at its headquarters in Düsseldorf as General Manager for Technical Development. He brought Oskar Siebler with him, once Chief Designer in Chemnitz. Werner's first decision, made together with Commercial General Manager Dr. Werner Henze, who had come to Auto Union in October 1956 at the instigation of Friedrich Flick and taken over Richard Bruhn's seat on the executive board, was to put a stop to the plastic car body project. This led to the departure of Prof. Eberan-Eberhorst, but went no further towards solving the question of Auto Union's future from a technical standpoint.

01 The DKW M (multipurpose vehicle) during a demonstration run in the winter of 1958
02 Testing the hill-climbing abilities of a DKW off-road prototype, 1955
03 In 1962 the DKW off-road vehicle was named the "Munga," the German acronym for "Multi-purpose universal off-road vehicle with all-wheel drive"
04 Chassis of the DKW off-road vehicle with three-cylinder two-stroke engine
05 The body of the STM II three-seater was assembled from individual plastic elements, 1955
06 The final version of the STM III four-seater, 1956
07 In May 1951 a full-scale model of the DKW FX was shown to the Auto Union Board of Management

05

06

07

Liaison with the three-pointed star
1958–1964

The company

Even after the takeover by Daimler-Benz, the central question governing the Auto Union's continued existence remained the future model policy. Solving this became rapidly more urgent as sales of motorcycles began to drop alarmingly and the motorcycle business was abandoned and sold off, despite the significant contribution it had made to the company's rebirth and revival. Since 1949, the Ingolstadt company had earned many times more from its motorcycles than from its cars.

On April 28, 1958, the partners' general meeting decided to start production of a new small car, and also to purchase an approximately 3.8 million square foot site in Ingolstadt and to build a completely new factory with an initial capacity of 250 cars per working day. The Bavarian State Bank backed this decision with an investment loan of 25 million Deutschmarks. The ground-breaking ceremony was held in July 1958, and scarcely more than a year later the first DKW Junior left the assembly line in what was then Europe's most modern car factory. In Düsseldorf, production of the existing DKW models, now upgraded and renamed Auto Union 1000, had been in progress since the end of 1957, and was continued.

DKW cars made under license abroad were also popular. Production of the DKW rapid delivery van had commenced in Belgium in 1935 and at the Imosa company in Vitoria, Spain, in 1955. From 1956 on DKW passenger cars and delivery vans were made under licence in the Netherlands, Brazil (Vemag), Argentina (Automotriz), Ireland, South Africa and for a short time in Mexico. Business boomed. The DKW Junior in particular was given a positively euphoric reception by the press and the general public, with customers standing in line to obtain cars from the dealers. Turnover doubled within three years, the best year in the reborn Auto Union company's post-war history being 1962, when turnover exceeded 800 million Deutschmarks.

Shortly before, on May 31, 1961, it had been decided to concentrate Auto Union/DKW production at a single location, with all the cars built at the new Ingolstadt factory. The entire site near Düsseldorf was later sold to Daimler-Benz and used from then on to manufacture Mercedes delivery vans and small trucks.

While William Werner and his team of technicians at Auto Union regarded the sales successes as proof that the correct follow-up model had been found in the guise of the DKW Junior, the parent company in Stuttgart called for further activity. They naturally favored the four-stroke engine and promised extensive help with the necessary development work. Time was pressing: sales of the larger DKW models were clearly dropping, and although the Junior was selling in large quantities, a small car such as this could not generate the necessary profits. Although William Werner accepted that the four-stroke engine had better long-term prospects, the Auto Union remained loyal to the two-stroke for the

01, 02

05

03, 04

06 Manufacturing the DKW
F 1000 L rapid delivery van at the
Imosa factory in Vitoria, Spain
(1964)
07 A DKW-Vemag "Belcar," the
Brazilian equivalent of the German
Auto Union 1000 S four-door
model, built in 1963 in São Paulo

06, 07

moment, and proposed waiting for a time before introducing a follow-up model. The Stuttgart group was irritated by what it regarded as a delaying tactic, and friction, mutual reproaches and a refusal to see the other side's point of view began to damage the relationship with the parent company. In due course Daimler-Benz decided to concentrate more on luxury car models and commercial vehicles, which in turn led to the decision to sell off Auto Union again.

Once again it was Friedrich Flick who paved the way for the necessary negotiations. In 1962 he met Heinrich Nordhoff, Volkswagen's Chief Executive, and discussed a possible takeover with him. The Wolfsburg management realized that this would give them an immediate increase in production capacity of 100,000 cars a year and

at the same time eliminate one of their strongest competitors from the market. For these benefits, a purchase price in the region of 300 million Deutschmarks did not seem too high.

From its liaison with Auto Union, Daimler retained certain material assets such as the Imosa delivery-van plant in Spain and the Düsseldorf factory that it had acquired in 1962. Of the non-material assets, it chose to keep control of the trademark that had once belonged to its previously more successful luxury-car competitor Horch. The Stuttgart company did on the other hand allow Technical General Manager Ludwig Kraus, born in Pfaffenhofen near Ingolstadt, to remain in his current job; he was to prove an innovative "secret weapon" in the years to come.

01

02

03

01 When developing the DKW
Junior, Auto Union's stylists were
clearly influenced by American
car design trends
02 Production of the DKW Junior
began in July 1959 at the new
factory in Ingolstadt
03 A small car with a big trunk
04 The Auto Union 1000 Sp was
exhibited as a roadster at the
Frankfurt Motor Show in September 1961
05 Auto Union models on display
at the Turin Motor Show in the
fall of 1961
06 An Auto Union 1000 Sp Coupé
in front of the Berlin Congress
Hall, 1960

154

The products

In the fall of 1957, visitors to the International
Motor Show in Frankfurt were able to inspect
the prototype of what was later to become the
DKW Junior. Only a short time after rejoining
the company, Technical Director William Werner
and his staff had developed a modern small
car with a pressed-steel body. It was exhibited
in Frankfurt as the DKW 660 and was intended
to occupy a position below the earlier DKW
3 = 6. The well-proven DKW front-wheel-drive
principle and the two-stroke engine were
retained. Unlike the 3 = 6, which still relied
on transverse leaf spring suspension and the

"floating" rear axle layout originating from the
1930s, the new small car featured a modern
chassis developed by Kurt Schwenk, with torsion-
bar suspension at the front and rear. However,
almost two years elapsed before the DKW Junior
reached the showrooms in August 1959, where
it was sold at 4,950 DM (compared with the
VW "Beetle" 1200 Export, which was listed at
4,600 DM).

The small DKW was not the only eye-catcher on
the Auto Union's motor show stand in the fall
of 1957. A breathtakingly beautiful two-seater
coupé in coral red with a white roof was attracting
as much if not more attention. Chief Stylist Josef

Dienst had given it a neat, vigorous and chic appearance, with certain markedly American features. The three-cylinder two-stroke engine had been enlarged to 1,000 cc and its power output boosted to 55 hp. To identify it quite clearly as the new top model, it was named the Auto Union 1000 Sp (Special). It was in fact the first of the company's cars to have "Auto Union" on its badge. The bodies were built in Stuttgart by the Baur company, but the cars were assembled at the Ingolstadt factory. From October 1961 the coupé was joined by an equally attractive roadster that was also greatly admired by the public.

05

06

01

02

03

01 The Auto Union 1000 Universal,
1960
02 At the IAA Frankfurt Motor
Show in September 1957, the
Auto Union 1000 Coupé de Luxe
was exhibited alongside the
1000 Sp two-seater. It was an
uprated version of the Type F 93
DKW 3 = 6. To draw attention to
the new top models, the "Auto
Union" brand name was used
for the first time as a product
designation

04

As well as the AU 1000 Sp, which the public nicknamed "Sputnik" on account of its futuristic appearance, the fall of 1957 saw the introduction of a version of the four-seater 3 = 6 deluxe coupé with an improved equipment specification and featuring the new 1,000 cc engine (here with an output of 44 hp). This model with the basic 3 = 6 body, the Type F 93, was sold as the Auto Union 1000 Coupé de Luxe.

In July 1959 the last DKW 3 = 6 passenger cars left the assembly line. These larger models remained on sale for several years as the Auto Union 1000. This was also when the two-door sedan and the four-seat coupé were given a boldly styled wraparound windshield clearly influenced by American car design trends. The final version of the AU 1000 S Coupé de Luxe, which appeared in March 1962, had front disk brakes – a significant step forward and one that many larger and more expensive cars had not yet adopted.

03 In the fall of 1959 the Auto Union 1000 (except for the Universal and four-door versions) were given a boldly styled wraparound windshield
04 The Auto Union 1000 reached the market as a four-door sedan in June 1958
05 The Auto Union 1000's wraparound windshield added a modern styling element

to the old DKW streamlined body
06 In March 1962 the AU 1000 Sp and AU 1000 S Coupé de Luxe were given front disk brakes. Auto Union was the first German automobile manufacturer to adopt this modern braking technology on midsize cars

06

05

01, 02

01, 02 The first DKW Junior 750 had left the assembly line at the new Ingolstadt factory in July 1959. In the summer of 1961 the Junior de Luxe was introduced with a 34 hp, 800 cc three-cylinder engine

03 The DKW F 12 was launched in January 1963. The engine was enlarged to 900 cc and now developed 40 hp

04, 05 The 1964 F 12 roadster with a 45 hp engine: the sportiest way to drive a DKW

As early as 1958 Professor Friedrich Nallinger, the Daimler-Benz Technical Director, had pointed out that in the opinion of his Board a successor for the 3 = 6 (the later AU 1000) would soon have to be found. He also felt that it should have a four-stroke engine, possibly of the horizontally opposed type, but should retain front-wheel drive. Werner thereupon instructed Siebler to design a modern passenger car with a load-bearing body-shell; this was known internally as the F 100. In the meantime, the Junior model range had been extended. In the summer of 1961, the Junior de Luxe was introduced with an upgraded equipment list and a three-cylinder engine increased in size to 800 cc. In a later development stage, the small DKW was given a modernized body with larger window area and a 900 cc engine that developed 40 hp. This new model was launched in January 1963 as the DKW F 12 and boasted a most unusual feature: inboard-mounted front brake disks. The F 12 model range was enlarged in 1964 to include a roadster with a 45 hp engine.

The next major development was the introduction in February 1964, after a long wait, of the DKW F 102. An initial pre-production batch had been

158

05

03

04

IN·T 991

01 When the DKW F 102 appeared in February 1964, the company had a model based on the latest automobile manufacturing principles. The engine was still a three-cylinder, two-stroke unit, but now developed 60 hp

built in the previous summer for road testing. This successor to the Auto Union 1000 S was a far more modern design, extensively tested by Daimler-Benz as well as by its manufacturer and incorporating a considerable number of improvements compared with its predecessor. To be frank, it had only one congenital shortcoming: it still had a two-stroke engine! This was in fact a new three-cylinder design with a capacity of just under

1.2 liters, rated at 60 hp – the largest DKW three-cylinder engine ever built.

The two-stroke engine had already lost much of the fascination evidently felt by the generation which had adopted it so enthusiastically in the 1930s, and which constituted DKW's loyal clientele for so long. They seemed unperturbed if their cars trailed a long plume of exhaust smoke behind them – after all, ageing four-strokes did

01

02

03

the same! Nor did the noise disturb them: this nervous two-stroke spluttering set them apart from the common herd. On the positive side, these engines started willingly, developed plenty of low-speed torque and were splendidly simple in construction, so that maintenance and repair costs were low – factors that genuinely mattered after the war.

But in that period and the 1950s, the four-strokes reached such a high standard that the younger generation could no longer be wooed with re-collections of DKW's better days.

Probably the main source of complaint, and the one that sealed the fate of the two-stroke engine, was crankshaft damage, particularly if the cars were frequently used for short journeys only. Corrosion attacked components in the crankcase and often caused the crankshaft to seize.

As far as the two-stroke's typical exhaust fumes were concerned, a separate lubrication system was considered as a possible answer. Together with the Bosch company, an automatic oil feed was developed, and installed on all Auto Union models from 1961 onwards. Unfortunately, the first of these devices often failed, especially in cold weather. In the winter of 1962/63, when temperatures reached record low levels, the number of crankshaft failures reached a new, but regrettably negative total. Sales responded with a sudden turn for the worse. The company's share of total new car registrations fell from 7.2 percent in 1961 to only 3.7 percent in 1964. Despite this, the Auto Union management clung

to its two-stroke policy and began to test the 80 hp, six-cylinder two-stroke engine developed in Andernach by the designer Hans Müller. This was indeed an engine with an impressive power output, but the senior management of Daimler-Benz had long since decided that the time had come to abandon the two-stroke. In October 1963 the Stuttgart company seconded the Head of its Passenger Car Pre-development Department, the graduate engineer Dr. Ludwig Kraus, to Ingolstadt as Technical Director. He came bearing gifts, notably a four-cylinder, four-stroke engine from the Daimler-Benz development department. Under the code name "Mexico," work started immediately on adapting this engine for the DKW F 102, on which development work has just been completed.

Everyone was aware from the outset that this new model with the internal code F 103 would not be marketed as a DKW. A new name had to be found, and one with a fine tradition was available: Audi. The first new Audi to be built by the Auto Union began to leave the assembly lines in Ingolstadt on August 13, 1965. By then, the Auto Union had a new parent company: Volkswagen, which only a few months before had arranged for a different car with a four-stroke engine to be built in Ingol-stadt: the VW Beetle. From May 1965 onwards it helped to increase utilization of the factory's production capacity. This sounded the ultimate death-knell for the two-stroke. The last car with such an engine, a four-door F 102 sedan, left the Ingolstadt assembly line on March 24, 1966.

02 When this picture for the DKW F 102 sales leaflet was taken, the follow-up model with a four-stroke engine was already being developed. The F 102 was the last model in Auto Union's history to be sold as a DKW

03 The Auto Union and DKW model range in 1964

Auto Union in motor sport

DKW motorcycles

In 1946, post-war Germany was still largely clearing away its war damage, but the first motor-cycle races were nonetheless being organized. DKW two-stroke bikes were in the forefront from the very beginning. A group of private entrants, among them former works rider H. P. Müller, gained the first successes for DKW on bikes dating from before the war. These were mainly the SS 250 and SS 350 Super Sport models that went on general sale between 1935 and 1939.

DKW took two German championship titles as early as 1948: Carl Döring won the 125 cc class and H. P. Müller the 250 cc class. In 1949 the DKW racing bikes were at the front of the starting grid again. In this season, Döring took the German championship again in the 125 cc class, and Sieg-fried Wünsche, who had fled from the Soviet Zone to Ingolstadt, captured the title for the larger bikes as a private entrant on his SS 350. In this year too Ewald Kluge, the "grandseigneur" of DKW motorcycle racing, returned to Germany as an ex-prisoner of war.

Auto Union was now giving serious thought to forming a new racing department. Carl Döring

and racing engineer Erich Wolf had developed a privately entered 125 cc racing bike with a charge-pump engine, which aroused considerable interest at the factory. For the 1950 season they were promptly hired and their design taken over. A factory racing bike was built, and in that year H. P. Müller secured a class victory in the hotly contended German championship.

In 1951 Auto Union announced officially that it had set up a racing department – and immediately found itself confronted with a major problem: two-stroke engines with charge-pump aspiration were banned from the racing circuits. DKW's racing bikes had to be converted more or less overnight to natural aspiration. The first to appear was a racing version of the DKW RT 125, now shorn of its charge pump, followed by a 250 cc class bike with a twin-cylinder engine. Erich Wolf's work was amazingly successful: before long, these designs were performing on a par with the previous charge-pump versions. Rudi Felgenheier and Karl Hofmann joined the DKW racing team as junior riders.

For the 1952 racing season, Auto Union surprised the experts by unveiling a new design. This "secret weapon" from Ingolstadt had a 350 cc three-

01

02

03

04 Karl Hofmann (center, with
start number 85) on the RM 350
at the start of a race at the
Hockenheimring in 1956
05 The 1955 DKW works team:
August Hobl, Karl Hofmann and
Siegfried Wünsche

04

05

cylinder engine and developed 38 hp at 12,500
revolutions per minute. Erich Wolf's design had
the centre cylinder positioned horizontally.
Thanks to the engine's characteristic sound, it has
gone down in the annals of motorcycle racing as
the "singing saw."
The new three-cylinder DKW (the RM 350) made
its debut in June 1952 on the Eilenriede circuit in
Hanover. And what a magnificent debut! The
competition was totally shattered. Kluge and Wünsche took the bikes to an unopposed one-two
victory, and in the course of the race Ewald Kluge
actually broke the lap record five times. The
RM 350 proved to be the fastest bike around,
even faster than the bikes in the 500 cc class.
Despite this success, 1952 was a year of transition.
H.P. Müller had left Auto Union and continued
his racing career initially on Mondial and Horex
bikes before signing up with NSU as a works rider
in 1954. In addition, despite various outstanding

victories the RM 350 proved to be less than totally
reliable and therefore unable to amass sufficient
championship points.
The 1953 season was overshadowed by Ewald
Kluge's severe crash in the Eifel race on the
Nürburgring, which obliged him to retire from
motorcycle racing. In the meantime the team
had engaged a promising young rider, August
Hobl, of whom much was expected. The season's
outstanding rider, however, was Siegfried Wünsche, who captured the 1953 German championship title for Ingolstadt in the 350 cc class.
In 1954 Erich Wolf's place was taken by the DKW
engineer Helmut Görg, who revised the RM 350
extensively. For the 1955 season it had more
power, swinging-fork front suspension, a five-
speed transmission and a streamlined fairing.
Riding the new bike, August Hobl came third in the
world championship rankings and took the German
championship title in the 350 cc class, with

01 With the new DKW 3 = 6, Auto Union scored overall victories in the 1954 German and European rally championships; the latter event was open only to standard production touring cars at that time

02 DKW works driver Gustav Menz in the 3 = 6 Sonderklasse in the 1954 Monte Carlo Rally

03 As the season's highlight for the many private DKW entrants, the Association of DKW Clubs organized races for a silver shield trophy at the Nürburgring between 1959 and 1965

04 A DKW F 91 sedan in the Austrian Alpine Run, 1954

01

DKW 3=6

CHAMPIONNAT D'EUROPE 1954
DE GRAND TOURISME ENLEVÉ PAR
1er WALTER SCHLÜTER 2e GUSTAV MENZ 3e HEINZ MEIER
SUR **DKW** TROIS-CYLINDRES DE SÉRIE NORMALES

CHAMPIONNAT D'ALLEMAGNE 1954
POUR VOITURES DE TOURISME ENLEVÉ PAR
1er HEINZ MEIER 3e WALTER SCHLÜTER
SUR **DKW** TROIS-CYLINDRES DE SÉRIE NORMALES

AUTO UNION G·M·B·H
INGOLSTADT ⬤⬤⬤⬤ AUTO UNION DÜSSELDORF

Wünsche and Hofmann as runners-up. Hobel even improved on this in 1956, as runner-up for the World Championship title in his class just behind Bill Lomas. In the German Championship he carried off not one but two titles: as well as the 350 cc class he rode the new 125 cc racing bike, developed from RM 350 components, to victory.
Despite these successes, withdrawal from road racing did not come entirely as a surprise, since other even more successful companies such as

NSU had already made the same decision. Motor sport success on its own was simply not enough to resist the collapse of the motorcycle industry.

DKW cars in racing and rallying
DKW cars too were active in motor sport in the immediate post-war years. Most of them were pre-war front-wheel-drive models or private entries for races and rallies using a DKW chassis. The first of the new DKW F 89 "Meisterklasse"

02

03

cars were seen in reliability trials in 1951. This two-cylinder model performed surprisingly well despite its low power output of only 23 hp. The first gold medal for a DKW F 89 driver went to Heinz Meier, Head of Auto Union's Factory Repair Department, as the winner of a winter trial in Garmisch-Partenkirchen.

When the DKW 3 = 6 "Sonderklasse" appeared in 1953 with its three-cylinder engine, it was seized upon immediately by dedicated motor sport enthusiasts as a promising competition car. In the fall of that year a new motor sport department was opened in Düsseldorf with the experience competition driver Karl-Friedrich Trübsbach as its manager. It was allocated six standard sedan cars with their engines specially selected and tuned by the factory's test department.

Drivers for the works team were Heinz Meier, who had participated in the 1939 Liege – Rome – Liege rally for Auto Union, the test engineer Gustav Menz, who had driven the company's cars successfully since 1929, and Hubert Brand from the testing department in Ingolstadt, who had earlier in the season scored some outstanding successes at the wheel of the "Meisterklasse," including overall victory in the International Austrian Alpine Run.

The factory's new motor sport department formed the basis for an unparalleled series of victories in the years that followed, as a result of which DKW cars enjoyed enormous popularity.

After a series of impressive successes, starting with Heinz Meier's class win in the Monte Carlo Rally, the first year of factory-sponsored motor

sport ended with a genuine sensation. The DKW "Sonderklasse" won its class in all the eight European championship heats for which it was entered, and also took the 1954 European Touring Car championship, driven by Walter Schlüter, who had enjoyed much success in the previous season together with Polenski at the wheel of a Porsche. Menz and Meier were second and third, the latter also taking the German Touring Car Championship in his 3 = 6.

This made the DKW "Sonderklasse" Europe's most successful touring car race entry. Not only was its roadholding excellent, it was also extremely fast: careful tuning had raised the power output to more than 50 hp. The unrivalled simplicity of the two-stroke engine tempted other prominent tuners on to the scene later, and in some cases up to 100 hp were obtained from this engine.

In 1955 Sven von Schroeter joined the DKW works team and took the German Touring Car Championship title in the three-cylinder DKW. The team was also able to secure third place in the European Touring Car Championship.

Auto Union's management greatly reduced the company's motor sport budget in 1956. As a consequence of this, only carefully chosen events likely to generate the greatest public interest were entered for, in most cases with the new "large 3 = 6," the Type F 93. At the end of the 1958 season, Auto Union ceased to participate actively in motor racing, but at the same time private entries were encouraged, and given support from the factory within Germany or from importers in other countries.

04

01

DKW

Geschichte einer Rekordfahrt

commissioned by Günther Ahrens and DKW tuner A. W. Mantzel, was designed and constructed by the Dannenhauer & Stauss company in Stuttgart. By 1959 about 230 of these most attractive sports coupés had been built, and sold as the DKW Monza. The Heidelberg DKW dealer Fritz Wenk had them built initially by the Massholder company in his home town, and later by Schenk in Stuttgart.

Even with the emphasis more on support for private entrants, the DKW brand's run of success continued. In 1959 Wolfgang Levy from Berlin, one of the most successful DKW rally drivers, only just failed to take the European Rally Championship title. In the same year Auto Union cars collected more than 300 class wins, 13 overall wins and 8 championship titles on the international rallying scene. Drivers such as Siegfried Eikelmann, Egon Evertz, Hans Wencher, Peter Ruby and Alfred Kling were the stars in these touring car races and in rallies. DKW tuners too – A. W. Mantzel, Gerhart Mitter, Alfred Hartmann and Johann Abt – kept the engines and chassis competitive. Auto Union supported these activities with technical know-how, sponsorship agreements and prize money from the Auto Union Sport Trophy.

Despite this gradual run-down, a very special event took place in 1956. On the "Motodrome" in Monza, Italy a plastic-bodied DKW 3 = 6 set a series of world speed records in the 1100 cc class, over distances of 4,000 miles, 5,000 miles and 10,000 km, and times of 48 and 72 hours. The drivers were Günther Ahrens, Heinz Meier, Georg Theiler and Roberto Barbay. The car's body,

02

03

04

When the DKW Junior reached the market in 1959, it proved to be a sporty model, potent, light in weight and maneuverable, with good roadholding and above all a very moderate purchase price: an ideal car for private entrants to race. The DKW Junior, and later the F 12, were much-feared opponents on the racing circuit and in rallies, and sparked respect even in the larger-engined classes. In 1962 the "Club International du Rallye Automobile" chose the small DKW as the world's best touring car for rallying.

Then came the end of the two-stroke era at Auto Union, and with it the end of a most successful period in motor sport. The last event tackled by a factory-supported Auto Union car was the Corsica Rally in November 1964. When Volkswagen took over Auto Union, the motor sport department was closed.

The ten-year period between 1954 and 1964, in which the Auto Union maintained an active factory presence in touring-car motor sport, had yielded a rich harvest: more than 100 championship titles, 150 overall wins and 2,500 class wins for DKW drivers.

Company chronicle

1945	Central Auto Union spare parts depot opened in Ingolstadt on December 19
1948	Auto Union AG deleted from the trade register of the town of Chemnitz
1949	On September 3, establishment of Auto Union GmbH in Ingolstadt as a new production company with an equity of three million Deutschmarks and Dr. Richard Bruhn as General Manager, with Dr. Carl Hahn as his Deputy
1950	Production facilities acquired on March 13 at the former Rheinmetall-Borsig factory in Düsseldorf. The first DKW Type F 89 P "Meisterklasse" was completed here in August
1958	On April 24, Daimler-Benz AG purchased 87.8 percent of the company's equity; it secured the remaining shares a year later
1959	New factory opened on the outskirts of Ingolstadt in July
1962	Düsseldorf factory sold to Daimler-Benz AG. 483,368 DKW cars had been built there between August 1950 and June 1962
1964	In December, the capital was increased to 160 million DM, of which Volkswagenwerk AG took up 50.3 percent, with an option on further shares
1965	Production switched to the VW Beetle (in May 1965) and the Auto Union Audi with four-stroke engine (in August 1965)
1966	After VW had acquired the remaining holdings, Auto Union GmbH became a wholly-owned subsidiary of the Wolfsburg-based group at the end of the year
1969	Backdated to January 1, Audi NSU Auto Union AG with headquarters in Neckarsulm was created by amalgamating Auto Union GmbH and NSU Motorenwerke AG

01 In December 1956, the drivers Heinz Meier, Günther Ahrens, Roberto Barbay and George Theiler set five new speed records with the plastic-bodied DKW sports coupé at the Monza Motodrome

02 The DKW sports coupé being prepared here for the record attempt on the Monza circuit in Italy was later named the "3 = 6 Monza"

03 A Silver Shield race on the Nürburgring in 1965; this is the start of the standard touring car race for licensed drivers in the up to 850 cc class

04 Privately entered DKW Junior and DKW F 12 cars were highly successful in touring car racing. In the foreground is the successful DKW dealer Günther Schreiber from Duisburg at the wheel of his F 12

05 An Auto Union 1000 Sp Coupé competing in the Tour de Corse, 1959

05

01

02

05

06

08

09

168

Auto Union –
an overview

03

04

07

01 DKW F 10 sedan, 1950

02 DKW F 89 Meisterklasse sedan (a pre-production car), 1950

03 DKW 3 = 6 Type F 91 S Universal, 1955

04 The large DKW 3 = 6 Type F 93 (left) was 3.94 inches wider: it is seen here with the previous model, the Type F 91 Sonderklasse, 1955

05 DKW 3 = 6 Type F 93 Sonderklasse, a two-seater convertible with body by Karmann, 1956

06 DKW F 94 Sonderklasse Universal, 1957

07 Film actress Romy Schneider with her DKW F 93 Sonderklasse, 1957

08 Auto Union 1000 Sp coupé, 1959

09 Auto Union 1000 Sp roadster, 1962

01

02

05

06

08

09

Auto Union – an overview

03

04

07

10

11

01 DKW Junior 750 (Type F 11/60) sedan, 1959

02 Auto Union 1000 Coupé de Luxe, 1959

03 Auto Union 1000 S Coupé de Luxe with wraparound windshield, 1963

04 DKW Junior de Luxe (F 11/62) sedan, 1962

05 DKW F 12 sedan, 1963

06 DKW F 12 roadster, 1964

07 DKW F 102 two-door sedan and DKW F 12 roadster, 1964

08 DKW F 89 L with four-speed transmission; luxury coach version, 1953

09 DKW 3 = 6 Type F 800/3 rapid delivery van as panel van, 1956

10 DKW Munga Type F 91/4 off-road vehicle, 1962

11 DKW F 1000 L rapid delivery van (Imosa production), 1963

NSU

Bicycles instead of knitting machines
1873 – 1918

01

01 Chassis for Daimler steel-
wheeled car, 1888
02 Sulmobil panel van, 1905
03 Dr. Schädel in Cameroon with
an NSU 3 hp, 1907

The company

In 1873 the mechanics Christian Schmidt and
Heinrich Stoll set up a workshop to build knitting
machines in Riedlingen, a German town on the
River Danube.

In 1880 the partners split up and Schmidt, with
seven workers and two salaried staff, moved to
larger premises in Neckarsulm and continued to
manufacture knitting machines. Shortly before
his untimely death in February 1884 he established "Neckarsulmer Strickmaschinen-Fabrik AG,"
with a capital of 140,000 marks. Management of
the business was taken on by his brother-in-law
Gottlob Banzhaf. In 1886 a new chapter in the
Neckarsulm factory's history began. The first
bicycle – the "Germania" penny-farthing – was
built. Banzhaf had identified a new trend at a very
early stage: two years later he began to build the
"safety cycles" which were already popular among
those who felt insecure on a bicycle with a front
wheel up to 4.82 feet in diameter. The demand
for bicycles boomed, and before long they were
the company's main line of business. In 1889 a
workforce of 60 built 200 bicycles.

At about this time, the Neckarsulm company
began to explore the automotive manufacturing
situation. Gottlieb Daimler and his design asso-
ciate Wilhelm Maybach were looking for a company to build the chassis for the first "Daimler
steel-wheeled car" that was to achieve fame later.
The Neckarsulmer factory's technical director
Ludwig Zeidler took this order on. In 1888 he
delivered 20 chassis with fifth-wheel steering and

an innovative form of water cooling. The vehicle
was exhibited at the 1889 World Exposition in
Paris; this led to a further order from Peugeot for
13 chassis.

From 1892 onwards, a lack of orders meant that
NSU knitting machines were no longer made; the
three letters were now understood as an abbreviation for "Neckarsulm," and from 1897 onwards
the company traded as a bicycle company, the
"Neckarsulmer Fahrradwerke AG."

From 1900, NSU was able to fulfill customers'
wishes all over the world as Germany's first
motorcycle manufacturer. NSU's two-wheeled
products of various kinds were sold through the
company's own branches in Düsseldorf, Hamburg,
Leipzig, Berlin, Königsberg, Moscow, London,
Paris and Zürich.

After only three years, two-thirds of the company's
output was being exported to neighbouring
European countries, but also to South America
and Southeast Asia.

At first the motorcycles were powered by a Zedel
engine obtained from Switzerland, but from 1903
onwards there were NSU engines of the company's
own manufacture, with outputs from 2 to 3.5 hp.
The advertisements stated, rather cryptically:

"We have decided to build a sturdy three-horse-
power motorcycle for riders with strong nerves. It
is extremely fast, but can also be ridden slowly!"

Business flourished and the company began
seriously to consider producing a car. By 1905,
these plans had borne fruit: the first car produced

02, 03

04 Poster for a Pfeil (Arrow) bicycle and an NSU 2.5 hp motorcycle, 1911

04

in Neckarsulm left the factory – a Belgian Pipe built under license. In parallel with this, NSU developed the "Sulmobil," a tricycle with the engine above the front wheel; it was not exactly a sales success. In 1905 the workforce of 786 built 7,000 bicycles and 2,228 motorcycles. The Neckarsulm engineers, however, were not averse

to tackling new challenges: in 1906 directors Carl Schwarz and Karl Schmidt, son of one of the company's original partners and later founder of the piston manufacturer Kolbenschmidt AG in Neckarsulm, developed the "Original Neckarsulm Motor Carriage." Larger and more powerful engines also appeared before long, and a full

173

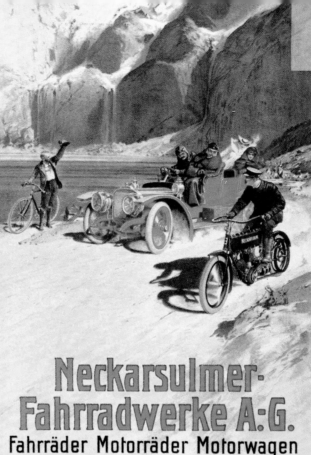

03

04

range of models was built up. Specific model names were not used: all the cars and motorcycles were simply labelled "NECKARSULM" in capital letters. From 1911 onwards the vehicles from Neckarsulm were referred to by the much more convenient three-letter abbreviation: NSU. Powerful twin-cylinder bikes and lighter tourers joined the motorcycle program. Rear suspension was available from NSU as early as 1911, together with chain drive (only on the 7.5 hp racing bike) or belt drive, a two-speed transmission and a sprung front fork. The NSU Pony was the smallest model, rated at 1.5 hp and weighing only 106 lb. It was nonetheless capable of reaching 37 mph and could cover 30 miles on 0.26 gallons of fuel. For the heavyweight bikes with 6.5 hp, 800 cc engine, which tipped the scales at 276 lb, the lightweight basketwork passenger accommodation soon gave way to a fully-fledged "phaeton" body. The tricycle concept – "runs like a car but is as cheap as a motorcycle" – was by no means defunct, though its place had clearly been taken by the motorcycle and sidecar outfit.

Before World War I, NSU was Germany's most active exporter of motorcycles and in fact built most of the motorcycles of German origin at that time. They were shipped to Russia, to most European countries, to Turkey and Scandinavia; even the Citizen's Guard of São Paulo in Brazil rode these bikes. But when World War I broke out in 1914, NSU was obliged, like all other manufacturers, to modify its product range in accordance with the demands imposed by the military authorities. Civilian home-market demand had in any case collapsed when hostilities commenced. The army's demand for NSU motorcycles and cars was enormous, and in fact before long it was taking the company's output almost completely. The export best-seller of 1913, the 3.5 hp twin-cylinder motorcycle, became the Army model of the war years. Of the cars, it was mainly the smaller models that continued in production, stripped of their luxury features and painted in field gray before being handed over to the army. Light trucks for payloads of 1.25 and 2.5 t were also built in Neckarsulm by order of the Imperial government. These orders enabled NSU to grow even during the war: in 1913 and 1914 more than 12,000 bicycles, 2,500 motorcycles and 400 cars were built by a workforce that reached 1,200.

03

Motor sport

In 1904 Martin Geiger won the Feldberg hillclimb on a Neckarsulm motorcycle, completing the 6.21-mile route, with its gradients of up to 12 percent, at an average speed of 24 mph. Also a source of public interest in these early years was Gertrud Eisemann, one of Germany's first and most successful woman motorcyclists. She established a number of speed records and recorded a considerable list of successes in long-distance events. She also drove Horch cars a number of times in competition events in this phase of her career.

The American rider Lingenfelder set the very first world speed record for motorcycles in Los Angeles, reaching 77 mph on a 7.5 hp NSU. Equally spectacular was the ride across the entire North American continent, from San Francisco to New York. William Streiff completed this 3,915-mile journey, largely on loose-surfaced roads, in 28 days, riding a 3.5 hp NSU. In 1911 Karl Gassert won a gold medal for NSU in the world's toughest motorcycle race, the Tourist Trophy. This event was a challenge that NSU faced constantly during the next 40 years.

Company chronicle

1873	Company founded by Christian Schmidt and Heinrich Stoll in Riedlingen to make knitting machines
1880	Move to Neckarsulm
1884	Neckarsulmer Strickmaschinenfabrik AG established on April 27 with a capital of 140,000 marks
1886	Production of bicycles starts (the "Germania" penny-farthing)
1892	Production of knitting machines ceases
1897	Name changed on September 24 to Neckarsulmer Fahrradwerke AG; capital 1 million marks
1900	Start of motorcycle production: Germany's first motorcycle manufacturer
1906	Production of the "Original Neckarsulmer Motorwagen" starts
1913	Neckarsulmer Fahrzeugwerke AG established on February 10; capital: 3.6 million marks
1914	In 1913 and 1914 NSU produced more than 12,000 bicycles, 2,500 motorcycles and 400 cars annually, with a workforce of 1,200 wage-earners and salaried staff in Neckarsulm

In 1914 the automobile engineers in Neckarsulm were the first to write a new chapter in automotive history: they built a car with a lightweight aluminum body. They had no means of knowing that weight-saving car design using this material would attain such importance for the Neckarsulm factory 80 years later. The company's carmaking successes led to a further change of name in 1913, to "Neckarsulmer Fahrzeugwerke Aktiengesellschaft."

In car racing, the Neckarsulm company soon began to match the successes it had already achieved with its motorcycles. In 1909 Director Karl Schmidt was as a member of a team driving three NSU 10/20 hp cars from what was still called the "Neckarsulmer Fahrradwerke AG" in the Prince Henry Run, an arduous event over a distance of more than 1,118 miles. They were awarded a silver plaque for completing the run without penalty points. For members of the Board of Directors to take part personally was a clear sign of the importance attached to the cars' quality and reliability. In 1914 the victorious 10/30 hp NSU was the only car to reach Marrakech after a journey through Morocco and across the Sahara Desert. In 1913 NSU cars triumphed in a considerable number of long-distance races, and 375 first prizes were awarded to NSU motorcyclists in Germany alone in the 1913/14 season.

01 A record performance by Gertrud Eisemann during the Eisenach – Berlin – Eisenach race: 373 miles, 1905
02 Otto Lingenfelder's world speed record in Los Angeles: 77 mph on an NSU 7.5 hp, 1909
03 William Streiff at the Neckarsulm factory after his San Francisco – New York journey, 1910
04 Winner of the Circuit of Morocco in 1914: an NSU 10/30 hp seen in Marrakech
05 During the Prince Henry long distance run, with Director Karl Schmidt and an NSU 10/20 hp, 1908

05

04

Crisis and success between the wars
1919 – 1945

NSU – the company

Like most manufacturers at the end of World War I, NSU survived by resorting to the products it had made before 1914. The first new vehicles, however, were in production by 1920/21: these were for the most part bicycles and motorcycles, in particular the well-proven 3.5 hp twin-cylinder "army bike." Demand for accessories also developed, and the production of freewheel hubs was steadily expanded until one was being completed every 30 seconds.

On the occasion of the company's 50th anniversary, which for business reasons was not celebrated until April 12, 1924, it was noticeable to what extent the factory had grown despite the inflation rampant in Germany at that time. A separate telephone exchange, laboratories and even its own photographic studio were installed. In the same year work began on a branch factory in nearby Heilbronn, though this was not completed until 1927/28.

In accordance with the tendency for German motor-vehicle companies to amalgamate at that time, NSU merged with Schebera Aktiengesell-schaft Berlin to form "NSU Vereinigte Fahrzeug-Werke AG." Unfortunately, the merger brought NSU nothing but severe losses and plunged it into a financial crisis. Production continued at the main factory in Neckarsulm, and the former Schebera company was involved in sales activities, concentrating in particular on the taxi business in Berlin. At that time NSUs were a frequent sight on the streets of Germany's capital as taxicabs. In 1930 the "Kraft AG" company took delivery of the thousandth Type 7/34 hp taxicab, but as more and more taxis were being driven, the individual owners' earnings dwindled and they were unable to pay the installments they owed to the manufacturer. In view of this, NSU itself incurred financial difficulties in 1926. Urgent reorganization measures were initiated in the following year, for example the adoption of assembly-line car production measures, but NSU's management was nonetheless forced in 1928 to cede the Heilbronn factory, erected only a short time before, to Fiat. A year after this, NSU stopped building cars of its own in Neckarsulm and supplied chassis to Fiat for the bodies to be added. The Fiat factory in Heilbronn operated under the name "NSU Automobil AG" and, until 1932, sold six-cylinder NSU models as the "NSU Fiat," a brand name that was retained when purely Italian cars such as the Ballila Sport and the Fiat 500, 1,000 and 1,100 models began to leave the assembly lines there.

» N S U «
Pfeil-Fahrräder

01

178

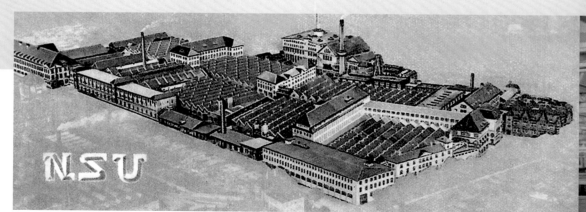

02

03

The world economic crisis from 1929 on led to mass dismissals and financial problems. Of the 5,000 people who had once worked in Neckarsulm, only 700 remained; of 60 German automobile manufacturers, only 16 survived. Even the sale of the Heilbronn factory failed to stop the downturn.

On January 1, 1930, Fritz von Falkenhayn was appointed Sales Director of NSU. In this function and later as the Chief Executive of NSU Vereinigte Fahrzeugwerke AG, he stepped up the rationalization process considerably and took measures to improve the sales situation. The after-sales service was expanded and, in 1930, a joint organization to promote motorcycle sales was established with the Wanderer company. As demonstrated by DKW with much success, regular training courses were held for mechanics. A service center was built, and the complete vehicle program was always on display in a large showroom. A further project for the coordination and amalgamation of production and sales was concluded in 1932 with Deutsche Industriewerke AG in Berlin (D-Rad) and led to the company's name being changed to "NSU-D-Rad Vereinigte Fahrzeugwerke AG."

04

NSU

DER STÄRKERE
7/34 PS-SECHSZYLINDER
MODELL 1929

NSU VEREINIGTE FAHRZEUGWERKE A.-G.
NECKARSULM
FABRIKNIEDERLASSUNG: BERLIN-CHARLOTTENBURG, SALZUFER 4

Internationale Automobil- und Motorrad-Ausstellung Berlin 1928
Automobile: **Halle I, Stand 44**, Motorräder: **Halle IV, Stand 706**

05

179

01

To prevent local residents from being exposed to excessive noise, a new 1-mile running-in and test track was built in 1929 in cooperation with the municipal administration. It was on the River Neckar, close to the factory, and was one of the most modern facilities available anywhere in Germany at that time. In 1936 a political decision led to NSU taking over bicycle production from Adam Opel AG; this made it the market leader in Germany. Two years after this, as a sales promotion measure, NSU formed a joint sales organization with Nuremberg-based motorcycle manufacturer Zündapp.

In 1936 the NSU Quick, a new type of small motorcycle, was exhibited at the International Car and Motorcycle Show in Berlin. It was so convincing that sales continued until well after World War II, with 250,000 units built by 1953. Now that

success had returned, it seemed likely to stay: between 1930 and 1936 the company increased its workforce five times over. 3,200 employees turned out 135,955 bicycles and 62,619 motorcycles. In 1940 the company's turnover, boosted by the war effort, rose from 33 to 53 million marks.

Motorcycles

When the first new design after the war appeared in 1921, it was clearly in keeping with the times. The 350 cc, single-cylinder engine developed 3 hp and drive to the rear wheel was by belt – a cheap, sturdy product.

Three years later chain drive, which had in fact been used on NSU motorcycles before the war, celebrated a comeback. There was a new front fork with parallelogram geometry and shock

180

N-38078

vertical shaft drive to the valve gear, a legend in its time. His handwriting could be seen not only on the NSU sports models but also on the OSL series with 200, 250, 350, 500 and 600 cc engines which dominated the range well into the 1930s. His predecessor Otto Reitz now made great efforts to penetrate the market segment consisting of lower-priced motorcycles for everyday use. This began with the NSU 201 R and continued in 1931 with the "Motosulm," a motorized bicycle with a 1.2 hp two-stroke engine above the front wheel. It was capable of reaching a surprising 22 mph. The ZDB models also began to appear in the early 1930s, all with a two-stroke engine that was easier and cheaper to manufacture. At the 1936 International Car and Motorcycle Show in Berlin, a small 100 cc motorcycle was to be seen: men's and women's versions were on display. It was named the "Quick" in accordance with an off-the-cuff suggestion made by a Berlin woman. It sold for 290 Reichsmarks and achieved fuel efficiency of just under 118 miles per gallon. The new model was an immediate and lasting success: NSU built and sold more than a quarter of a million.

03, 04

01 NSU Type 251 R with belt drive, 1928
02 Motosulm motorized bicycle, 1931
03 Ladies' model of the Quick light motorcycle, with dropped frame and inclined fuel tank, 1941
04 Gentleman's model of the Quick light motorcycle, 1941

absorbers. From 1927 onwards, NSU motorcycles had the engine and three-speed transmission combined into a single unit that also contained the primary transmission, magneto drive and oil pump.
The dimensions were standardized in order to permit the cylinder of either a side-valve tourer or an overhead-valve sports model to be attached. In 1928, when engines of up to 200 cc were exempted from tax, NSU launched a suitable model (the NSU 201 R) and added a 300 cc bike (the NSU 301 T) to the range. In 1930 the first 175 cc two-stroke (the NSU 175 Z) was introduced.
In 1929 NSU appointed a new Chief Designer from England, Walter William Moore. He had previously worked for Norton, where he drafted out the famous single-cylinder engine with

POSTAMT N
X STADT
Y STRASSE

02

01

02

01 NSU Type 7/34 hp large
touring sedan, 1929
02 NSU Type 5/25 hp touring
sedan, 1928

Cars

Nothing significantly new was to be seen at the 1921 Berlin Motor Show. Most of the cars looked the same as they had before the war, with a pointed radiator grill. This was true of the three NSU exhibits too. They had acquired electric lighting and a starter motor, but were otherwise new versions of pre-war designs: the 5/15 hp, 8/24 hp and 14/40 hp models. The last of these was soon replaced by a 5/30 hp model.

All these cars had a four-cylinder engine. A 2.5-tonne truck was also exhibited, but did not remain in the sales catalog for long.

The luxury version of the 5/15 hp NSU model was known as the "Dove" and had a sedan body with a detachable upper section, so that the car could be transformed into a phaeton. After this, too much attention was clearly devoted to motorcycle development in Neckarsulm, since successors to the cars mentioned above did not materialize until 1928! For all this intervening period, the company evidently believed that it could live off the substance accumulated before the war.

The eventual replacement was a 6/30 hp car with a six-cylinder engine and a three-speed transmission. NSU hoped to break into the taxi trade with this car. In the same year a version with the engine bored out to 1.8 liters and developing 7/34 hp was added. But all these moves came too late: although Fiat continued to build these models unchanged after acquiring the factory from NSU, the Neckarsulm brand vanished from the car scene for many years from 1928 onwards.

In 1932 NSU broke away completely from the Fiat Group and regained its independence. A year later Fritz von Falkenhayn issued a design order to Ferdinand Porsche's Stuttgart office for a new, low-priced NSU small car. NSU built three prototypes of this "Porsche Type 32," a forerunner of the Volkswagen Beetle.

The engine was a 1.5-liter flat four, rear-mounted and rated at 30 hp. The car's top speed was 71 mph. For reasons of finance, it never went into production, and only one of the prototypes has survived. It belonged to an NSU employee, who traded it in for a new Beetle in 1953.

Chain reaction

The NSU Type HK 101 half-tracked vehicle had a front end and steering layout derived from the OSL series of motorcycles. Its development was supervised by Ewald Praxl and it was built from 1940 to 1948 at the Neckarsulm factory and also under license by Stoewer in Stettin. It was the German Army's smallest half-tracked tractor vehicle, driven by a 36 hp, 1.5-liter Opel Olympia engine and possessing quite remarkable maneuverability. Its turning circle was a mere 9.84 feet, aided by the fact that the crawler-track brakes could be used to make the vehicle turn more sharply. The maximum gradient without a trailer was 45 degrees, and the fording depth 17.32 inches. Yet on a flat road, the half-tracked vehicle could be driven at up to 50 mph!

After World War II, NSU was granted a special permit by the American occupying forces to build the half-tracked vehicle for use exclusively in vineyards and for other agricultural and forestry tasks. Since it was only 39 inches wide, it could be driven between the grape vines on steep slopes. Its all-terrain capabilities in forests made it an invaluable tool for the timber trade.
The NSU half-tracked vehicle was the only German military vehicle for which permission was granted for production to continue after World War II.

05

04

03 Porsche Type 32 prototype
and the follow-up version, 1955
04 Porsche Type 32 prototype,
1933
05 NSU half-tracked vehicle, 1941

02

03

Motor sport

When motor sport events began to be organised again after World War I had come to an end, numerous private entrants were eager to take part. Although NSU's motor sport reputation was based on its motorcycles, it was in fact an NSU 8/24 hp car that earned the company its first laurels, a class win at the opening race on the Berlin Avus circuit in 1921. Drivers Klöble and Kist, already well known for their prowess on motorcycles, also recorded the day's second-best lap time. Whereas their two-seater was only a slightly modified production car, NSU decided only two years later to pull out all the stops.

In 1923 1.3-liter cars derived from the 5/15 hp model (1,230 cc, 50 hp), but with a supercharger to extract additional power, were entered for a race on the same circuit, and took the first three places in the small-car class. A 30 hp non-supercharged version could be purchased by the man in the street, and proved to be in exceptional demand. The Neckarsulm team, incidentally, repeated its success in the following year, but the designers in the town where the Rivers Neckar and Sulm meet were already hard at work sketching out a new model. Intended initially for competition and later for series production, it was to have a six-cylinder engine that would be supercharged for the racetrack and would then develop 60 horsepower. The prototype was entered for the very first "German Sports Car Grand Prix" in 1925. It was entrusted to a driver who later achieved considerable fame at the wheel of Wanderer and Auto Union sports cars, August Momberger. At that time a student completing a placement with NSU, he astounded the experts by winning the race outright. The sensation could hardly have been more perfect: NSU had taken on all the entire elite, with resounding names

01 NSU 6/60 hp supercharged racing car, 1926
02 Wartberg race meeting: NSU Type 10/30 hp, 1913
03 NSU 8/24 hp with drivers Klöble and Kist, 1921

185

01

02

Company chronicle

1926	Merger with Schebera AG in November to form NSU Vereinigte Fahrzeugwerke AG, with a capital of 12.5 million Reichsmarks
1928	Car production abandoned
1932	NSU-D-Rad Vereinigte Fahrzeugwerke AG established on 3 September
1938	NSU Werke AG registered on June 8, with capital of 3.6 million RM. A workforce of about 3,000 produced 63,000 motorcycles and 136,000 bicycles

01 Successful drivers of the supercharged NSU 6/60 hp (from left to right): Scholl, Islinger, Klöble and Müller, 1926
02 Tom Bullus on the NSU 500 SS, 1933
03 Böhm/Fuchs on the super-charged NSU 500, 1950
04 NSU Supersport 500 SS, 1933

such as Mercedes and Bugatti, and left them behind. A year later the company carried off the first four places in the 1.5-liter class, the drivers being Georg Klöble, Josef Müller, Ernst Islinger and Jakob Scholl. On the AVUS circuit in Berlin, the cars were reaching top speeds of more than 109 mph. A year later, the car went into series production, and in this guise set up an impressive endurance record: at the end of 1928 it covered 12,427 miles without a breakdown during the 18-day uninterrupted 24-hour event on the Nürburgring. Two years later, in the ADAC long-distance run, the NSU team took the principal gold medal with the same car.

When car production ceased, the motorcycles again took the limelight. NSU's Chief Designer William Moore persuaded his fellow countryman Tom Bullus, one of the best English riders, to come to Germany and ride a new 500 cc supersport bike

that Moore had just developed. Bullus accepted, and on June 29, 1930, won the Motorcycle Grand Prix on the Nürburgring circuit. From that time on NSU seemed to possess almost unbeatable status in this engine-size category. After his initial triumph, Bullus rode the same bike to victory at the Solitude race meeting, the Eifel race, the Klausen Pass hillclimb, the German Hillclimb Grand Prix, the Gaisberg race near Salzburg and the International Grand Prix in Monza. This made him one of the most successful racing riders of all time. As for the motorcycle, the vertical-shaft valve gear and the well-chosen center of gravity which made for excellent roadholding were just two of the features that predestined the SS 500 to be a winner wherever it was entered. The first major design rework took place in 1937, whereupon Heiner Fleischmann, riding a 350 cc version with an output of 36 hp, took the German Championship title in his class at the end of the

186

03   04

season. Moore was then obliged to leave the country for political reasons, his place as NSU's Chief Designer being taken by Albert Roder, who developed a double overhead-camshaft, super-charged engine that developed 44 hp straight off

the drawing board! This time it was the outbreak of war that put paid to further development work, but between 1931 and 1937 NSU riders had won eleven German and five Swiss Championship titles in the 350 to 1,000 cc classes.

1845 – 1969 NSU – From two-stroke motorcycle to Wankel-engined car

From two-stroke motorcycle to Wankel-engined car
1945–1969

The company

The years immediately after World War II were no different for NSU than for most of Germany's industrial companies: the first step was to clear away dust and rubble and get production going again at a low level, using pre-war designs. Later came the German currency reform, and a boom set in, giving manufacturers a chance to satisfy pent-up demand. This focused in particular on anything connected with mobility that could be obtained at a reasonable price in those arduous post-war years: bicycles, motorcycles, scooters and cars, especially small cars.

NSU started production again at the end of 1945 with a workforce of 843; the pre-war Quick, 125 ZDB and 251 OSL models were assembled in small quantities from existing parts. This was only possible because important documents and machines had been brought to places of safety in good time. Altogether, 8,822 bicycles and 98 motorcycles were built. Slowly but surely, the recovery set in.

Walter Niegtsch became the company's Chief Executive on July 1, 1946. He not only took steps to build up motorcycle production as rapidly as possible, but also approved the plans of his Chief Designer, Albert Roder, for the development of new models. Niegtsch began exporting the company's products at a very early date, and can truly be said to have laid the foundation stone for NSU's growth after the war. By 1948 the workforce numbered 4,462. Demand for NSU two-wheelers rocketed, with 135,480 bicycles

and 37,929 motorcycles produced. Motorcycle sport was also revived. At the end of 1948, NSU introduced its first post-war model, with a 100 cc engine. This was the "Fox," sold under the slogan "Fixe Fahrer fahren Fox" (approximately translated as "The Fox is for Clever Riders"). Other successful models, the "Max" and the "Lux" followed in rapid succession, as well as the "Quickly" moped, of which more than a million were sold, and Germany's favorite motor scooter, the "Lambretta."

After Niegtsch's death in 1951, Gerd Stieler von Heydekampf took over, and maintained the company's growth policy. In 1954 the Neckarsulm factory was building 250 bicycles, 350 motorcycles and scooters and 1,000 Quickly mopeds every day. In the following year, output reached an absolute peak, with more than 50,000 bicycles and 300,000 motorized two-wheelers leaving the assembly lines. NSU was the largest manufacturer of two-wheelers in the world and Germany's top-selling motorcycle brand. But despite this fame and the associated rewards, the Neckarsulm management had to face the fact that the prolonged boom in motorcycle sales was coming to a close, and that urgent action would be needed to keep turnover at its present high level. The logical solution was to recommence production of NSU cars, since as the German economic miracle proceeded the car was gradually becoming the public's chosen means of transport. In 1957 NSU developed a small, sporty model. A major difficulty nonetheless had to be overcome before

02

03

01

02

the Fiat group was prepared to permit the renewed use of the NSU name on cars. Back in 1929, NSU had signed a contract agreeing never to manufacture cars under this name again, in order to prevent competition with those built in Heilbronn by the new owners of its plant, and still being badged as NSU/Fiat. Since there were no signs of an amicable settlement, the Neckarsulm management decided to create a new brand: the "Prinz." All the "Prinz" models sold extremely well, and brought NSU steady increases turnover as well as successes in motor sport.

It was not until 1966, after lengthy legal proceedings, that NSU was able to use its own name on its cars. The "Prinz" officially became an NSU, and the original name gradually vanished from the model program. Nonetheless, it is still remembered today as a synonym for NSU's modern small cars.

Together with its inventor Felix Wankel, the rotary-piston engine concept had been actively explored since 1953. In the Technical Development department Neckarsulm's designers made many a quantum leap forward and were soon able to take a decisive step into a secure future: on February 1, 1957 a Wankel rotary-piston engine was started up for the first time on the NSU test rig – and ran!

The Wankel was the first internal combustion engine to generate its power by rotary rather than reciprocal movement. This pioneering invention made the Neckarsulm design team leaders in engine development and brought the company international respect and a high income in the form of license fees. A large number of automobile manufacturers, among them Daimler-Benz, Rolls-Royce and Mazda, purchased licenses for this novel and highly promising form of propulsion, which was also used for motor boats, motorcycles and aircraft. The NSU/Wankel Spider was exhibited in 1963 at the IAA Motor Show in Frankfurt – the world's first series-production car with a Wankel engine. The engine's advantages were obvious: it occupied very little space, was light in weight and, with very few moving parts, ran extremely smoothly.

When car production was restarted in 1957, the company's turnover was 148 million Deutschmarks (DM); by 1968 it had risen to 566 million DM. The company changed its name in 1960 to "NSU Motorenwerke AG Neckarsulm." In 1965 it employed more than 10,000 people, who produced 6,000 motorcycles, 3,700 motor scooters, 28,924 mopeds – and 81,757 cars. In 1966 the impressive era of two-wheeler production came to an end in Neckarsulm after 80 years, and after 1.75 million bicycles and 2.3 million motorized two-wheelers had been built. The bicycle production plant had been sold previously, in 1963. During the economic boom period, NSU purchased the Drauz coachbuilding company's factory in Heilbronn in 1965, and a year later had produced its 500,000th car since restarting the production of four-wheeled vehicles.

In the spring of 1969, excitement was rife in Neckarsulm. First came rumors, then headlines in the tabloid press, and finally the facts: the giant VW Group was about to take over the dwarf NSU company. Other news from NSU was equally stimulating: even an output of 590 cars per day was not enough to satisfy demand without lengthy delivery delays. Turnover was up by 23 percent on the previous year, the pioneering Ro 80 was selling well and its Wankel engine concept was attracting more and more licensees. There were of course areas where action was needed: the Prinz models needed to be replaced by a larger midsize car, the later K 70: the Ro 80 had been given a bad press recently on account

03

04

TUNDRAGRÜN

02

of the intensive detail work it still needed, and although additional models were essential the necessary investment capital was lacking. In 1965 the Dresdner Bank, NSU's main shareholder, had urged the company's Chief Executive to look for a larger partner. Exploratory talks were held with Ford and Fiat, but it was VW that eventually showed interest. NSU's capital was increased from 87 to 215 million DM by the Wolfsburg company, and it was decided at the same time to amalgamate it with VW's other wholly owned subsidiary, Auto Union GmbH in Ingolstadt. The new company was named "Audi NSU Auto Union AG" and had its headquarters in Neckarsulm. The first aim was to combine the two companies' marketing and sales operations and coordinate the markedly different technical concepts of Audi and NSU. This led to the NSU K 70, which was ready for production, being taken over by the parent company in Wolfsburg and launched in the fall of 1970 as the VW K 70.

The products: motorcycles

NSU launched its first post-war motorcycle design in 1949, the NSU Fox. It had a 98 cc OH four-stroke engine that developed a remarkable 5.2 hp. In 1950, at the Frankfurt Trade Fair, the Lambretta scooter, referred to from 1951 onwards as an "Autoroller" ("auto-scooter") with an NSU engine went on display, It was built under license from Italy, but improved in some respects by the engineers in Neckarsulm and rendered easier to

operate. It was powered by an NSU 125 cc, 4.5 hp two-stroke engine, with shaft drive to the rear wheel, and was one of Germany's very first motor scooters. It was developed and improved on several occasions, and nearly 120,000 had been built by 1956, when it superseded by the company's "Prima" model.

The 200 cc "Lux," with a two-stroke engine, appeared in 1951. At that time too, the NSU motorcycle program was enlarged by the introduction of two versions of a larger model, the Konsul I with a 350 cc and the Konsul ll with a 500 cc four-stroke engine. In 1952 the NSU 251 OSL, the last model of pre-war design, went out of production. In the same year the "Max" was launched, a historic design in several respects. Its engine was again a four-stroke overhead-valve unit, but Albert Roder had dispensed with costly vertical-shaft drive to the valve gear and developed a special form of pushrod operation instead, which was given the name "Ultramax." Before the intake air formed the combustion mixture with the fuel, it had a lengthy path to follow on the "Max," the aim being to suppress turbulence. This air settling system was not new, although unusual on a motorcycle. NSU used it to set new noise suppression standards.

A successor to the "Quick" was launched in 1953: the "Quickly," a smaller (only 50 cc) engined version with pedals, weighing only 72.75 pounds and authorized for use without road tax, number plate or driver's license. "Give up walking, ride a

01 NSU Prima V motor scooter, 1958
02 NSU Max and Maxi, 1956
03 NSU Lambretta exhibition display, 1954
04 NSU Lambretta assembly line, 1955
05 Actor Peter Alexander with the NSU Quickly Type N, 1953

03, 04

05

01   02

03

Quickly!" was the advertising slogan that indicated that NSU was trying to interest customers new to motorized transport. In the mid-1950s, the NSU motorcycle range was enhanced in both performance and comfort, with the word "Super" placed in front of the existing model names: "Super Fox," "Super Lux" and "Super Max." Two-color paintwork had been available on many NSU motorcycles from 1954 on, but the great days of motorcycle sales were clearly over, despite encouraging news items such as the production of the millionth Quickly, now Germany's number one moped. The last new NSU two-wheeler design, the Quick 50, appeared in 1962. It had a 50 cc, 4.3 hp two-stroke engine. It went out of production when the motorcycle era ended in Neckarsulm four years later.

Cars

The "put a roof over your head" movement did not reach NSU until relatively late, undoubtedly because the company was enjoying such excellent results with its motorcycles. Plans to build a car originally centered on a vehicle with much of the character of a motorcycle: a three-wheeled cabin scooter with pivoting engine and rear swinging arm that would appeal to the more comfort-conscious motorcyclist. However, the common-sense view that a "proper" car should stand on four wheels soon prevailed. It was to be driven by a rear-mounted, 600 cc 20 hp engine based on the new Max engine with its rod and crank valve gear. The car was light in weight, and proved

capable of reaching 65 mph without difficulty. The then fashionable rear engine meant that luggage space had to be provided at the front. Named the "Prinz," the new car was launched in three equipment and engine versions.

Then came 1963, and the world's first Wankel-engined production car was exhibited at the IAA Motor Show in Frankfurt: the NSU/Wankel Spider. Externally, it resembled the Sport Prinz that had been in production for some years, but the rear engine cover concealed a 50 hp Wankel engine that achieved a top speed of 93 mph. The Prinz 4 had already been launched in 1961 with a totally new body that appealed to the modern customer much more than the previous curvaceous styling. The air-cooled OHV engine developed 30 hp and was still at the rear. The car was a success and by 1963 about 74,000 units had already been sold.

A year later, when the NSU Prinz 1000 L was first seen, dealers and technical staff alike were extremely optimistic. Its performance and vitality were aimed at the more demanding driver. The new 43 hp engine was expected to contribute to this: it was mounted transversely at the rear, but retained its air cooling. Then, at the 1965 Frankfurt Motor Show, NSU once again had two new models on its stand: the NSU Type 110 with 1,100 cc engine and enlarged body was the more spacious and the more expensive of these; the other was the NSU Prinz 1000 TT, a sports version of the Prinz 1000 with a power output of 55 hp.

04

05

01

A successor was introduced in 1967: the NSU TT with 1,200 cc, 65 hp engine. The last new model in this series was the NSU TTS powered by a 1,000 cc, 70 hp engine (also in 1967).

But there was another good reason why everyone's attention was riveted on the NSU motor-show stand in 1967. The Ro 80 not only featured a 115 hp rotary-piston (Wankel) engine that was revolutionary in every sense of the term, but was an advanced design in many other respects, as confirmed by its elegant body with excellent aerodynamics. With superb suspension and front-wheel drive, this totally new car also marked NSU's departure from the rear-engined layout with its considerable disadvantages.

In 1968 the Ro 80 was voted "Car of the Year." This was indeed a major triumph for NSU's engineering team. With this car they rewrote motoring history – certainly not for the first, but unfortunately for the last time.

02

03, 04

Motor sport

In the summer of 1947, when the first racing motorcycles returned to their traditional circuits, the NSU brand was among them. Wilhelm Herz, for instance, had built himself a 350 cc supercharged bike, and rode it to victory in the 1948 German Championship's 350 cc class. At the end of that year, NSU's directors resolved to go racing again with a works team. This consisted of Wilhelm Herz in the 350 cc class, Heiner Fleischmann on a 500 cc bike and Böhm/Fuchs in the up to 600 cc sidecar class. 1950 was the last season in which superchargers were permitted, and resulted in further post-war triumphs for NSU. Böhm/Fuchs won the German championship in the sidecar class and took the title in the 350 cc category.

On April 12, 1951, NSU undertook its first motorcycle record-breaking attempts since the war. On a streamlined 500 cc bike, Wilhelm Herz reached a genuine 180 mph, capturing for the Neckarsulm company the record set 14 years before, when Henne on a BMW recorded 174 mph. Böhm added sidecar speed records to the total of eight that were obtained on this occasion. Encouraged by the sales success of the "Fox," it was decided to enter races in this category as well. The OHC engine revved to an amazing 11,000 rpm and had a power output of 11 hp.

A notable first-time victory was scored on July 20, 1952: the first world championship race that Germany was allowed to hold after the war was run on the Solitude circuit near Stuttgart, and the new 125 cc NSU "Rennfox" racing bike, ridden by Werner Haas, was also on the starting line for the first time in its career. Haas outdistanced the world's elite riders and brought the NSU home to an impressive, well-earned victory.

01, 02

01, 02 H. P. Müller with the Baumm II, which set a new speed record for the 125 cc class in 1956 at 150 mph

The next racing bike, the 250 cc "Rennmax," appeared in 1952. Its parallel-twin engine had double overhead camshafts driven by two vertical bevel-gear shafts. This bike too was an immediate success on the racing circuits. Haas rode it to victory on the Grenzlandring in its first season, but also took it to the starting line in the larger 350 cc class, and outclassed his rivals there too. NSU resolved to enter world championship events in the 1953 season, despite the considerable funds, technical resources and personnel that the project would tie up. The reward was not long in coming: Werner Haas ended the season as twofold world champion, in the 125 and 250 cc classes. He also secured the German Championship titles in the same two engine-size categories.

New riders joined the NSU works team in 1954. The best-known newcomer was H. P. Müller, known to his fans as the "Racing Tiger," who had previously ridden for DKW and then for a short time as a private entrant. Hans Baltisberger and Rupert Hollaus completed the team, which was still headed by Werner Haas.

The Fox and Max racing bikes were given a new fairing that earned them the nickname "Dolphins." The Rennfox engine developed 19 hp, the Rennmax 37 hp. The season's biggest success was in the English Tourist Trophy (TT) race. Hollaus defeated the Italian rider Ubbiali in the 125 cc class, and in the 250 cc class the NSU team took the first four places, the riders being Haas, Hollaus, Armstrong and Müller.

NSU racing bikes appeared with a "new look" in July 1954. The fairing had lost its dolphin's beak and was wider at the front. The brake cooling apertures now suggested quite a different aquatic mammal, and the fans therefore began to speak of NSU's "Blue Whales." Once again the world championship titles in the 125 cc and 250 cc classes were secured, but the Neckarsulm team also suffered a tragic setback: Rupert Hollaus, one of its star drivers, crashed in Monza and suffered fatal injuries. The season's results were if anything more impressive than ever: 24 starts, 24 victories! For two years running NSU had won

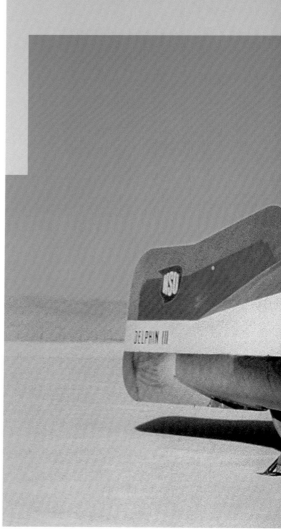

03

the manufacturers' world championship and the German championship. Nonetheless, company management now felt that it was time for a change of policy.

At the end of 1954 the company made an announcement that amounted to a bombshell in the motorcycle racing world: NSU would not be competing in any more races. Its official works team would be wound up and from now on it would only provide support for promising private entrants. However, if people thought that the brand's run of success would dry up as a result, they were wrong: in 1955 "Racing Tiger" H. P. Müller pulled off a unique masterstroke, becoming the first private entrant ever to take the 250 cc world championship title. At this time NSU switched its activity to world speed record attempts.

Gustav Adolf Baumm was a graphic artist by profession. With the help of NSU's technicians

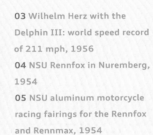

04

03 Wilhelm Herz with the
Delphin III: world speed record
of 211 mph, 1956
04 NSU Rennfox in Nuremberg,
1954
05 NSU aluminum motorcycle
racing fairings for the Rennfox
and Rennmax, 1954

he sketched out and built his own unusual, highly
aerodynamic vehicle, powered by a rear-mounted
50 cc Quickly engine developing 3.4 horsepower:
the "Flying Deckchair." With this contrivance, and
with another version of similar design powered
by a 100 cc, 7 hp Fox engine, Baumm captured
eleven world records in 1954.

After the New Zealand rider Wright had surpassed
Herz's world motorcycle speed record in 1955
on a 1,000 cc Vincent, NSU's engineers developed
a truly outstanding, fully streamlined record-
breaking motorcycle with a 500 cc engine. Wilhelm
Herz rode it on the Bonneville salt flats in the
state of Utah in July and August 1956, and put
the record up to 211 mph. H. P. Müller took a
Baumm "Flying Deckchair" up to 122 mph with a
50 cc engine and up to 150 mph with the 125 cc
engine installed.

NSU thus held all the world speed records that it
was possible for a two-wheeled vehicle to set.

NSU-Delphin
Anfang 1954

120

Übergangsform
Großer Preis von Holland

NSU-Blau-Wal
Solitude 1954

05

01

02

A five-year period of abstinence then set in, until in 1960 the NSU Board of Management decided that motor sport with the company's cars should be given more attention. Although no new works team was set up, the intention was to provide private entrants in touring-car racing with more effective support.

Car racing

An NSU Trophy was therefore presented to the most successful competitor at the wheel of one of the company's cars. The compact rear-engined cars were in their element when entered for hillclimbs. In 1962, for example, Karl-Heinz Panowitz was German Hillclimb Champion in every category, outperforming many a rival in a larger-engined car.

In the following season Behra/Behra won their class in the Monte Carlo Rally, and a year later Siegfried Spiess was German Hillclimb Champion in his NSU Prinz II.

Company chronicle

1960 NSU Motorenwerke AG established on August 5; capital: 27 million DM. From the end of the war until production ceased in 1963, 1,034,277 NSU bicycles were made. Annual motorcycle output exceeded 100,000 units in 1953, and reached an absolute peak in 1956 with 236,132 units. From 1957 to the end of 1968, NSU built approximately 760,000 passenger cars. The workforce rose from just over 5,000 in the 1950s to more than 7,000 in the 1960s

1969 Audi NSU Auto Union AG established on August 21. At that time, NSU had 11,504 employees

03

With a larger trochoid, an inlet manifold with Stromberg carburetor, a special transmission and improvements to the suspension, the racing version of the NSU Wankel Spider developed 90 hp, unlike the production cars with their power output of only 50 hp.

In 1966 Karl-Heinz Panowitz/Rainer Strunz entered their racing Spider for eight heats of the German GT Rally Championship and took first place five times and second place three times. This title win was the first ever to be obtained by an NSU Wankel-engined car. In the same year Siegfried Spiess was runner-up to a Porsche in the German hillclimb championship for GT and sports cars, surpassing his own achievement a year later by capturing the German Car Hillclimb Championship in all classes and categories, a success he repeated in 1968, giving the NSU Wankel Spider three championship victories in three successive years.

In other countries too the NSU Wankel Spider carried off championship titles: Alexander Maniatopoulos was the 1966 Greek Car Champion and Christine Beckers the 1967 Hillclimb Champion in Belgium.

The standard NSU TT remained in production from 1967 to 1972, and had a power output of 65 hp from its 1,200 cc engine. For motor sport, the engine's swept volume was increased to 1,300 cc, and Weber carburetors with a special inlet manifold, twin-spark ignition and enlarged inlet and exhaust ports made it competitive. In 1967 Günther Irrascher was the overall winner of the Tour d'Europe in an NSU TT, in 1968 Bill Allen took the American championship in the South Pacific region and in 1974 Willi Bergmeister was German hillclimb champion. Between 1971 and 1974 the NSU TT was the most successful German car in national hillclimb events. It also won no fewer than 29 national circuit racing championships in Europe and North America.

01 – 03 The NSU TTS had won 29 national championships by 1977

01

02

04

07

10

NSU – an overview
Bicycles

03

05

06

08

09

01

02

05

06

07

12

1873 – 1969 NSU – Motorcycles – an overview

NSU – an overview
Motorcycles

01 NSU 1.75 hp, 1903
02 NSU 1.25 hp, 1907
03 NSU 8 hp twin, 1914
04 NSU Motosulm, 1931
05 NSU Fox four-stroke, 1952
06 NSU Geländemax off-road
model, 1955
07 NSU Super Lux, 1954
08 NSU Max, 1956
09 NSU Super Max, 1957
10 NSU Quickly S with legshields,
1956
11 NSU Maxi, 1958
12 Quickly Cavallino, 1957

03

04

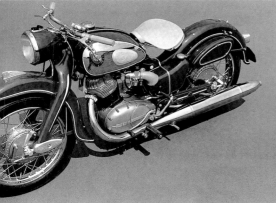

08

09

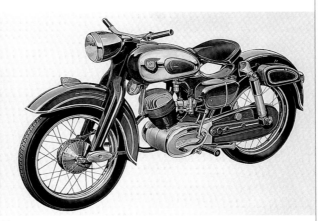

10

11

01

02

05

06

09

10

206

NSU – an overview
Cars

03

04

01 The Sulmobil, NSU's first car, 1905

02 Enesumobil prototype, 1913

03 NSU Type 10/20 hp car, 1909

04 NSU 5/15 hp, 1914

05 NSU 2.5 t truck, 1921

06 NSU 7/34 hp delivery van, 1929

07 NSU Prinz III, 1960

08 NSU/Wankel Spider, 1964

09 NSU Type 110, 1967

10 NSU TT, 1969

11 NSU Ro 80, 1975

07

08

11

207

A new profile for the Four Rings

Takeover and merger
VW, NSU and elective affinities

The 1960s began for Germany with a political earthquake – construction of the Berlin Wall. Not long after this, the Cuba crisis threatened the security of the entire world and appeared likely to transform the Cold War into a much hotter one. By the end of the decade, too, the character of the United States' involvement in the Vietnam war was becoming increasingly obvious. In the West, cracks began to develop in the pattern of economic growth. Germany was not immune to spectacular insolvencies such as the Borgward carmaking empire in Bremen, and old-established shipyards began to fade from the scene, although there was still full employment. Adenauer's chancellorship in Germany came to an end; Ludwig Erhard, father of the economic miracle, took over, but his period of office was not a success. He appealed in vain for moderation, resigned in due course and made way for a grand coalition of the two major political parties. This was an era of change, and also the time in which Auto Union GmbH was restructured.

In 1965, the situation as it involved Auto Union was far from clear. The owner, Daimler-Benz, was selling its holding in several packages to the Wolfsburg-based Volkswagenwerk. Financial complications slowed the process down, whereas in contrast the technical and staff changes were all the more radical.

By the end of 1964 the VW Group had acquired 50.3 percent of Auto Union's equity, but when it came to reorganizing its acquisition, the management in Wolfsburg found the task more demanding that it had originally expected. Nonetheless, complete takeover of the Ingolstadt carmaker went ahead as planned; in the following two years, the remaining 49.7 percent of the shares were bought in. By the end of 1966, Auto Union GmbH had become a wholly owned VW subsidiary.

01

01 Heinrich Nordhoff, Volkswagen's Chief Executive from
1948 to 1968

12,000 employees in Ingolstadt and 1,200 Auto Union dealers were urgently waiting for a new perspective for the future and a change of course in the direction of new products with greater market appeal. The two-stroke engine's reputation was already damaged to such an extent that the

02

cars built in Ingolstadt could scarcely be sold at any price. In 1965, there were 30,000 of them undelivered. As the new owner, VW had deleted a number of models from the DKW program, but new cars were still being produced and stock-piled. Work went ahead at a frantic pace on the F 103 – the DKW F 102 with a new four-stroke medium compression engine – but it was impossible to estimate when the car would reach the dealers, and still less whether the customers would like it. The factory was in a precarious situation, and an urgent solution was needed. This was found without delay in the guise of the VW Beetle: between May 1965 and July 4, 1969, between 300 and 500 Beetles were assembled at the Ingolstadt factory. Total output of this model was no fewer than 347,869 cars. This wise decision helped to make use of the factory's spare capacity and safeguard employees' jobs.

After taking over Auto Union, VW Chief Executive Nordhoff's main worry was not keeping production moving; he also took immediate steps to renew the entire management team. In the weeks that followed completion of the takeover process, all the top executives were dispatched into retirement or persuaded by some other means to resign their positions. Nordhoff then appointed the best person in his team to run the company: Rudolf Leiding, manager of the Volkswagen factory in Kassel. His task was to dispose of the stockpiled new cars and at the same time initiate a funda-mental reorganization process. He described the situation as follows:
"All the spirit had gone out of the workforce [...]. Cost-related thinking is an almost unknown concept in many departments throughout the company [...]. Hard work will be needed every-where before all departments understand the principle of cost-saving."
Nordhoff's declared intention was to run Ingol-stadt just as rigidly as the VW factories in Wolfs-burg, Hanover, Braunschweig and Kassel. Leiding was also instructed to take down the flag with the four-ring emblem in Ingolstadt.

02 The last Beetle built in Ingolstadt. It helped Auto Union through very difficult times

211

01

01 The first new Audi, accompanied by (from left to right) Dr. Ludwig Kraus, Rudolf Leiding, Volkswagen's Marketing and Sales Director Fritz Frank, and the Auto Union Sales Director Emil Gräbner

Daimler-Benz AG had left draft designs with Auto Union for a four-cylinder, four-stroke engine intended for a military project. Ludwig Kraus, also seconded to Auto Union in 1963, was told to develop this engine to series-production maturity and implant it in an existing car. By mid-1965 the 1.7-liter medium compression engine was ready for production: it was installed in a modified DKW F 102 and presented to the public in September 1965 as the first car with a four-stroke engine to emerge from Ingolstadt. Nobody was enthusiastic about marketing the new model under the DKW brand name, encumbered as it was with memories of recent unsuccessful models. The new car therefore went on sale as an Audi.

The public took to the new model enthusiastically, and its sales figures made good progress – until the company and indeed the entire car industry was dealt a severe blow by the first recession since the end of World War II. An average drop in output of some 20 percent was the result. In Ingolstadt, the losses were at least partly contained by carefully planned changes and additions to the model program.

Wedding bells
During this difficult phase, Heinrich Nordhoff died on April 12, 1968. He was succeeded by Kurt Lotz, who lost no time in pressing ahead with the acquisition of NSU AG in Neckarsulm. In Nordhoff's era the question of taking over this carmaker in the Swabian region of Germany and combining its sales program with that of Auto Union had already been considered. Despite reports verging on euphoria in the press, neither Nordhoff nor Lotz was very impressed with the Wankel engine or its future prospects. The main argument in favor of taking a share in NSU was a different one: making it easier to fend off competition. In Neckarsulm it had been obvious for some time

The new company

Audi NSU Auto Union AG adopted a policy of growth from the very start. This not only called for a total sum in the billions to be made available for investment, but also involved corporate restructuring. Whenever possible, the Volkswagen Group purchased the shares of such NSU shareholders as were so far uncommitted, and in due course became the almost 100-percent owner of the joint stock company with its factories in Ingolstadt and Neckarsulm. The previous NSU Chief Executive, Gerd Stieler von Heydekampf, was appointed Chairman of the Board of Management, followed again for a short period in 1971 by Rudolf Leiding.

The Chief Executives in later years – Leiding was followed by Dr. Gerhard Prinz, Dr. Werner Schmidt, Gottlieb Strobl and Dr. Wolfgang Habbel – completed the company restructuring process. Together with VW they put together a sales organization, ensured that an attractive product program was built-up and updated and formulated penetration of the large-car market as a strategic objective.

The most effective instrument in upgrading the Audi brand was the advanced technology incorporated into the cars bearing the four-ring badge. The plan was to be subsequently at the forefront of technical progress in many areas of automobile manufacturing. After NSU and Audi had merged, an advertisement for the new company summed up everything that the two brands had contributed to the wealth of motor-vehicle technology. It was then only a small step to the advertising slogan that appeared for the first time in a double-page ad and since then has accompanied the progress of the cars with the four-ring emblem all over the world: Vorsprung durch Technik.

03

02 The Audi Variant station wagon seen at the Paris Motor Show in 1966
03 A pre-production Auto Union Audi, still with trim and rear panel from the DKW F 102, photographed in early 1965

02

that the company's meager capitalization would force it to seek shelter with a larger company before very long. To survive on the market, large-scale strategies were needed, but these in turn called for high levels of investment.
Possible hindrances to amalgamation were felt to be the NSU share price, which fluctuated wildly due to the activities of speculators, and the fact that the company had so many small shareholders. After lengthy negotiations, the two management teams had a clear picture of the procedure that they would have to follow, and on March 10, 1969, the merger agreement between Auto Union GmbH and NSU Motoren-werke AG was signed. At an extraordinary general meeting on April 26, after twelve hours of heated discussion, the shareholders also accepted the merger. The new Audi NSU Auto Union AG came into effect retrospectively from January 1, 1969, onwards. Its headquarters were initially in Neckarsulm.

01

01 Audi 75 Variant station wagon: a remarkable amount of space was available when the rear seat was folded

The importance attached to technical research and development was underscored in Ingolstadt in the spring of 1969 when the foundation stone was laid for Technical Development's own complex of buildings. The initiative for this project came from the company's Technical Director, Dr. Ludwig Kraus. At Group Management meetings he had unceasingly put forward the idea that Audi should have its own independent development facilities. The years that followed were ample confirmation of his far-sighted approach. Many of the ideas conceived and developed to series-production maturity in Ingolstadt appeared not only in Audi models but in various VW models too. Cooperation in the research, development and production areas became closer. The sales area was restructured as well. By the mid-1970s, a joint VW/Audi dealer organization with sufficient freedom for Audi to develop an independent image had been built up.

Products in the early years

After the first new Audi had gone into production in the fall of 1965, the direction that development was to take in the future could be clearly seen. The first new Audi was to father a whole family of cars, beginning with a station wagon based based on the DKW F 102, which had already been developed almost to production readiness. This preparatory work was now transferred to Audi. The cars' new four-stroke engine was always described in advertising as a medium compression engine, although in strict technical terms this was inaccurate or even misleading. The term was originally coined to indicate that the compression ratio lay between that of a gasoline engine and that of a diesel. In other words the engine had an unusually high compression ratio for a gasoline engine and was therefore highly efficient.
It was as if people had just been waiting for the company to say farewell to the two-stroke engine: 16,000 of the new Audi model were built in the first three months of its career. Its technical features formed the basis for a varied range of models, not only with different body styles but in particular with various power outputs.

02

The family grows

When the new Audi was introduced in 1965 it needed no specific model designation. Later, when a family of models was built up, it was called the Audi 72, as an indication of how many horsepower the engine developed. The station wagon version appeared in the spring of 1966, and was marketed as the "Variant," the term used by VW. The sedan model was available with two or four doors and with the option of a luxury equipment specification.

214

03

69   68

02 Audi Super 90, top model in the range from 1966 onwards
03 Audi Super 90, distinguishable from other models by the chromed wheel arch cutouts
04 An Audi 60 Variant in the summer of 1970

05 (p. 216/217) The Audi NSU Auto Union AG model program for 1970

HN - JL 859

04

01 Front-wheel drive for
directional stability
02 A cutaway view of the facelifted Audi models sold from
August 1970 onwards

In September 1966 the Audi 80 was introduced, with an 80 hp medium-compression engine as the name implied, and only three months later the top model was announced: the Audi Super 90. With 90 hp from its engine, it could reach a top speed of 99 mph, a distinctly impressive figure at that time. The lower end of the range was completed in January 1968 by the Audi 60, with a 55 hp engine. This was intended as the high-volume entry-level model. At the end of the year the Audi 72 and 80 models were replaced by the Audi 75. As predicted, the smallest-engined car, the Audi 60, was the most successful, accounting for more than 50 percent of first-generation Audi output.

The development department remained extremely active: Kraus kept the pressure on his staff. The successful launch of the first-generation models encouraged him to develop a "genuine" Audi, free of DKW genes. Kraus often described the F 103 series, with its DKW body and Mercedes engine, with a mixture of affection and disapproval, as "the bastard." Group management in Wolfsburg, however, was opposed to his plan to develop a totally new car, and had limited Kraus's brief to work on the current models. Ingolstadt was forbidden to undertake new development work, which was the sole prerogative of Volkswagen in Wolfsburg.

03 Arduous testing in the Alpine foothills
04 The advertising dream: a 1970 Audi 60, the perfect second car for the aircraft owner
05 Audi 60 L – the high-volume model. More than 215,000 were built between 1968 and 1972

Kraus, on the other hand, had plans to build an Audi 100, a much larger car than the current Audi, with a powerful but economical engine and weighing less than its competitors so that acceleration would be superior. The car would also have a more streamlined body with a lower drag coefficient.

Disregarding the directives from Wolfsburg and with Volkswagen's management kept in the dark, work began in secret on this upper-midsize model. Leiding's first inkling of the project was when he saw a clay model in the Ingolstadt styling department. He was delighted with it, but Nordhoff's agreement was essential. This was obtained by a tactical masterstroke. Leiding arranged for Wolfsburg to issue a development order under the heading of "Body modifications," and suggested that the Group's Board of Management might care to inspect the results. The car pleased the Board members – Nordhoff in particular – so much that they decided to build it as a Volkswagen model. This called for another round of diplomatic negotiation before the Group managers could be dissuaded. In the end, the Ingolstadt team's missionary work bore fruit, and development of the Audi 100 went ahead as the Type 104 project.

01 In the 1970s, 90 percent of all cars were bought by men. The advertising industry was obviously aware of this
02 A 1971 Audi 100 LS – in the heyday of miniskirts and knitted dresses
03 Audi 100 LS, 1972 model
04 The Audi 100 LS at the launch ceremony in 1971

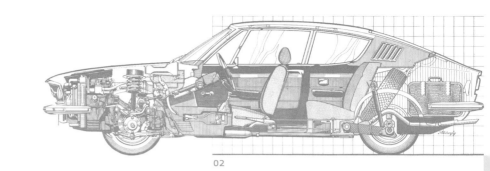

01 Audi 100 Coupé S, 1973
02 A cutaway view of the first-series Audi 100 Coupé S. It still had inboard brake disks next to the transmission, and torsion-crank rear suspension

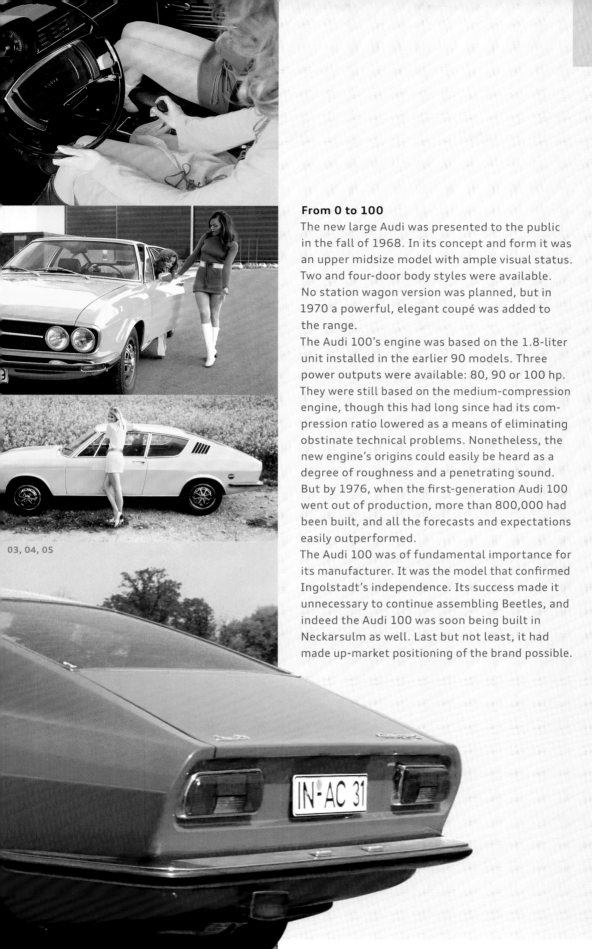

From 0 to 100

The new large Audi was presented to the public in the fall of 1968. In its concept and form it was an upper midsize model with ample visual status. Two and four-door body styles were available. No station wagon version was planned, but in 1970 a powerful, elegant coupé was added to the range.

The Audi 100's engine was based on the 1.8-liter unit installed in the earlier 90 models. Three power outputs were available: 80, 90 or 100 hp. They were still based on the medium-compression engine, though this had long since had its compression ratio lowered as a means of eliminating obstinate technical problems. Nonetheless, the new engine's origins could easily be heard as a degree of roughness and a penetrating sound.

But by 1976, when the first-generation Audi 100 went out of production, more than 800,000 had been built, and all the forecasts and expectations easily outperformed.

The Audi 100 was of fundamental importance for its manufacturer. It was the model that confirmed Ingolstadt's independence. Its success made it unnecessary to continue assembling Beetles, and indeed the Audi 100 was soon being built in Neckarsulm as well. Last but not least, it had made up-market positioning of the brand possible.

03, 04, 05

03 Interior of the Audi 100 Coupé S with photo models in contemporary style
04 Audi 100 Coupé S in Tibet orange; the occupants have chosen contrasting colors
05 Banana yellow – a striking color at extra charge for the 1975 and 1976 model years

01 1973 Audi 80 GL with 85 hp
engine, making it one of the
fastest cars in its class

In the summer of 1972 the next entirely new model, the Audi 80, was introduced to supersede the original cars with their medium-compression engines after a seven-year production period. The concept of a modular-element design came from Ludwig Kraus, with a four-cylinder OHC engine as the intended power unit. This engine, developed under the supervision of Franz Hauk, was referred to internally as EA 827, and was to become the highest-volume unit built by the Volkswagen Group. The Audi 80's suspension also set fresh standards in car design with its negative steering roll radius. This front-axle layout prevented the car from veering off its chosen course if poor road surfaces, tire damage or braking problems occurred. It had already been described in technical publications, but Audi was the first manufacturer to interpret it successfully on a high-volume model. The Ingolstadt-based engineer Detlef Banholzer earned special praise for his contribution, and was awarded Vienna Technical University's Porsche Prize in 1977 "as a tribute to his exceptional scientific achievements in the field of motor-vehicle suspension development."

The Audi 80 was a classic example of skilled weight-saving design. The technical limits for every assembly or component group were explored: wall thicknesses, production effort and space required in the car. The resulting unladen weight of under 1,984 pounds permitted vigorous performance accompanied by moderate fuel consumption.

The Audi 80's body was coated at various points with zinc powder paint to resist corrosion, the first time that Audi had used this technique. PVC underseal was also applied. The new car was a sales success from the very start. Including a mild facelift in the course of its career, it sold more than a million in the six years that followed. VW "adopted" the Audi 80, so to speak, and sold it with only marginal changes – apart from the fastback body style – as the VW Passat, the first model to emerge from Wolfsburg with a water-cooled engine and front-wheel drive. The station wagon version of the VW model, on the other hand, was sold in the United States as the Audi Fox Station Wagon – the wheel had come full circle.

01

02 Audi 80 GL, 1973 model year

03 With front-wheel drive, McPherson front suspension struts and negative roll radius, road behavior was exemplary

04 Audi 80 GT with sport package. The 100 hp version was built from the summer of 1973 to the fall of 1975

05 Audi 80 LS, 1972. More than 355,000 were sold in its six years of production

02

03

04

05

01

The Audi sales program in the early 1970s was completed two years after the appearance of the Audi 80 by the launch of a small car. The Audi 50 was in fact the smallest-ever Audi model. Ludwig Kraus was of the opinion that every brand should have its entry-level model, and that after the rear-engined NSU models had ceased production the company had seriously neglected the small-car market. At that time observers felt that customers were favoring larger, more powerful cars, but the situation in the early 1970s, which culminated in an energy crisis, reversed this trend.

Energy versus crisis

In October 1973 the OPEC nations imposed an oil embargo against all countries that dealt with Israel. Within six months there was a fourfold increase in the price of crude oil. The sacrifices that the energy crisis entailed were felt by the motor-vehicle industry as a severe recession. In addition to economic problems, the automobile had to fight against a general decline in sympathy. It was accused of squandering energy, burdening the environment and causing accidents, though curiously enough the public's craving for mobility remained as strong as ever. The lack of new orders

03

04

accompanying these reproaches confronted the industry with many an economic problem but also with a challenge: to improve future cars in certain very specific ways.

Concentrated effort was therefore devoted to reducing fuel consumption, minimizing pollutant emissions and improving active and passive safety. The state of California played a leading role in legislating for reduced exhaust emissions. Its statutory limits were the toughest in the world, and obliged Europe's automobile manufacturers to come up with new solutions. As a result, pollutant emissions were cut by two-thirds in the next 15 years. New cars' handling and ride quality reached levels previously considered impossible to attain, noise levels and aerodynamic drag coefficients dropped to equally unexpected values.

Small cars to combat the crisis

When it was obvious that the trend toward smaller, more economical cars was here to stay, Kraus was ready to produce the answer with a flourish: a car with a low-consumption four-cylinder inline engine mounted transversely at the front of the car and developing 50 horsepower – hence the

name Audi 50. The overall length was initially only 11.48 feet, but extremely clever use was made of the interior space, and the body had impact-absorbing zones at the front and rear and a large tailgate, which convinced many customers of its virtues as a miniature station wagon. Presented to the media in 1974 on the island of Sardinia, the Audi 50 was in fact the first modern German car in this size category. It aroused immediate public interest and sold well despite the prevailing atmosphere of crisis. The Audi 50 was built from the very start on the assembly lines in Wolfsburg, and it was an open secret that a VW model based on the small Audi would soon appear as well. This proved to be the VW Polo, with a 40 hp engine – also developed in Ingolstadt – and rather spartan interior equipment and trim. Since Audi was determinedly moving up market at this time, the marketing strategists felt that there was no place in the product program for a small car. The concept of premium small cars would have to wait another 20 years to become reality. Production of the Audi 50 came to a halt in 1978, after over 180,000 units had been built. The VW Polo continued in production until the fall of 1981, and proved to be a top seller.

03 Audi 50 CL, 1975
04 Audi 50 GL, 1974

227

01

The way to the top

By the mid-1970s, the Audi 50, 80 and 100 models meant that small and midsize cars were well represented in the "four-ring" program. A final step into the upper midsize category was taken in 1976, when the second-generation Audi 100 was announced. The top version of the new model line, which went on sale in April 1977, was propelled by a 2.2-liter five-cylinder inline engine rated at 100 kW (136 hp). This unusual number of cylinders, which had involved much technical work to master the difficult problem of mass inertial balance, proved to be ideal in conjunction with another design principle favored by Audi NSU Auto Union AG: front-wheel drive with the engine ahead of the transmission and differential. The meaty sound of the five-cylinder engine had a certain resemblance to that of a V8, and was

soon to be heard from a large number of next-generation models. Apart from technical innovations, a new body style with a sloping tailgate joined the program in August 1977 and was sold as the Audi 100 Avant.

September 1979 saw the introduction of the Audi 200, two versions of which reached the market in the spring of 1980. The Audi 200 5E had the 100 kW (136 hp) five-cylinder engine, the turbocharged Audi 200 5T developed 125 kW (170 hp). The latter unit fathered a whole generation of turbocharged engines, which remained in production after several design revisions until the second half of the 1990s and was used to propel the especially sporty Audi models. The Audi 200 was also Audi NSU Auto Union AG's first direct onslaught on the large car market.

02

03

04

05

01 Audi 100, 1976
02 Audi 100 GL 5E facelift, 1980
03 Audi 100 Avant – ideal for winter sport, with its large tailgate and ski bag
04 Audi 200 5E, 1980
05 An Audi 200 headlight unit – attractively styled, but the light output was rather weak

01

02

230

The Audi 80, Ingolstadt's success concept, appeared in the fall of 1978 as a totally redesigned second-generation model. The appearance of this high-volume model matched that of the Audi 100, and it was in strong demand right from the start, with up to 800 being built every day. Starting in the fall of 1981, the Audi 80 could also be ordered with an 85 kW (115 hp) five-

03

cylinder engine. In 1984 the model line was face-lifted and this version sold as a separate type known as the Audi 90.

Ten years after production of the DKW Munga, which was primarily supplied to the German Army, had ended, Ingolstadt was again involved in building an off-road vehicle. In November 1978 the first all-wheel-drive VW Iltis (Polecat) was formally handed over to a German Army contin-gent in front of the City Theater in Ingolstadt. This vehicle had in fact been developed by Audi and was being built in Ingolstadt, but since Audi had no commercial-vehicle sales organization, the Iltis was sold as a VW. Later, the production equipment was moved to the VW factory in Brussels, and after fulfillment of the German and Belgian Army contracts, sold to Bombardier, a Canadian conglomerate.

Permanent all-wheel drive in a sports coupé – this was the sensation at the Audi stand at the Geneva Motor Show in March 1980. The Audi quattro

created new accents worldwide on the automobile scene, and started a boom in all-wheel-drive cars that has persisted right up to the present day. The Audi quattro was a quantum leap forward that identified the Audi brand as a supplier of technically innovative vehicles. In the fall of the same year the Audi Coupé was introduced; its body design closely resembled that of the Audi quattro.

As a response to the shock caused by increased crude oil prices in the 1970s and the resulting steep increase in the cost of motor-vehicle fuel, Audi NSU Auto Union AG exhibited the Audi "research car" at the Frankfurt Motor Show in 1981. Its development had been grant-aided by Germany's Research Ministry. This study was aimed at achieving distinct improvements in energy and raw material consumption, environmental acceptability, safety, overall economy and user benefit. Many of its features were seen in practice only a year later, when the third-generation Audi 100 reached the market.

01 An Audi 80 GLS at the Danube Gorge near Weltenburg monastery in 1978
02 The first five-cylinder engine for the Audi 80: 1,921 cc, 85 kW (115 hp)
03 Audi 80 GLS, built from 1978 onwards
04 Audi 90 and Audi Coupé GT, 1985. Both these models were based on the platform of the Audi 80 introduced in 1978
05 Audi Coupé GT quattro, 1984

04, 05

231

The results of this research work were most impressive. Led by Technical Board Member Ferdinand Piëch, Audi's development engineers had succeeded in uniting state-of-the-art technical know-how in this car. With an aerodynamic drag coefficient of $c_d = 0.30$, the new Audi 100 had better aerodynamics than any other production sedan in the world when it was announced. Many international prizes and a major sales success confirmed that Audi NSU had found the correct answer to current motoring needs.

Successful premieres

In 1983 a new Avant model was added to the 100 series. Its elegance and practicality appealed to a large number of customers, with the result that this station wagon with its fastback styling became a firm feature of the Audi product program. Next to appear was the new-generation Audi 200, in the fall of the same year. The 200 turbo version of this attractive, aerodynamically efficient car now developed 134 kW (182 hp) and achieved a top speed of 143 mph. At the end of 1984 the Audi 200 became available for the first time with all-wheel drive. From 1985 onwards, the bodyshells were fully galvanized, not only for the Audi 200, but also the Audi 100 and, starting in 1986, the third-generation Audi 80 and its derivatives.

When it became known that from 1986 onwards the German government was planning to make catalytic converters compulsory on all new cars for environmental protection reasons, Audi took firm action without delay. Audi NSU was the first German automobile manufacturer to be granted a general operating permit for vehicles with exhaust emission control by catalytic converter; this was in 1983. At that time too, permanent all-wheel drive gradually became available on all Audi models. The remaining step towards large-scale production was taken in the fall of 1982, when the Audi 80 quattro was launched. By 1984, customers could obtain any Audi model with all four wheels driven. Only a few years had been needed to create an attractive, technically advanced model program that satisfied the needs and wishes of a wide variety of customers.

03

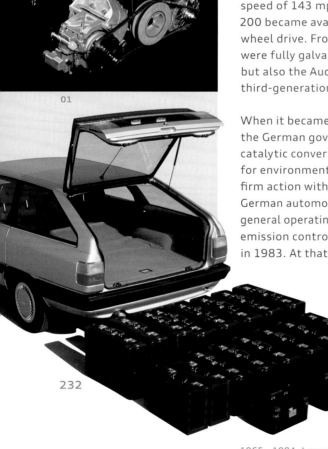

01

02

232

01 The first five-cylinder TDI
engine was premiered in 1989 in
the Audi 100

02 With the rear seats folded,
the Audi 100 Avant impressed
with its gigantic load volume

03 With a drag coefficient (c_d) of
only 0.30, the Audi 100 had the
best aerodynamics of any standard
sedan car in the world when it
was introduced

04 Audi 100 CD, 1982

05 Audi 100 Avant quattro, 1987

quattro – a hand with four aces

01

Work on the Iltis off-road vehicle led to Ingolstadt's technical staff considering the prospects
of making and selling cars with all-wheel drive
more closely. The initial incentive for the development of a powerful sports car with permanent
all-wheel drive came from Jörg Bensinger, an Audi
engineer in charge of suspension testing. He had
accompanied an all-wheel-drive Iltis to Northern
Finland for winter testing. Despite its high ground
clearance and relative lack of power, the vehicle
handled exceptionally well on ice and snow and
was actually faster in these conditions than the
first prototypes of the forthcoming turbocharged
models. How would an all-wheel-drive car with a
much more powerful engine perform?

After returning to Ingolstadt, Bensinger put this
idea to his superior, Ferdinand Piëch, who agreed
that an experimental car should be built. The
aim was not to develop another luxury off-road
vehicle such as the British Range Rover. What
the two engineers had in mind was a sportier,
attractively styled package with a powerful engine
that would reveal the true benefits of permanent
all-wheel drive. To save time, but above all
because there was in-house access to mechanical
assemblies from various models, items from

various Audi cars were adopted. The five-cylinder
turbocharged engine came from the Audi 200,
the floor pan and various suspension components
from the Audi 80. A front-axle assembly from
the same car was used as a basis for the driven
rear axle; for the rear differential, light alloy
castings were produced using the Iltis as a model.
The body came almost completely from the Audi
80 Coupé, which was about to enter production
at that time.

Test work began in March 1977. For initial trials
of the concept, the Iltis drive train was transplanted into a standard Audi 80 sedan, though
the use of 16-inch wheels indicated that there
were differences under the skin. From the very
outset it was decided that all-wheel drive should
be permanent; a driver-engaged layout was ruled
out. One of the main design problems that had
to be solved was the center differential, which
had the task of equalising differences in front-
and rear-axle speeds of rotation. The solution
surely deserves to be regarded as a stroke of
genius: a compact, lightweight hollow-shaft
layout. The shaft driving the front wheels ran
inside the hollow transmission output shaft and
had a differential at its rear end that distributed
power in equal proportions to the front and rear

02   03

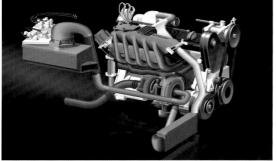

04

05

axles, but also allowed the axles to rotate at different speeds, for example when cornering. The center differential was given a mechanical lock for use in extreme driving conditions. Trials of this still unnamed all-wheel-drive coupé were so encouraging that it was given the status of an official development project at the Ingolstadt factory in 1977. Road testing began in November of that year, and when it proved successful the Board of Management decided to include the car in the production program.

The next step was taken in January 1978, when the engineering team took the car to the Turracher Höhe mountain pass in Austria and demonstrated it to VW's Head of Sales Dr. Schmidt. The manner in which the car coped with gradients of up to 23 percent on Europe's steepest Alpine pass was totally convincing. The prototype stormed up the pass with no traction problems, with summer tires and no snow chains. In April, at the Hockenheimring, the 160 hp quattro showed that it need have no fear of competition even as potentially threatening as the Porsche 911. In view of this Prof. Fiala, the VW Group's Head of Development, gave the go-ahead in May 1978 for series production.

Before this stage was reached, the quattro's power output was boosted again quite considerably, thanks to the adoption for the first time on this model of a 13-row charge air intercooler, which lowered the intake air temperature by between 122 and 140 degrees Fahrenheit and thus improved cylinder filling. The standard version of the turbocharged five-cylinder engine had an output of 147 kW (200 hp) at the moderate engine speed of 5,500 rpm.

04 The intake side of the Audi quattro's turbocharged and intercooled engine
05 A prototype Audi quattro being tested in Northern Scandinavia, 1979

Ausgenommen
PKW mit Allradantrieb
Winterreifen u. PKW mit Spikes

01 The first Audi quattro's driveline

02 Audi quattro 20V, 1990, the first quattro with catalytic converter

03 Advanced technology as an advertising icon

01

02

03

During the Geneva Motor Show in March 1980 the Audi quattro was presented to an international public in an ice skating stadium, and attracted an immense amount of attention. Until then, only thoroughbred off-road vehicles had been given this kind of drive train. Ferdinand Porsche had adopted all-wheel drive for a high-performance car, the Cisitalia racing car he designed immediately after the war, but this had never proved its worth in actual practice. The British Jensen FF was a technically complex niche-market model of which only a few were sold. The Audi quattro's styling, with its sharp edges and corners, appealed to some people more than others. Hartmut Warkuss, VW's Head of Design, called it "cute." The flared wheel arches soon appeared as a styling feature on various production cars from other manufacturers. Aware of the technical

effort that had gone into the quattro, the trade press was unanimous that the Audi brand had taken a giant step forward with this model. The "Vorsprung durch Technik" advertising slogan applied in a double sense to the quattro.

The Audi 80 quattro reached the market in 1982 as the first high-volume model with all-wheel drive. Two years later it was joined by the Audi 200 quattro and Audi 100 quattro. From 1984 onwards the Audi Coupé was also available with permanent all-wheel drive, and by 1985, there was at least one car with all-wheel drive in every Audi model line. Audi stirred up the competition quite noticeably with its quattro concept. Before very long, there was scarcely any car manufacturer without at least one all-wheel-drive model in its program. The quattro idea was making waves!

236

04

05

06

07

04 Audi 80 quattro – the first high-volume model with this drive train appeared in 1983
05 The 1984 Audi 100 quattro: star of the legendary ski-jump commercial
06 The Audi 200 quattro, a car built after the 1989 update
07 Walter Röhrl at the wheel of an Audi Sport quattro

01

From racing circuit to gravel track – successful ye
1965–1987

Very soon after the Audi brand was revived, it began to make the headlines in motor sport. Private entrants tuned the Audi Super 90 and drove it successfully in rallies. A year later, an Audi 80 GTE took the European Touring Car Championship after the final race in Zolder. These private entrants received worthwhile support from the factory. Starting in 1973, a factory trophy was awarded to the best private entrant with a front-wheel-drive Audi. As the Audi 80 piled up one success after another, a motor sport department was organized in Ingolstadt. It maintained close contact with the drivers and assisted them wherever possible. Leading motor sport personalities contributed their know-how and experience, and in this way helped to make the rally cars successful in competition. From the 1978 season onwards,

the factory entered a 160 hp Audi 80 in German rally championship events, and acquired plenty of experience that stood it in good stead later, when the Audi quattro was entered.
The most important precondition for acceptance of quattro technology in rallying was for it to be authorized by the FIA (Fédération Internationale de l'Automobile). There was some doubt as to whether this approval would be granted, but the vital decision became effective as of January 1. At this point in time, the FIA officials probably considered it unlikely that an all-wheel-drive concept would function properly.

The quattro was first tried out as a route marshal's vehicle during the European Rally heat held in Portugal, in the fall of 1980. The Finnish driver Hannu Mikkola, the first to be hired by Audi, had taken part in all the rally quattro test runs. Although a non-competitor, he pushed the quattro around the rally route to such good effect that he reached the finishing line almost half an hour earlier than the actual winner!

After this, Audi entered works cars for rallies and in 1981, in its first season, won the Scandinavian Rally, the San Remo Rally and the British RAC Rally. As well as Hannu Mikkola, the French woman driver Michèle Mouton was a member of the team. Mikkola's navigator was Arne Hertz; for Mouton, this vital task was performed by the Italian Fabrizia Pons. The ladies were always good for a surprise, for instance an outright win in San Remo in 1981 – the first time that a women's team had ever won a World Rally Championship event.

Audi carried off the manufacturers' World Rally Championship title in 1982, and Michèle Mouton was runner-up in the drivers' championship. A triumph, equaled if not surpassed just a year later by a drivers' title for the Finn Hannu Mikkola and a runners-up title in the manufacturers' category. In the years following 1983, Audi collected 13 national rally championship titles in Europe and overseas. The ultimate climax came in 1984,

02

motor sport

03

04, 05

06 Michèle Mouton

07 Fabrizia Pons

06, 07

when Audi took the Manufacturers' World Rally Championship title and Stig Blomqvist, only recently hired as a works driver, won the drivers' title. Audi's pioneering work on quattro driveline technology was acknowledged by granting the company the title "Motor Sport Car of the Year 1984." The year's ultimate triumph was a one-two-three victory for Audi in the Monte Carlo Rally, with first place for Walter Röhrl.

239

03

01

02

01 Stig Blomqvist with navigator
Björn Cederberg: they were
World Rally Champions in 1984
02 Stig Blomqvist in the 1985
Monte Carlo Rally. He drove the
Audi Sport quattro into fifth place

240

Mountaineers, sprinters, marathon runners

1982, the year in which Audi won the Manufacturers' World Rally Championship title for the first time was when the company's series of supreme rally wins got under way. A year later, Hannu Mikkola became the first winner of the drivers' title at the wheel of an Audi. After more outstanding successes in 1984, including both championship titles, Audi was runner-up in the manufacturers' category in 1985. In the drivers' category, the Blomqvist/Cederberg works team was second and Röhrl/Geistdörfer third. With 23 wins in only five years, the Audi quattro was one of the most successful rally cars since the world championship had been inaugurated. In the Far East too, hundreds of thousands of spectators watched these events enthusiastically. The first Hong Kong – Peking relay, held in 1985, was a triumph for Hannu Mikkola and Arne Hertz, a success convincingly repeated a year later by the Blomqvist/Berglund quattro team. The 1986 season, unfortunately, was overshadowed by a tragic accident in the Portugal Rally: the Portuguese driver Joaquim Santos swerved to avoid spectators on the road, lost control of his Ford RS 200 and plunged into another group of spectators. Since the organizers of the various world rally championship heats declared themselves unable to ensure either drivers' or spectators' safety by taking suitable measures along the rally route, Audi decided to withdraw from Group B rallying.

04, 05

Company chronicle

In due course, the potent Group B cars disappeared from rallying, and only Group A cars were licensed to participate. Audi therefore returned to world championship rallying in 1987. At the wheel of the Audi 200 quattro, Hannu Mikkola gained Audi its first win in the notorious Safari Rally in Kenya. His team colleague Walter Röhrl was meanwhile creating a sensation at the Pikes Peak Hillclimb in Colorado. Driving a 598 hp Audi Sport quattro S1, he stormed to the top of this mountain in record time. This was the third time in succession that an Audi driver had taken the winner's position on the podium: Michèle Mouton in 1985 and Bobby Unser a year later had hurled the Audi Sport quattro S1 up this steep hillclimb course and set new best times.

1987 was also a year to remember for Audi private entrants Armin Schwarz and H.J. Hösch. They won the drivers' and manufacturers' titles in the German Rally Championship.

1965	On January 1, Volkswagen AG acquired 50.3 percent of Auto Union's shares; in September production of Auto Union's Audi started, with a 72 hp four-stroke medium compression engine
1966	On March 11, the last DKW passenger car with a two-stroke engine, an F 102, left the assembly line; at the end of the year Auto Union became a wholly owned subsidiary of VW; in Ingolstadt, a workforce of 12,000 produced about 110,000 cars a year
1969	The merger between Auto Union GmbH and NSU AG was initiated on March 10
1969	Audi NSU Auto Union AG, with head offices in Neckarsulm, was established on August 21
1977	In March the last NSU Ro 80 was built, after which the NSU name was no longer applied to production vehicles

03 The 1985 San Remo Rally was won by Walter Röhrl in the Audi Sport quattro S1
04 Walter Röhrl taking the Audi Sport quattro S1 up Pikes Peak in record time
05 Walter Röhrl off-duty for a change
06 Winners of the 1987 Safari Rally: Mikkola/Hertz in the Group A Audi 200 quattro

06

01

04

05

08

09

242

Audi – an overview

02

03

06

07

10

11

01 The first new Audi – a pre-production car in the styling studio, 1965
02 Audi 80 L Variant station wagon, 1966
03 Audi Super 90, a four-seater convertible prototype built by Karmann, 1967
04 Audi 60 L sedan (facelift), 1971 model
05 Audi 100 LS sedan, 1970
06 Audi 100 GL two-door sedan, 1972
07 Audi 100 Coupé S, 1973
08 Audi 80 L sedan, 1973
09 Audi 80 GLS sedan (facelift), 1976
10 Audi 80 GTE sedan (facelift), 1977
11 Audi 50 LS sedan, 1976

01

02

05

06

07

244

Audi – an overview

03

04

08

09

10

11

The way to the top

1985–2000

Turbulent times

Increasing awareness of the environment on the other side of the Atlantic, public discussion of the need to use resources economically and new legislation by governments – all these developments strongly influenced motor-vehicle development in the 1980s. Experts are of the opinion that technological development made greater progress in this period than at any other time in its history. This was well and truly evident in the terms that made the headlines: "downsizing" in the United States, "exhaust emission control" and "passive safety" in Europe. But despite all these innovations, there was no denying that a degree of market saturation had set in everywhere on the sales side. Restrictive regulations slowed the car boom down, especially in the United States. In Great Britain and in Italy, independent manufacturers that were formerly famous names fell victim to the trend towards concentration that was closely associated with these limited market prospects.

The political break-up of the Soviet Union and the resulting upheavals in Poland, Czechoslovakia and Romania, culminating in the formal opening-up of the border between Hungary and Austria confronted the populations of these countries within a very short time with the need to radically reconstruct a view of the world that had been carved in stone for the past 40 years. For the Federal Republic of Germany, the climax came in the autumn of 1989 with the fall of the Berlin Wall. At one stroke, these happenings gave access to a market that planned socialist economies had never been able to satisfy. In Germany in particular, industry and commerce found themselves facing a wave of purchase demand such as they had never experienced before. Vehicle population growth rates of 40 percent annually or more brought the infrastructure in East Germany, always thin at the best of times, rapidly to its capacity limits.

In Germany, a political and economic recovery program for these areas was drawn up on the crest of a wave of euphoria. Its aim was for the reunited country – although this would run counter to the current world economic climate – to enjoy a boom in the next few years.

The Audi terminal in Tokyo, with new brand architecture

Up and away to new dimensions

In March 1977 the last Ro 80 was built, and the NSU brand, with its long tradition, ceased to trade as a separate entity. From this time on much thought was given to the fusion of brand and company into a single concept. In 1985, Audi NSU Auto Union AG therefore changed its name to AUDI AG. At the same time two subsidiary companies, Auto Union GmbH and NSU GmbH, were established in order to provide legal protection to the extensive assets associated with these names. Since then, the two companies have been responsible for upholding brand traditions and protecting the name and brand rights of earlier, now inactive, companies and their products. When the change of name took place, the company moved its head offices from Neckarsulm to Ingolstadt.

01

01 The Audi oval, introduced in May 1978, was erected at a prominent point on the highway near Ingolstadt in 1984. Since 1995, the Four Rings have been the dominant feature of the company's visual identity

Product process means progress in production technology as well. This was particularly relevant when the B3-series Audi 80 went into production in the fall of 1986. It had a fully galvanized, aerodynamically efficient body for which the manufacturer was prepared to grant a ten-year warranty against penetration by rust. This set new standards in the car's market segment, but also called for an investment of several hundred millions for production and product-related measures. Starting at the end of 1985, Audi 100/ 200 models had appeared with fully galvanised bodies that promised optimal corrosion protection and retention of the car's value. This was the first time that a volume manufacturer has used galvanized sheet metal on all its model lines. Improved sheet forming methods and welding and painting techniques were essential before this technical innovation could be introduced.

The new production methods were paralleled by restructuring measures in the production logistics area. The term "just in time" began to be heard more and more often. Outside suppliers organized the delivery of pre-assembled components directly to the conveyor lines. More and more suppliers moved to premises close to the actual car factory. At the same time, this trend reduced the manu-

02

facturer's in-house production depth, and the number of vehicle parts of Audi's own manufacture dropped steadily. At the end of 1995 the GVZ Logistics Center went into operation directly adjacent to the Ingolstadt factory, as a means of ensuring reliable supplies of parts. In addition to permitting closer cooperation with system suppliers, which for a long time had also included the joint development of outsourced components, the GVZ was an opportunity for up to 80 percent of the necessary freight traffic to be handled by rail – a worthwhile reduction of the burden on the roads that would otherwise have arisen. A similar project was implemented at the Neckarsulm factory in October 1996.

03

02 The Audi 80, 1986 model.
With a drag coefficient of
$c_d = 0.29$, it even outperforms
the Audi 100

03 The Audi 80's fully galvanized
bodyshell

04 The GVZ Logistics Center in
Ingolstadt. The factory buildings
begin at the left margin of this
picture

04

01

01 2,057 trainees were included in the Group's complete workforce of 57,533 in 2008

02 Of 5,000 applicants for training in 2008, 682 were selected. 453 start their careers in Ingolstadt, the other 229 in Neckarsulm

02

Enlargement and extension

Increased awareness of quality went hand in hand with the new production methods and procedures. In 1986, a new Quality Center in Ingolstadt combined the activities of all the existing quality assurance departments. In October 1993 AUDI AG was the first German automobile manufacturer to receive certification according to the DIN ISO 9001 industrial standard for overall quality management systems. Work sequences and processes in all the company's divisions complied with the extremely strict requirements imposed by this standard.

New training centers in Neckarsulm and Ingolstadt, together with new organizational models, ensured a high level of employee training. In recent years, new job specifications have arisen, and provided an additional incentive for in-company training to be reorganized. AUDI AG recruits the bulk of the workforce it needs from among those it has trained.

Steps were taken to increase training capacities, and the Technical Development department (TE) built up in 1969 close to the Ingolstadt factory was considerably extended, with new buildings and staff. The most obvious external sign of this was Building T 22, a steel and glass structure that has dominated the TE site since December 1988. In 1990, after a lengthy search for a suitable plot of land, Audi began to build its own testing and proving ground near Neustadt (Danube). It went into operation in a series of stages by the mid-1990s. Problems encountered by competitors were taken into account: local authorities, environmental protection and nature conservation organizations and committees formed by local citizens were all actively involved in the planning stage.

Since the fall of 1999 the Ingolstadt factory has also operated its own Wind Tunnel Center. This can generate a wind speed of up to 186 mph, and is not only one of the most powerful wind tunnels in the world, but also the quietest.

03 Dual vocational training leading to a technical university entrance qualification is now possible in four career areas. Training for more than 20 careers takes place at the two Audi sites
04 View of the front of Technical Development building T22 in Ingolstadt
05 A Q7 in the AUDI AG wind tunnel, one of the most powerful and also the quietest facilities of its kind anywhere in the world

03, 04

05

Customer loyalty

When a step was made into the large luxury segment of the car market by launching the Audi V8 in October 1988, the sales and marketing areas were restructured at the same time. As a means of strengthening customers' bonds with the company, they were now offered an opportunity of collecting their new cars personally from the delivery center in Neckarsulm.

The Audi Piazza was built at the head offices in Ingolstadt to act as a reception area for visitors to AUDI AG and also as the company's architectural calling card. The Audi Forum, the museum mobile and the Market and Customer building, all of them featuring a modern, transparent formal idiom, are grouped together in an open square surrounded by trees. The Audi Center, part of the present-day Forum, was completed as the first construction stage in May 1992. Here purchasers of models built in Ingolstadt can take possession of their new cars, visit the factory in which they took shape and trace the history of AUDI AG and the companies that preceded it in the museum.

In the Market and Customer administrative building, visitors and business associates can contact representatives of the Sales, Marketing and Public Relations departments and also obtain information about a large number of services associated with the products and the company. The company history collection, known as the "museum mobile," was opened at the end of 2000, and portrays the history and development of AUDI AG from the earliest times until the present day. There are presentations devoted to the

02

01 Audi Forum Ingolstadt. On the far left is the pick-up center for new cars, next to it the Forum with Market Restaurant and the Avus Restaurant on the first floor. The circular building in the center houses the museum mobile with museum shop. The Market and Customer building is on the far right

03

01

progress of mobility, the urge for freedom and individuality and the relationship between human beings, the automobile and technology in general over the course of a tradition that now goes back more than a hundred years. A special area of the museum is reserved for changing exhibitions on various themes.

Completed in 2005, the Neckarsulm factory now has a suitably impressive Service Center with steel and glass architecture, resembling the Audi Forum in Ingolstadt. Its opening marked the end of the period in which customers were able to collect their cars from the first Audi delivery center. On the top floor of the Audi Forum in Neckarsulm an exhibition recalls the history of the NSU brand, the name borne by the motorcycles and cars built at this factory until 1977.

05, 06

02 An Audi Type A, the brand's oldest surviving car, as part of a special exhibition in the museum mobile
03 The museum and Forum run special programs for the youngest visitors
04 View from the uppermost galley of the museum mobile. The disk-shaped structure is reminiscent of a tree's annual growth rings
05 The program for visitors includes tours of the factory's production areas
06 Interior of the Market and Customer building
07 Audi Forum Neckarsulm was opened on May 10, 2005

04

07

A new identity

In 1988 the first Audi Centers were opened in the German cities of Koblenz, Hanover and Munich, in close cooperation with the local dealers. They strengthened the independent status of the Audi brand, and were soon followed by further Audi Centers at selected locations within Germany and abroad. Starting in 1997, an unusual "hangar" architectural style was introduced as a corporate design element for all subsequent Audi Centers, the aim being to enhance visual communication of the premium claim of the Audi brand. At this time, Audi and Volkswagen dealers in Germany were offered separate dealer contracts and the previous joint sales channels, publicized by the "VAG" logo, were abandoned. The number of Audi dealers in Germany was reduced.

For image and marketing reasons, the company was given its own sales profile; a new Marketing Department had already been created in April 1991 in Ingolstadt. On January 1, 1993, the sales responsibility that had been in the hands of Volkswagen AG in Wolfsburg since 1974 was transferred back to Ingolstadt. The Audi logo was abandoned in October 1994 – since then the four rings alone have been used as a sign of corporate identity.

Audi worldwide

Production of the Audi 100 C3 began in October 1988 in Changchun, after negotiation of a cooper-

ation agreement with the Chinese FAW (First Automobile Works) company. With a 10-percent share of the equity, AUDI AG joined the existing joint venture between FAW and Volkswagen AG in November 1995. The factory in Changchun began to build a special long-wheelbase version of the C5-series Audi A6 for the Chinese market in September 1999.

Increasingly close international trade links, the European Union and the adoption of a unified currency have led to changes of many kinds in commerce and industry. For Audi, worldwide purchasing of outsourced parts and services is an important factor, but there have also been new departures in the development and production areas. Design centers in Spain and California, the Audi assembly plant for engines and complete cars in Győr, Hungary, and the start-up of the Audi factory in Curitiba, Brazil, in January 1999 were some of the measures taken to ensure the company's ability to remain competitive in the long term. Another element in this global strategy was the establishment of regional offices to strengthen the company's presence in growth-market countries, for instance those opened in Singapore and Bangkok. Other activities included and still include the assembly of CKD vehicles in South Africa, Malaysia, the Philippines and Thailand. The cars built there are supplied as completely or partly knocked down component and assembly sets from Germany.

03, 04

AUDI AG becomes a group

The first step in the direction of an international group of companies took place in April 1993 with the establishment of a wholly owned subsidiary, Audi Hungaria Motor Kft., in Győr, Hungary. This was followed in 1997 by the Brazilian subsidiary Audi do Brasil, with its head offices in Curitiba, in the Brazilian state of Paraná. The Curitiba factory, built jointly with Volkswagen do Brasil, produced its first Audi, an A3 model, in mid-1999.

Two further companies were taken over in 1998 and joined the Audi Group. Automobili Lamborghini S.p.A., based in the Italian town of Sant' Agata Bolognese, is a well-known manufacturer of high-performance sports cars, and Cosworth Technology Ltd. in Northampton, Great Britain, specializes in the design, development and assembly of future-oriented powertrain concepts.

06, 07

05

Fallen, recovered, ready to go – recession and its consequences

Dr. Wolfgang R. Habbel retired from his position as Board Chairman at the end of 1987. He had supervised Audi's step forward into the upper midsize car category. Dr. Ferdinand Piëch took over as his successor in January 1988. Apart from expanding the Audi product range and securing a share of the luxury market segment, he saw one of his primary tasks as improving AUDI AG's profitability.

A "Corporate Concept 1988" was drawn up, for which the management obtained the cooperation of the General Works Council, now chaired by Erhard Kuballa, who had taken over in May 1987 from his long-serving colleague Fritz Böhm. A series of measures was devoted to improving the cost and results situation, including lean production and lean management, but also socially acceptable adjustments to the workforce, which was to be reduced by eight percent. Cost-cutting and restructuring had the effect of boosting the pre-tax operating margin from 1.8 to 3.6 percent; turnover rose by 1.5 percent to 11.5 billion Deutschmarks. In the year that followed, turnover went up again and the operating margin rose beyond the forecast level.

The fall of the wall separating the two German states, their reunification and the currency union led to a revival on the domestic market, though at the same time there were initial signs of an economic crisis. 1991 proved to be a record year on the evidence of both total vehicle output and the launching of new models. In the course of a year, almost the complete model range was renewed. This generated strong market demand, which was reflected in record turnover. In 1992 it proved possible to increase production volume again, but after this an international business recession caused sales to stagnate. Within Germany, the extra business stimulated by reunification gradually lost its impetus. In 1993 the picture changed: unsold cars were stockpiled, production was run down and shortened working times had to be introduced.

In May 1992, Franz-Josef Kortüm came to Ingolstadt as the Board of Management Member for Marketing, a newly created division. On January 1, 1993, he took over as Board Chairman from Dr. Ferdinand Piëch, who became Chairman of the

The two luxury cars that are capturing the German imagination.

There they were, West and East Germany's finest. Poignantly, standing along a stretch of the fast-disappearing Berlin Wall.

Throughout the day, a steady stream of East Germans came along to sit in it, admire it, wonder at it, touch it – the latest Trabant 601 de-luxe, that is.

The £40,000 worth of high technology next to it may just as well have come from another world as another country.

Curiously, the two cars have striking similarities. For example, the Trabant's bodywork is a combination of cotton and plastic, which renders it rust-proof.

The new Audi V8 too, has a rust-proofed body, although Audi has opted for more substantial galvanized steel instead. And, by zinc galvanizing all the bare metal, Audi is able to offer a 10 year guarantee against rusting, which should see you nicely into the next millennium.

The Trabant features a new 1100cc environmentally-friendlier engine. (In comparison to the old 2-stroke power plant, which ran on a combination of petrol and oil.)

The engineers at Audi, too, have cast an eye to the environment. As with all Audi models, the V8 comes with the latest 3-way catalytic converter technology as standard, which reduces toxic pollutants by up to 95%.

For the past six years they've spent time perfecting the revolutionary 3.6 litre, 32 valve, V8 engine.

This is arguably the quietest, smoothest, most advanced engine in any saloon today.

When it comes to luxury fittings both cars have their share. The Trabant, for example, boasts textile floor covering and a two-tone horn.

Standard equipment on the V8 includes quattro four-wheel drive with electronic automatic transmission, ABS, cruise-control, climate control air-conditioning, leather upholstery, on-board computer and six-speaker stereo system.

Not forgetting Audi's unique Procon-Ten safety system. This pre-tensions the seat belts and pulls the steering column away from the driver in the event of a frontal impact.

Apparently none of this means too much to the East Germans at the moment, but we're sure it's just another barrier that they'll soon surmount.

THE AUDI V8 FROM £40,334.

For further information on the new Audi V8 please complete the coupon or send your business card to: Audi Information Department AB, FREEPOST, Yeomans Drive, Blakelands, Milton Keynes MK14 5EE Or dial 100 and ask for FREEPONE AUDI.

Mr/Mrs/Ms   Initials   Surname
Address
                              Postcode
Phone   Phone
Home   Business

VORSPRUNG DURCH TECHNIK.

02

Volkswagen Group Board of Management. However, Franz-Josef Kortüm left AUDI AG in February 1994. His place was taken on March 22, 1995, by Dr. Herbert Demel, who had been Board Spokesman from February 1994 until then. In July 1997 he was invited by Group Management in Wolfsburg to take on the Chairmanship of VW do Brasil. Dr. Demel was succeeded by Dr. Franz-Josef Paefgen, a Member of the Board who had until then been responsible for the Technical Development area.

In the second half of the 1990s, the economy recovered rapidly, and this was reflected in AUDI AG's results. Turnover and sales volume rose year by year, and the call for greater vehicle output made it necessary to enlarge the workforce. In the period that followed, the company adopted a strategic goal of strengthening the brand still further and improving its market position rather than aiming for short-term profits.

Overcoming conflicts by cooperation

The structural changes to industry and the economy that accompanied the ongoing globalization process also confronted the Works Council with major tasks. Adolf Hochrein was elected Chairman in July 1993, followed in May 1994 by Xaver Meier as Chairman of the General Works Council. The nature of work and the forms of organization applied to it were topics that called for extensive rethinking; other matters too represented a

constant challenge to the workforce's representatives, for example the outsourcing of certain production areas or the granting of development orders to outside suppliers, the operation of production facilities abroad and competition between individual factories and companies within the VW Group.

An important task for the Works Councils has always been obtaining long-term guarantees for the Ingolstadt and Neckarsulm locations. To satisfy this demand, an agreement entitled "Audi for Secure Jobs and Production Locations" was signed in May 1996 between company management and the General Works Council. This was an important means of guaranteeing and promoting job security at Audi until the year 2000 and beyond. An important statement in this agreement confirmed that the European volume markets would continue to be supplied for the most part from Ingolstadt and Neckarsulm. Success in assuring job security, similar successes in negotiating working conditions and ensuring freedom from accidents: it was announced with some pride that Audi had the lowest rate of industrial accidents in the entire German automotive industry. Against the background of a modern workforce involvement policy, constructive dialog between company management and the Works Council proved to be an important factor in successful company development in the late 1990s and the period at the start of the new millennium.

03

02 Prof. Dr. Martin Winterkorn addressing the AUDI AG Annual General Meeting in 2008
03 Presentation of the new Audi R12 TDI Le Mans racing car

257

01

02

03

1985 – 2000 The way to the top – Fallen, recovered, ready to go – recession and its consequences

04

The product program in the 1990s

After a year of recession in 1993, all hopes were concentrated in the second half of 1994 on the launch of the Audi A4, which was presented at the end of October in Berlin. The new model exceeded all expectations. The customers were exceptionally interested in it, with the result that the sales curve following the new Audi A4's introduction rose more steeply than ever before. In view of the demand encountered for the sister models A6 and A8 and the sporty S models as well, output volume had to be boosted considerably in 1995. The newspapers soon began to comment: "Audi is in the fast lane!" As already implied, this positive trend was the beginning of AUDI AG's transformation into a globally active company. A start was made on building other production facilities abroad and expanding the worldwide sales network. In parallel with this, the model program was systematically enlarged.

The products – 1985 to 1990

A notable trend in the second half of the 1980s was the increase in ecological awareness. Audi did not have to respond to this development for the simple reason that the Ingolstadt-based company had already played a pioneering role in many of the relevant areas. In the fall of 1985, when the 1986 model year was introduced, the Audi 100 and Audi 200 were given fully galvanized bodies. This saw the introduction of highly effective corrosion protection on production cars, and a guarantee of maximum long-term quality and retention of value. At the same time, the IAA Frankfurt Motor Show was used to announce an extensive program of low-emission Audi models.

The third-generation Audi 80 (known internally as the B3) appeared in September 1986, and was followed in May 1987 by the second-generation Audi 90, which had a five-cylinder engine. These models also had a fully galvanized bodyshell. At the

01 The quattro model range in 1991 (from left to right): Audi S2 Coupé, Audi V8, Audi 80 quattro, Audi 100 quattro, Audi quattro 20V
02 Seeing double – the B3-series Audi 80 as exhibited in 1986 at the IAA Motor Show in Frankfurt
03 With sales of more than 630,000, the Audi 80 1.8S is the best-seller in this model line
04 The Audi 80 driver's area from 1986 onwards

259

01

Birmingham Motor Show in 1988, Audi launched the Audi Coupé as an addition to the model range. At the same time, intensive work was taking place in Ingolstadt on the development of a convertible. This open four-seater was exhibited as a design study at the IAA Frankfurt Motor Show in the fall of 1989, and went into production two years later.

The new-model launches reached a climax in the fall of 1988, with a clear indication of the path the company had decided to pursue. The occasion was the presentation of the Audi V8, which was Audi's decisive step forward into the premium category. It was exhibited to the public for the first time at the Paris Motor Show in September 1988, powered initially by a 184 kW (250 hp) 3.6-liter engine with a light alloy block. The Audi V8 possessed a whole series of innovative details, including permanent all-wheel drive, four valves per cylinder and a four-speed electronically controlled automatic transmission. It was the flagship of the Audi program, and like the Audi 100

and 200 models, was built in Neckarsulm. New engines were also added to the range available in the smaller models. These engines had four valves per cylinder. From the fall of 1988 the quattro versions of the Audi 90 and the new Audi Coupé were also offered with a 123 kW (170 hp) five-cylinder naturally aspirated engine. This turbocharged unit also had four valves per cylinder, and developed 162 kW (220 hp). In the summer of the same year it had already taken the place of the previous two-valve turbocharged engine in the Audi quattro. At that time the quattro was the last model in all the Audi model lines not to be available with a catalytic converter; the Audi quattro 20V meant that the company now offered all its models with exhaust emission control by catalytic converter.

In 1990 the Audi 80 rounded off the B-series program, with a sports specification and a four-valve version of the 2-liter, four-cylinder engine. This agile midsize car had been exhibited the previous year at the IAA Frankfurt Motor Show.

02

03

04

05

06

05 The Audi 200 quattro 20V, with 220 hp turbocharged horsepower, the top 200 model from the fall of 1988 to midway through 1991

06 The 1988 Audi 90 quattro 20V, the first five-cylinder engine with four valves per cylinder, but still without turbocharging

TDI – the diesel revolution

Audi has sold diesel-engined cars since 1978. Like the other diesel-engined passenger cars on the world market, the company's compression-ignition models were economical but not especially noted for their vigor. Performance levels went up distinctly with the advent of turbocharging, but the turbodiesel still led a shadowy existence, favored only by drivers who covered enormous mileage or by technology freaks. All this was to change radically, however, in the fall of 1989.

Environmental pollution, acid rain and its effect on our forests, the demand for more careful use of the earth's natural resources – all this had long since given rise to a demand for more economical cars and to the desire for a car that could deliver fuel efficiency of 78 miles per gallon. In a period of growing ecological awareness, considerations such as these began to influence potential car buyers more and more.

Audi came up with the answer after 13 years of research and development work, and called it "TDI" (Turbocharged Diesel with Direct Fuel Injection). The Audi 100 TDI made its debut at the IAA Frankfurt Motor Show in September 1989. Its 2.5-liter, five-cylinder diesel engine had direct fuel injection, a turbocharger with charge-air intercooler, and

02

extensive noise insulation measures. The first version developed 88 kW (120 hp). Road testers and journalists were greatly impressed by this fast, comfortable and remarkably economical car, and began to refer to a "diesel revolution." Nothing stood in the way of the TDI engine's all-conquering progress.

Before the Audi TDI made its appearance, almost all passenger-car diesel engines used the indirect fuel injection principle; the company's own Audi 80 and 100 diesel models also had pre-combustion chamber engines. Audi's technical staff devoted their lengthy development work to the refinement of many details of the direct injection principle already used on trucks and other commercial vehicles, with such success that it became suitable for use on passenger-car diesel engines. In an Audi TDI engine, fuel was injected at high pressure directly into the bowl-in-piston combustion chamber, the quantity being accurately metered by electronic control of the distributor-pattern injection pump. The combustion air, first precompressed by the turbocharger, had its temperature lowered again in the charge-air intercooler and then flowed through a specially shaped inlet port into the combustion chamber. This port caused the air to rotate; the resulting intensive turbulence ensured the best possible ignition of the fuel-air mixture. The typically aggressive combustion noise associated with direct injection engines was rendered smoother by separate pre-injection of a small quantity of fuel. Compared with other principles, the Audi direct injection system caused the lowest combustion losses. The fuel consumption of cars with a TDI engine was exceptionally low, a user benefit that was referred to extensively in advertising and confirmed by a number of test runs:

European record run by a modified Audi 100 TDI; at an average speed of 37.4 mph, it covered more than 2,994 miles on one tank of fuel = 133.64 miles per gallon (1989)

Around the world in a standard Audi 80 TDI, a total distance of 25,024 miles at an average speed of 53.3 mph = fuel consumption of 62.23 miles per gallon (1992)

ADAC test run with an Audi 80 1.9 TDI: 1,256 miles at an average fuel consumption of 69.18 miles per gallon (1993)

Economy run from Vienna to Geneva in an Audi 80 1.9 TDI: 670 miles at an average speed of 43.5 miles per hour, total fuel consumption 7.9 gallons, equivalent to 84.92 miles per gallon (1994)

04

01 Audi's first TDI engine was introduced in the fall of 1989 for the C3-series Audi 100
02 Sectioned model of the 2.5-liter, five-cylinder TDI; this is the first version with a power output of 120 hp
03 Swirl-action air inlet port, bowl-in-piston combustion chamber and – shown in white – the position of the injector in the TDI engine
04 Before the start of the low-consumption record run across Europe: the quantity of fuel has been precisely measured and the filler cap sealed officially. Now the journey can start!

03

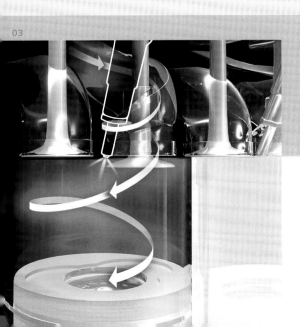

02

01 The first Audi duo, at the
Geneva Motor Show in March
1990

02 An Audi A4 Avant duo – this is
the duo III – at the solar-energy
filling station in the Ingolstadt
factory

Audi was thus the first German car manufacturer
to tame the direct injection diesel principle suf-
ficiently for it to be used in a premium passenger
car with no severe loss of refinement. In less
than ten months, 4,764 of the C3-series Audi 100
TDI were sold. Of the next model, the C4 series
introduced in 1990 as the Audi 100 TDI and later
the Audi A6 TDI with a choice of two power outputs, 133 068 cars were sold with five-cylinder
TDI engines.

Early hybrids
The Audi duo of 1989 adopted a totally different
approach to environmental acceptability. Shown
at the Geneva Motor Show in March 1990 and
based on the C3-series Audi 100 Avant, it was
the first-generation Audi duo: an Audi 100 Avant
quattro with a 100 kW (136 hp) five-cylinder
fuel-injection engine. A DC electric motor rated
at 12.6 hp was installed to drive the rear wheels
and demonstrate the feasibility of the hybrid car
and its ability to cover short distances with zero
exhaust emissions. The electric section of the
driveline was fed from a nickel-cadmium battery.
This first-generation car had to be brought to a
standstill before it could be switched over to the
other form of propulsion.

01

Two years later, again in Geneva, Audi exhibited
another alternative concept for the passenger
car. This new Audi duo, with a C4-series Audi 100
Avant quattro body, again had two forms of propulsion: an internal combustion engine driving
both axles and an electric motor that could be
connected to the rear axle when needed. The
two-liter, four-cylinder engine developed 85 kW
(115 hp) and drove all four wheels through a
manual-shift five-speed transmission. In the
electric mode, a 21 kW (28.5 hp) water-cooled
three-phase synchronous motor with permanent
excitation drove the rear wheels. The electric
motor was installed in unit with the rear-axle differential and its rotor used to connect the car's
propeller shaft with the differential's input pinion.

The Audi duo could reach 40 mph when propelled by the electric motor, and its sodium-sulfur battery, operating at 252 volts, gave it an action radius of approximately 50 miles. The Torsen center differential disconnected the power flow to the front axle automatically when the electric motor was in use. The batteries were housed in the spare wheel well of the station wagon body. In mid-September 1996, for the AAA in Berlin, Audi revealed the third and last Audi duo generation. This time the technical basis was the Audi A4 Avant, powered by the well-known 66 kW (90 hp) four-cylinder TDI engine and a water-cooled three-phase synchronous electric motor rated at 21 kW (29 hp). In contrast to the previous designs, the electric motor was flanged to the five-speed transmission and only the car's front wheels were driven. A lead-acid battery and the complete control system were housed in the spare wheel well, and could be recharged when necessary from any household power socket, by way of a built-in charger. In the electric operating mode, a small electric pump maintained pressure in the car's hydraulic system, so that the power steering, brake servo and ABS continued to operate normally. A fuel-burning heater was fitted. Energy could be recuperated when the diesel engine was in use or when the brakes were applied. The lead-acid battery's capacity was sufficient for a journey of about 31 miles on urban roads. To obtain more extensive test data, 90 cars in all were built and some of them leased to customers.

01

*From a discussion with Industrie-
magazin at the end of 1990*

Dr. Ferdinand Piëch talks about the Audi 100 C4

"A fanfare or a roll of drums has to suit the times, and at the moment the order of the day is most definitely 'evolution.' In 1982, when we intro- duced the C3, it was something that people were waiting for. They responded very sensitively to every occurrence in the technical world. Our car

with its world-record aerodynamics suited that scenario very well. The situation is rather different today: the classic buyer group for this class of car is looking for careful attention to detail, optimal settings throughout the car and an altogether better ambience."

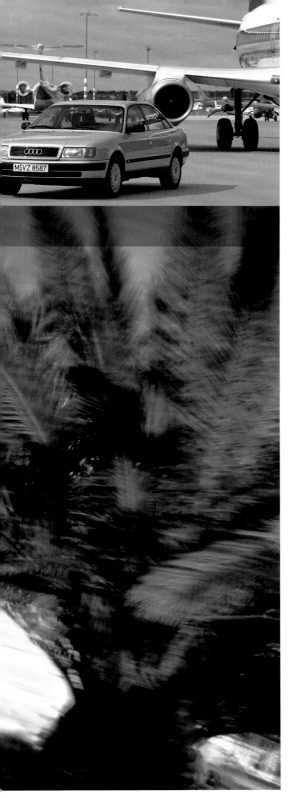

The early 1990s

1990 was a year in which several Audi anniversaries were celebrated. 25 years had elapsed since the re-establishment of the Audi brand in 1965. On January 9, 1990, the seven millionth Audi built since 1965 left the assembly line. The original Audi quattro – the "Urquattro," as it was now known – was in its tenth year of production. At first it had been planned to build only a short production run of 400, but this forerunner of all later quattro cars gained such popularity among drivers with sporting ambitions that it remained as the top sports model in the Audi sales program for many years. The "Urquattro" was largely hand-built in Ingolstadt, away from the remaining assembly lines. The 11,452nd and last car was built on May 17, 1991, and taken directly to the AUDI AG historic vehicles collection. With its eleven-year production period the Audi quattro still holds the record for the longest production time of all Audi models. In October 1990, before production of the first quattro model ceased, a potential successor was introduced in the guise of the Audi S2 Coupé.

Then came 1991 – an important year for Audi, and one in which almost the entire product programme was modernized. For the 1991 model year, the new Audi 100 (internal code: C4) was introduced, with a six-cylinder version available for the first time. This engine, a V6 with a displacement of 2.8 liters and a power output of 128 kW (174 hp), was shorter and lighter than any comparable engine in its class. A variable-length intake pipe increased torque at low engine speeds, but could be shortened for maximum power in the upper engine-speed range.

01 The final version of the Audi S2 Coupé, with 230 hp turbo-charged five-cylinder engine and newly styled wheels
02 An Audi quattro 20V with a sporty driver at the wheel. He's still a long way from the car's handling limits!
03 A fourth-series Audi 100 2.3E, built from the fall of 1990 to the summer of 1994

03

When the Geneva Motor Show opened its doors in the spring of 1991, the Audi Cabriolet was the focus of public attention. In the summer of the same year it was followed by the top model in the Audi 100 line, the Audi S4, which was powered by the successful turbocharged five-cylinder engine with four valves per cylinder. At the IAA Frankfurt Motor Show in the fall, the new Audi 80 (internal code: B4) went on display, together with the Avant version of the Audi 100. But the true sensation at this IAA was a low-built orange sports coupé with a V6 mid-engine and a sensationally styled aluminum body: the Audi quattro Spyder. The rumor soon spread that Audi was seriously thinking of putting this design study into production, and Audi dealers were bombarded with purchase options. Unfortunately, the target price of less than 100,000 Deutschmarks could not be met, and only the two prototypes of the quattro Spyder were ever built.

A month later, at the Tokyo Motor Show, Audi amazed the experts in the automobile world yet again. This time the public was amazed to find a futuristic sports car study with a body in highly polished aluminum and a W12 mid-engine on the exhibition stand: the Audi Avus quattro. Although the engine of the car on display was only a mock-up, keen observers of the car-industry scene knew what was to be expected.

For some years prior to this, Audi had been cooperation with the Aluminum Company of America (ALCOA) on the development of a production car using a weight-saving aluminum construction principle. The approach was summed up as follows: only systematic weight saving could achieve a distinct reduction in fuel consumption with no loss of comfort or performance. Compared with a pressed-steel body built to the same specification, an aluminum body would weigh between 30 and 40 percent less. Furthermore, aluminum is a material that can be re-used almost indefinitely without any loss of quality. Conditions for recycling it are ideal: less than 20 percent of the energy needed for the original smelting of aluminum is consumed when this lightweight metal is re-melted (for scrap steel 50 percent), and it therefore has an excellent overall energy balance sheet.

02

01

1985 – 2000 The way to the top – Fallen, recovered, ready to go – recession and its consequences

The age of aluminum

The outcome of this year-long research work was exhibited in the fall of 1993 at the IAA Frankfurt Motor Show. The ASF (Audi Space Frame) sedancar study not only fascinated visitors on account of its aluminum body. A V8 TDI diesel in the engine compartment was a further sign of what developments could be expected soon. If any manufacturer could succeed in making the diesel engine acceptable in a large luxury car, then it would surely be Audi! To drive home the company's claim to large premium-model status, the Tokyo Motor Show stand in October 1993 featured a second breathtaking Audi Space Frame concept car study, powered this time by a 4.8-liter W12 engine; its power output was given as 260 kW (354 hp).

In cooperation with ALCOA, a structure had been developed in which loads were also shared by the panels. Extruded aluminum sections were joined together by pressure-cast nodes, and the large-area aluminum panels integrated into the resulting frame – the Audi Space Frame. Such new construction methods naturally called for innovative production technologies: improved light

alloys and process techniques were developed. In addition to welding and adhesive bonding, punch rivets were used for the first time in car construction at certain joints. These innovations resulted in a series of patent applications and the award of more than 40 patents – evidence of the remarkable new thinking that had gone into the Audi Space Frame.

The aluminum Audi, successor to the Audi V8, made its debut in March 1994 at the Geneva Motor Show. It was called the A8 and was the first model to make use of a completely new Audi identification system. The facelifted Audi 100 followed in the summer of 1994 and was known as the Audi A6. In November, the Audi 80 was replaced by the new Audi A4. This new car was the trump card in Audi's already successful hand. Available only as a sedan initially, its public acceptance surpassed all the manufacturer's hopes. The Avant version was launched in February 1996, and on June 17, three years and six months after production of B5-series cars had begun, the one-millionth Audi A4 left the assembly line – a proud day for the production engineers.

01 Audi Space Frame concept car, with a W 12 engine, exhibited in October 1993 at the Tokyo Show. It closely resembled the Audi A8, which reached the market six months later

02 Audi A8, 1998

03 A glance inside the aluminum Audi Space Frame reveals the load-bearing extruded sections and the cast nodal joints that connect them together

04 The Audi A8's 12-cylinder production engine: a masterpiece of engineering

05 The Audi A4 sedan. It superseded the previous Audi 80 in 1994. This is a facelifted car dating from 1997

06 "Beautiful station wagons are called Avant." Advertising knows how to awaken desires

01

02, 03

for the Audi TTS Roadster at the Tokyo Motor Show. Both these cars were built on the platform developed for the forthcoming VW Golf IV, and were highlights of the exhibitions at which they were displayed. In December 1995 the Board of Management made the decision to build and sell both these sports cars. The Audi TT Coupé reached the market in the fall of 1998, the TT Roadster in the summer of 1999. Both models were largely similar in appearance to the design studies seen three years earlier. The Audi TT was built by an alliance consisting of the Ingolstadt factory and Audi Hungaria Motor Kft. Painted TT bodies

Design and emotion

The image of a car brand is not only governed by objective technical data but to an ever-increasing extent by softer, more emotional factors. Using the slogan "Arouse emotions," Audi exhibited design studies for the Audi TT Coupé at the IAA Frankfurt Motor Show in the fall of 1995, and

01 The first rendering for the later Audi TT

02 The original shape of the Audi Coupé quattro TT. It was exhibited as a design study under this name at the 1995 IAA Frankfurt Motor Show

03 The Audi TTS Roadster was seen two months later, also as a design study, at the Tokyo Motor Show in November 1995

04 Initially, the Audi TTS Roadster's interior was sporty but spartan without compromise

05 Production version of the Audi TT Coupé, here with optional S line equipment

04

272

05

07

traveled by rail from Ingolstadt to Győr, Hungary, where final assembly took place.

By now, the Audi brand was extremely well positioned in the mid-size and large-car categories, and the next target was to secure market share in the small-car sector. An entry-level model was therefore developed on the platform intended for the forthcoming VW Golf IV – the first "small" Audi since the Audi 50 went out of production in 1978. The three-door Audi A3 was introduced in September 1996, and immediately began to conquer new customer groups in the compact car

class. A version with four doors followed in the spring of 1999. And also a sports derivative with all-wheel drive, marketed as the S3. In this model a 154 kW (210 hp) engine propelled the car with ease up to the impressive top speed of 148 mph, but when a facelift took place in the summer of 2001, the S3 acquired even more power: 165 kW (225 hp), enough for a top speed of almost 155 mph. Audi had clearly gained a most gratifying foothold in the premium small-car market segment with its A3 model line. In a production period of just under seven years, almost 800,000 of these first-generation A3 cars were built.

06 The five-door Audi A3 as introduced in 1999
07 Audi A3: from 1996 to 1999 only the three-door model was available, but this had no adverse effect on the model's success

01

01 The German Sunday paper
Bild am Sonntag awarded the
new Audi A6 its "Golden Steering
Wheel" as the "Runaway winner in
the large car class." The Industry
Design Forum in Hanover chose
the sedan as "Best in category."
and in the German ADAC car club's
breakdown statistics the A6 was
able to claim the title of "Most
reliable large car in 2000"

The new Audi A6 sedan made its debut at the
Geneva Motor Show in March 1997. This new
model, the fifth generation in the C model line,
had a domed roof and rounded-off rear end –
evidence of courageous design. The A6 Avant
followed a year later. In October 1999 Audi once
again demonstrated its technological leadership
as summed up in the slogan "Vorsprung durch

Technik" by introducing its "multitronic" continuously variable transmission. Consisting of a
special multi-plate chain and two conical drive
discs (variator), it selected the optimal gear
ratio from the infinite number actually available;
cars equipped with multitronic recorded fuel
consumption lower than with conventional automatic transmission or even with a manual-shift

04

02, 03

transmission. Numerous patents were applied for, and this innovative technology was awarded various prizes – renewed evidence of Audi's role as a technological trendsetter.

At a later Geneva Motor Show, in March 2000, the public was introduced to the Audi allroad quattro, a version of the Audi A6 Avant with fundamental visual and technical changes. The allroad quattro succeeded in combining apparently contradictory virtues: it was a large luxury car with technical features that allowed it to match the performance of many an outright off-roader. Among the technical features aimed at enhancing its off-road capabilities beyond anything that the average SUV could offer were air suspension and extra-low gearing.

02 The C5 series Audi A6 Avant, built from 1998 onwards
03 The Audi A6 C5 sedan went on sale in May 1997. The new design idiom, with domed roof and rounded rear end, was a complete contrast to the previous model. In the fall of 1997, the A6 was awarded the "Good Design Gold Prize" in Tokyo
04 Selector lever for the Audi multitronic continuously variable transmission
05 With its advanced technologies, the Audi allroad quattro continued to perform excellently where paved roads came to an end
06 An "SUV" (sports utility vehicle) can scarcely be portrayed better than this

05

06

01

02

03

04

05

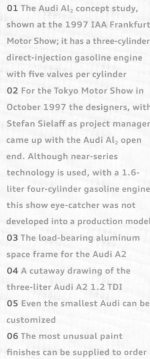

01 The Audi Al₂ concept study, shown at the 1997 IAA Frankfurt Motor Show; it has a three-cylinder direct-injection gasoline engine with five valves per cylinder
02 For the Tokyo Motor Show in October 1997 the designers, with Stefan Sielaff as project manager, came up with the Audi Al₂ open end. Although near-series technology is used, with a 1.6-liter four-cylinder gasoline engine, this show eye-catcher was not developed into a production model
03 The load-bearing aluminum space frame for the Audi A2
04 A cutaway drawing of the three-liter Audi A2 1.2 TDI
05 Even the smallest Audi can be customized
06 The most unusual paint finishes can be supplied to order by quattro GmbH

07

From Al₂ to A2

The Audi Al₂ design study had already aroused great interest at the IAA Frankfurt Motor Show back in 1997; it was the first small car in recent automobile history to have an all-aluminum body-shell, the only exception being the French Panhard, a five-seat sedan of the 1950s. An engine with direct gasoline injection provided a glimpse of the technology that could be expected later, though in fact five years elapsed before a production car appeared. The Al₂ was a sign that Audi planned to use its patented Aluminum Space Frame techno-logy for the first time for a model located farther down the size scale than the A8. The Audi A2 made its debut in June 2000; with an overall length of only 12.53 feet and a weight of 1,885 lb, it com-bined intelligent weight-saving construction with

good space utilization, bold design features and above-average performance. From the start of production, a version of the A2 with extra-low fuel consumption was offered to the public. The A2 1.2 TDI had its weight and aerodynamics optimized and featured aluminum suspension components, tires with low rolling resistance, an automatic-shift manual transmission and auto-matic engine start-stop. Special wheel covers and a spoiler package kept the aerodynamic drag coefficient down to a remarkable $c_d = 0.25$. This five-seat car with its ingenious technical features was the world's first full-scale car with a fuel consumption of 78.4 miles per gallon. Produced for nearly five years, this version's share of total A2 output was just under four percent.

07 The colorful Audi A2 color.storm model introduced in 2003. The car illustrated has the optional S line package and other items of optional equipment such as the Audi open sky system, a panoramic glass sunroof

277

01 The V6 TDI engine appeared in
1997; this is the first version,
with an output of 150 hp from a
displacement of 2.5 liters
02 Five B-series generations
(clockwise from left to right):
Audi 80 B4 (1991 – 1994),
Audi 80 B3 (1986 – 1991),
Audi 80 B2 (1978 – 1986),
Audi 80 B1 (1972 – 1978);
and in the center, the Audi A4 B5
(1994 – 2001)

Model types and series

Ever since the 1970s, Audi had retained the Audi
100 and Audi 80 names consistently through
several model generations. The first-generation
Audi 100 appeared in 1968, the second in 1976,
the third in 1982 and the fourth in 1990.

The first-generation Audi 80 of 1972 was followed
by the second in 1978, the third in 1986 and the
fourth and last bearing this name in 1991.

To distinguish the various model cycles more
easily, internal B, C and later D codes were used.
The first Audi 80 of 1972 was the B1, the first
Audi 100 of 1968 the C1. When the Audi V8 was
introduced in 1988, it was known internally as the
D1. The aluminum-bodied luxury car announced
in 1994 was logically known as the D2 series, but
at this point Audi broke with tradition and named
it the A8, after which all the remaining models
were renamed as well. A4 stood for the previous
B-series (Audi 80) types, initially available with
either four or six-cylinder engines. The new engines
with five valves per cylinder used in the B5-series
version of the A4 were supplied from the new

engine factory in Győr, Hungary, which also opened
in 1994.

A6 was the new designation for the previous Audi
100 models. These were mostly powered by the
V6 engines which went into production in 1992.

A8 therefore stood for the second-generation
premium luxury-class cars. The D2-series Audi A8
had also been available since June 1997 with a V6
TDI diesel engine, a choice which confirmed that
diesels were now socially acceptable, so to speak,
in the top motoring category. In the spring of
2000, a 3.3-liter V8 TDI engine was added to the
range, and since the fall of 1999 a long-wheelbase
version of the A8 with 4.2-liter V8 engine had
been available.

The A3, announced in September 1996 marked
Audi's debut with a premium model in the compact
car class. A further step in the same direction was
the Audi A2, launched in June 2000; it used the
patented Audi Space Frame structural principle
and was the first volume-produced small car with
an aluminum body.

03 The Audi 100 family tree
(from left to right):
Audi 100 C1 (1968 – 1976),
Audi 100 C2 (1976 – 1982),
Audi 100 C3 (1982 – 1990),
Audi 100 C4 (1990 – 1994)
04 Also an Audi 100: the
technically and visually revised
Audi A6 dating from the fall of
1994. It remained in the program
until 1997 and, like the Audi A8
and Audi A4, was given a new
model designation

02

03

01, 02

S for sport

Audi attached a red and silver "S" emblem to its selection of sporty, high-performance cars with quattro all-wheel drive as standard equipment. Precursor of the S models was the Audi Sport quattro Evolution S1 dating from 1985, a car built specifically for use in rallies. The 1990 Audi Coupé S2, the first car to bear the S emblem, was initially planned to follow in the footsteps of the "original"

03

04

05

quattro; from 1993 onwards the S2 Avant and sedan were added, both of them based on the B4-series Audi 80. Another sports sedan appeared in May 1991: the Audi S4, using the body of the Audi 100. An Avant version was introduced in September 1991. All S4 models were initially powered by the turbocharged five-cylinder engine with four valves per cylinder, but a 4.2-liter V8 was offered at the end of 1992 as an alternative for the S4 Avant, and in the following March for the S4 sedan as well.

The Audi Avant RS 2, an exclusive high-performance station wagon, was developed jointly with Porsche. 2,891 were built altogether between the fall of 1993 and July 1995, all of them based on the Audi 80 S2 Avant. With a power output of 232 kW (315 hp), this was the most powerful model in the entire Audi car program throughout its production period.

Introduction of the new A4, A6 and A8 model names in 1994 meant that the S models had to be renamed as well. When the Audi A6 was launched in June 1994 the sports models were accordingly named S6 (sedan and Avant). This first-generation S6 was available with a 4.2-liter V8 engine or with the turbocharged five-cylinder unit, the long and successful era of which came to an end only when this model went out of production in the spring of 1997. For ten years, the S6 was the only remaining Audi with a five-cylinder gasoline engine.

For the 1996 model year, the power output of the S6 4.2 was increased to 213 kW (290 hp), and it was available with either a six-speed manual-shift transmission or a four-speed automatic transmission. In June 1996 quattro GmbH introduced a further version of the S6 4.2, with the power output boosted to 240 kW (326 hp). These models were referred to as the S6 plus and S6 plus Avant. At list prices exceeding 116,000 Deutschmarks, these versions were a genuinely exclusive offer, of which fewer than 1,000 were made.

The sporty derivate of the Audi A8 made its appearance at the Geneva Motor Show in the spring of 1996. This was the Audi S8, powered by a 4.2-liter V8 engine rated initially at 250 kW (340 hp). Introduction of the V8 engine with five valves per cylinder in 1999 permitted a moderate boost in the S8's power output to 265 kW (360 hp).

06

01 Truly exclusive and packed with power. Only 300 of these Audi S2 sedans, propelled by a 230 hp turbocharged five-cylinder engine with four valves per cylinder, were built
02 Audi S4 Avant. The most sporty version of the Audi 100 was available from 1991 onwards, powered by the well-proven turbocharged engine. In 1992 a 4.2-liter V8 was added
03 315 horses that need to be saddled. The Audi RS 2 was developed jointly with Porsche in 1994, and began the tradition of high-performance Audi models
04 Wolf in designer's clothing: this Audi S8 was sold between 1996 and 2002, powered by a 340 hp engine with four valves per cylinder. In 1999 a newly developed 360 hp V8 with five valves per cylinder was installed
05 The 1999 Audi S8
06 In 1996, quattro GmbH began to sell the Audi S6 plus. A high-performance station wagon with a 326 hp engine, it remained in production for a year

01, 02

01 A B5-series Audi S4 Avant, as built between 1997 and 2001. The appropriate high level of performance came from a twin-turbo six-cylinder engine
02 The Audi S3, a compact, sporty car built between 1999 and 2003. 210 hp (from the fall of 2001 onwards 225 hp) were trans-mitted to the road through all four wheels
03 A C5-series Audi S6 sedan. The S model, which was in production from 1998 to 2004, can be identified by the aluminum-colored mirror housings, the radiator grill emblem and the flared wheel arches
04 The Audi S6 Avant combines the load capacity of practical family transport with the performance figures of a genuine sports car

For the 1997 IAA Frankfurt Motor Show, Audi announced a systematic development of the "S" concept: the S4 and S4 Avant, developed from the Audi A4. These new S models featured a twin-turbo 2.7-liter V6 engine with an output of 195 kW (265 hp), a new development that once again drove home Audi's "Vorsprung durch Technik." The S4 badge had previously been applied to the sports versions of the last Audi 100, the C4-series model. This duplication of the names still causes occasional confusion today, ten years after both models went out of production.

There were further additions to the S model pro-gram in 1999. When the four-door A3 hatchback was launched, it was accompanied in the spring by an S3 with a 154 kW (210 hp) turbocharged four-cylinder engine – the sports version of Audi's compact-class model. In September 2001 the S3 was given a minor facelift and its power output raised to 165 kW (225 hp).

Audi displayed the second-generation S6 at the IAA Frankfurt Motor Show in September 1999. A month later the S 6 became available, with either a six-speed manual transmission or tiptronic auto-matic transmission. This model was based on the A6 4.2 of the C5 series, but with the suspension modified and 17-inch wheels fitted. The front wings were flared out to accommodate eight inch wide 16-inch wheels if necessary. The bumpers and side sills were painted in the main body color. Aluminum exterior mirror housings and a stainless steel sports exhaust system with oval tailpipes were further external features that distinguished the S6 from other A6 models.

In 2002, quattro GmbH introduced the Audi RS 6, with biturbo 4.2-liter V8 engine, sports suspension, flared wheel arches at front and rear and a sports exhaust system with oval tailpipes. Avant and sedan RS models were available.

The RS 6 plus replaced the RS 6 models shortly before the C5 series ceased production in 2004.

03, 04

Fine tuning and water-cooled turbochargers enabled the power output to be boosted to 353 kW (480 hp). A limited edition of 999 cars, all of them in fact with an Avant body, was offered for sale. Apart from the mirror housings, all the normally chrome-plated parts were given an anodized matt black finish – even the exhaust tailpipes. The sports suspension was equipped with electronic Dynamic Ride Control to eliminate body pitch and roll. The RS 6, which featured a high-performance brake system from Brembo, did not have its top speed governed electronically.

For the B series, the RS 2 high-performance sports

05

06

station wagon concept of 1993 was revived, and the RS 4, based on the S4 Avant, presented to the public in the fall of 1999. With a 280 kW (380 hp) V6 twin-turbo engine, the RS 4 was the first model to be conceived by Audi's quattro GmbH subsidiary and developed jointly with AUDI AG. Engine development was entrusted to the reputable British engine construction company Cosworth, a member of the Audi Group since 1998. The RS 4 was produced jointly by the Ingolstadt factory and quattro GmbH in Neckarsulm, where final assembly and finishing work were undertaken by hand and only a few cars completed per day.

Dr.-Ing. Franz-Josef Paefgen on the company's position

"Public approval of a brand, its products and the people associated with it is a decisive competition factor. We have worked hard for many years on improving our image, but this is a long drawn-out process. We have now reached a stage where we can reap the benefits of the task we began so many years ago."

From an interview with the magazine Audi mobil, *March 1998*

05 Performance – in the stadium and elsewhere. As part of the partnership between Audi and FC Bayern Munich, the soccer club uses Audi company cars **06** The Audi RS 4 resulted from cooperation between quattro GmbH and Cosworth, and was listed in the product program only in 2001. The 380 hp developed by the fully revised engine ensured breathtaking performance and captivated more than 6,000 customers

01 Hans-Joachim Stuck at the wheel of the Audi 200 quattro TransAm

02 The 1988 TransAm Series race in Sears Point

03 Hans-Joachim Stuck on the Miami racetrack with the Audi 90 quattro IMSA-GTO

01, 02

03

TransAm, IMSA-GTO, DTM and Le Mans – on the world's racing circuits
1988 – 2009

TransAm and IMSA – Audi in America

The Audi quattro's supreme performance is not limited to gravel tracks, mud, snow or ice. To demonstrate this, Audi entered for the American TransAm series in 1988. The Audi team, with drivers Hurley Haywood, Walter Röhrl and Hans-Joachim Stuck, drove modified Audi 200 quattro cars in this American production car championship, which consisted of 13 races in all. As was to be expected, local competition was severe, but despite having to accept various restrictions, for example an increase in the cars' minimum weight, Audi had secured the championship title by the time the tenth race had been run, and also the driver's title for Hurley Haywood. Back home in Germany, Armin Schwarz at the wheel of an Audi 200 quattro was able to defend his previous season's championship title successfully.

The Audi team returned to the United States in 1989 for a new challenge: the IMSA-GTO series. For this demanding production-car race series, Audi's sport department had developed a car based on the Audi 90 quattro. Its five-cylinder engine with four valves per cylinder had a healthy output of no fewer than 620 hp – enough to give a car weighing 2,646 pounds a top speed of 193 mph. With seven wins, including five in first and second place, Audi was championship runner-up at the end of the series. Stuck and his Audi only failed to carry off the title because a decision was made not to enter the Sebring and Daytona long-distance races.

Motor sport success with the V8

In 1990 Audi concentrated its motor-sport efforts on Germany and began to enter the Audi V8 quattro for races. Not having been conceived initially as a sports model, it was mocked mercilessly as a "chauffeur's car." Then the seemingly impossible happened: in an exciting series of races culminating in a dramatic final at the Hockenheimring, Hans-Joachim Stuck captured the German Touring Car Championship (DTM). Four Audi V8s were on the starting grid when the next season began. Stuck's colleagues in the team were Biela, Jelinski and Haupt. Once again, the very last race on the Hockenheimring was decisive. In a dramatic contest, Biela was able to win both heats and carry off the title for Audi – the first manufacturer ever to defend its title in the German Touring Car Championship successfully.

After winning the DTM title twice, with Hans-Joachim Stuck at the wheel in 1990 and Frank Biela in 1991, Audi was prepared to regard the 1992 DTM season as something of a transitional period, while preparing cars for the changed rules that would apply in 1993. The Ingolstadt-based company did not expect to carry off the title yet again. Then, midway through the 1992 season, came a decision from the Supreme National Motor Sport Authority (the ONS): the crankshaft used in the Audi V8 quattro's engine did not conform with the rules. Audi was unable to participate any further, yet before the 1992 race season started, the ONS

04 Hans-Joachim Stuck
05 Stuck drives the V8 at the Zolder DTM race in 1990
06 The 1991 DTM Championship: Frank Biela, German champion in that season, in action
07 Stuck, Röhrl and Jelinski in close formation during the finale of the 1990 DTM season in Hockenheim

04, 05

06

07

01

01 Frank Biela won the British
Touring Car Challenge in 1996

had approved this crankshaft – not once but twice! To make the best of this situation, Hans-Joachim Stuck and Frank Biela drove successfully during the second half of the season in Touring Car Championship events in South Africa and France.

France, as one of Audi's most important export markets, was also where Audi undertook its racing activities in 1993. Frank Biela was entered for the French "Supertourisme" touring car championship, driving a 272 hp Audi 80 quattro, and took the title at the end of the season. Together with team colleague Marc Sourd he also secured the manufacturers' title for Audi, though this was in doubt right up to the last determinedly contested race.

Two-liter touring car racing all over Europe

From this time on, Audi concentrated on the two-liter class in its motor sport activities. For the D1 ADAC Touring Car Cup, held for the first time in 1994, the Ingolstadt-based company appeared once again in front of its home-market public with the Audi 80 competition. With supreme victories at the start of the season Frank Biela impressively demonstrated his intention of taking the title, but after the final race he had to admit defeat, taking second place just behind Johnny Cecotto's BMW.

Team colleague Emanuele Pirro had better luck: in the Italian Touring Car Championship that was run in parallel, he too drove an Audi 80 competition

286

02

03, 04

and took both the driver's championship and, another triumph for the brand with the four-ring emblem, the manufacturer's title for Audi. Ten years after the successes enjoyed by Audi rally driver Michèle Mouton, Audi entered another woman driver for events in the 1995 season. Tamara Vidali, the speedy Italian, strengthened the Audi team at the wheel of the new Audi A4 Supertouring model in the D1 ADAC Super Touring Car Cup and in the Italian BIU Touring Car Championship. Once again the season began well for Audi, which dominated the Super Touring Car Cup until halfway through the season. After this, that vital element of luck deserted the team, and after the last race Biela, Stuck and Heger had to be content with third, fourth and fifth places. In Italy, on the other hand, it was success all the way. Emanuele Pirro won eleven of his 20 races – a new record, and was able to defend his championship title with the greatest of ease. The manufacturer's title went to Audi once again. Championship runner-up was Pirro's team-mate Rinaldo Capello. Frank Biela also scored a major triumph as the season came to an end: he won the International Final of the FIA Touring World Cup on the Paul Ricard Circuit in the South of France, and became Super Touring Car Champion for the first time, followed by Emanuele Pirro as runner-up in the overall rankings.

Seven at one fell swoop
For the 1996 racing season, Audi's Head of Motor Sport Dr. Wolfgang Ullrich decided to enter the German and Italian championships, and also for the British Touring Car Championship. With support from the local importers, Audi also entered for the national Touring Car Championships in Belgium, Spain, Australia and South Africa, as a means of strengthening its presence in worldwide motor sport. This decision was rewarded with success: Audi carried off the national championship titles in seven countries!

After this achievement, the results in the 1997 season were more modest. The rule change that imposed an additional weight penalty of up to 209 pounds on cars with all-wheel drive could hardly fail to take effect. Despite this weight handicap, the Audi A4 quattro's performance potential was demonstrated clearly enough by several notable victories, but at the end of the season the Audi team had to be content with relatively thankless results: Pirro was fifth in Germany, Biela second in the British Touring Car Championship and Capello third in Italy.

"Bye, bye, quattro" was the rather depressing message for the 1998 touring-car racing season. The powers-that-be had declared an end to the era of the Audi quattro in circuit racing. The FIA (the international motor sport authority) banned all-wheel-drive touring cars in its 1998 rules. More convincing evidence of the superiority of the quattro driveline would have been hard to find! During the previous season, Audi had begun to enter front-wheel-drive A4s additionally, as a means of gaining experience. In the 1998 season itself, Audi fell on hard times: the A4s entered in Germany, England and Italy scored no victories at all. This was despite the fact that the Audi Sport team had mastered the changeover to front-wheel drive much more successfully before the season came to an end. Small consolation, but better than none at all: in the Central European and Australian touring car championships, where cars with all-wheel drive were permitted, the teams sponsored by the local importers were victorious with the A4 quattro.

The STC organizer moved the goalposts again for 1999. The big surprise was a renewed change in the rules, so that cars with all-wheel drive were now allowed to start, but even this was unable to persuade Audi to return to the championship with a works team. However, the ABT-Sportsline

02 Frank Biela
03 Emanuele Pirro
04 Rinaldo "Dindo" Capello

287

01

01 Laurent Aiello in the Abt TT-R,
winner of the 2002 DTM
02 Mattias Ekström in the Red
Bull Audi A4. In 2004 he won the
driver's championship, and Audi
took the manufacturers' title

team did compete, as did the private AZK Phoenix
Racing team, which entered two Audi A4 Supertouring quattro cars. They were both "secondhand"
in the sense that they had been raced actively
since 1996. It was a tough, merciless season, but
the privately entered Audis put up a strong fight
and relegated the factory-entered Opels to the
lower places. ABT-Sportsline became the first
private team to win an STC title.

Wound up in 1996, the DTM was reborn under a
different name, "German Touring Car Masters,"
for the 2000 racing season. This was intended to
demonstrate that the organizers had learned
from past mistakes. Complex technical developments were prohibited by the new rules. Standard
parts had to be used for the brakes, tires and transmissions; these were provided by suppliers within
the industry. Only cars with rear-wheel drive were
allowed to start. Strict technical limits were imposed on the V8 engines, with maximum power
governed by restrictors in the air intake system.

Racing with the Audi TT

Audi had no suitable car available for the new race
series, but the ABT-Sportsline team was eager to
continue working with Audi Motorsport, and was
in due course granted an exemption by the ITR
which allowed it to enter a car based on the Audi
TT. Audi approved this project, but emphasized
nonetheless that ABT would be participating as
an entirely private team. Three cars were built in
a very short time with the eight-cylinder, 3,998 cc
engine, a new development with a power output
of 450 hp. The season proved to be a year of
apprenticeship for the team, which collected only
a meager 19 points in the championship rankings.

For the 2001 season, the rules were modified
slightly, enabling the TT-R's wheelbase to be
lengthened by a modest 6.69 inches. The longer
body was more suitable for fine aerodynamic
tuning, and changes to the rear wing increased
downthrust at the rear wheels. Christian Abt,
Laurent Aiello, Martin Tomczyk and Mattias

Ekström were the drivers. By the end of the
season, ABT-Sportsline had overtaken Opel but
found Mercedes-Benz impossible to defeat.
Laurent Aiello was the best non-Mercedes driver,
in fifth place.

Before the 2002 season started, the cars underwent a number of detail modifications. Power
output went up only slightly, to 455 hp, but more
power was available at the lower end of the
engine speed scale than in the previous season.
Two lips were added to the rear wing as a further
aerodynamic improvement. The four drivers from
2001 remained with the team, and were joined
by the Austrian driver Karl Wendlinger. By the
time the last race but one had been run, Laurent
Aiello had the champion's title safe and sound.

The previous year's title winner was a hunted man
in the 2003 season. To strengthen the team still
further, Peter Terting was commissioned to drive
one of the previous year's cars. Detail work on the
engine, the cooling, lubricating and exhaust
systems and the aerodynamics rendered the TT-R
fit for the task of defending its title. A new rule
called for two pit stops during the race, and for
points to be allocated in the same way as in Formula One. Try as they may, the TT-R team was
unable to defend its title: the Mercedes CLK cars
were simply all-powerful. Three Mercedes drivers
occupied the winners' podium at the end of the
season, with Mattias Ekström in fourth place as
the best Audi driver. The manufacturers' title
also went to Mercedes-Benz with Audi as runner-
up. This marked the end of the Audi TT-R's racing
career: as early as the fall of 2003 Audi had
decided to rejoin the DTM with a works team.

On the track again as a works team

The special permit that enabled the Audi TT-R to
go to the start expired at the end of the 2003
season, so that the car was no longer suitable for
DTM events. Audi resolved to develop an entry of
its own, based on the Audi A4. The ABT-Sportsline
team was given factory status and the Joest team

02

prepared and entered two further Audi A4 DTM cars. Christian Abt, Mattias Ekström, Tom Christensen, Martin Tomczyk, Frank Biela and Emanuele Pirro drove for these teams. Test driving sessions had already demonstrated the A4's potential, and as the season got under way Audi optimized the aerodynamics again, as revealed by a complex assembly of wings and spoilers behind the wheel arches. The Motor Sport Department in Ingolstadt was able to transfer much of the know-how

acquired in Le Mans to the new car. Only the engine was retained from the previous season's TT-R, but with the intake and exhaust systems modified in detail to boost power to about 460 hp. By the time the next to the last race of a turbulent, toughly contended season had been run, the title was already safely in the hands of Martin Tomczyk. At the final event in Hockenheim, Audi also assured itself of the team prize and the manufacturer's title.

01

02

In 2005 the ABT-Sportsline and Joest teams continued to enter the Audi A4 DTM: ABT went to the start with four new cars built exclusively for the team, Joest fielded four of the previous season's cars. ABT's drivers were Ekström, Tomczyk, Kristensen and McNish. The Joest team consisted of Kaffer, Capello, Stippler and Abt. The cars for the 2005 season were modified visually to match the new Audi A4 with single-frame radiator grill, and optimized once more in the wind tunnel. A worthwhile weight saving was made by installing a Hewland six-speed trans-mission; competitors initially remained loyal to the older x-trac transmission. Audi was unable to defend the previous year's title despite determined efforts by the teams. When the final rankings were known, Mattias Ekström took second place on the podium in the driver's championship.

The 2006 season again came to an end with Audi empty-handed, apart from a third place for Tom Christensen. Fourth place in the drivers' rankings went to his team-mate Martin Tomczyk. The A4

DTM cars were again modified only in detail for the 2007 season. This proved to be extremely exciting, and it was not until the very last heat that Mattias Ekström could be sure of success in the drivers' rankings, with Martin Tomczyk taking third place. The Audi Sport ABT-Sportsline team took first place in the team rankings by a con-siderable margin.

Audi had every cause to be satisfied with the 2008 season as well. With Timo Scheider first and Mattias Ekström third in the drivers' rankings, the title was confidently defended, with a lead of four points at the end of the season over the runner-up Mercedes driven by Paul di Resta, who had dueled mercilessly with Scheider. In the season's team rankings, Audi came second, third, fifth and seventh.

01 Audi A4 DTM, Type R11: the 2004 championship car
02 Perfect choreography – Martin Tomczyk comes into the pits in 2007
03 The pressure's on Christian Abt (2007)
04 Timo Scheider in the Audi A4 DTM R13, 2008

03, 04

01

01 R8 Le Mans, 2001 model
02 The cars that won Le Mans in
2000, 2001 and 2002

Audi at the Le Mans 24-hour race

In 1999, Audi was looking for a new challenge. The choice fell on an international motor sport classic, the Le Mans 24-hour event. This covers a distance comparable with fifteen Formula One Grand Prix races, and can be regarded as a sprint and a marathon at one and the same time. The speeds are high, so that success depends equally on technical reliability and human endurance.

Audi developed a totally new sports racing car when it decided to enter this most famous of all long-distance races. After a development period of 15 months, the Audi R8 was shown to the media for the first time in October 1998: a low-slung, potent creation with a carbon-fiber body. The twin-turbo V8 engine, with a displacement of 3,600 cc and a power output of 450 kW (610 hp) at 6,300 1/min was brought to life by Dr. Baretzky in Neckarsulm. Chassis development took place in Ingolstadt and the monocoque carbon-fiber body came from Italy. The result: a mid-engined roadster designed and built from scratch, with none of its assemblies inherited from any other model. Later in the fall a coupé version of the R8 was also completed. The GTP rules permitted the coupé to run at higher boost pressure and with a larger intake air restrictor. This meant a power increase of 30 hp, but also a vast amount of chassis tuning work.

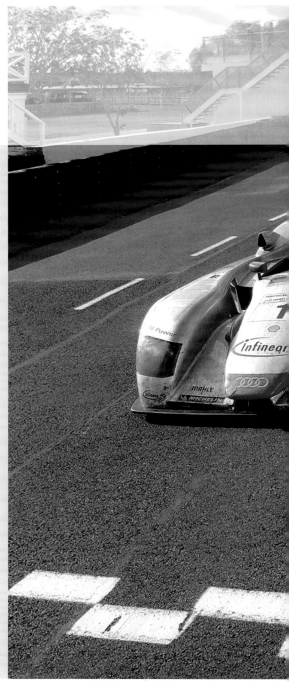

02

Audi enlisted the aid of experienced, long-time partners for its long-distance championship attempt. The Joest team was responsible for entering the R8R, the British Audi UK team managed by Richard Lloyd took the two R8C cars under its wing. No fewer than twelve drivers were hired, including regular Audi stars such as Frank Biela, Emanuele Pirro and Rinaldo Capello. They were joined by Christian Abt, who had strengthened the Audi Team in the previous season and, in parallel with his Le Mans outing, was already

driving an Audi A4 quattro successfully in the German Super Touring Car championship.

The 1999 marathon event began at the usual time of 4 p.m. on June 12, 1999. The drivers were facing a distance of almost 3,107 miles, and as many laps of the circuit as there are days in the year. Would Audi's concept prove correct? Would the multitude of theoretical calculations prove accurate in practice? Both the R8C cars retired with transmission problems. But the two remaining

R8 roadsters kept going determinedly, lap after lap, and crossed the finishing line to enthusiastic applause in the Audi pits. Third and fourth places after 24 hours, in this, the toughest of all long distance races, and at the very first attempt! Only BMW and Toyota were faster.

A year later, the Le Mans challenge was tackled again. All or nothing was the unspoken slogan for the 2000 race. A clearly defined target for the R8R cars that Audi Sport had been developing still further with top priority. Aerodynamic drag had been reduced: the drivers could sense this immediately. Know-how acquired from the 1999 race was applied to the R8, and in fact 80 percent of its technical content was new. Even the carbon-fiber monocoque body was 55 pounds lighter. The side panels were raised for greater driver safety. Radiators moved to the side panels kept cockpit temperatures down to a bearable level. Development work on the Coupé version was halted, however, and it vanished into oblivion.

293

The dress rehearsal, so to speak, was held on March 18, the date of the twelve-hour race in Sebring, Florida, the first event in the American Le Mans Series (ALMS), for which Audi had entered as in the previous year. A complete success: the new Audi R8 s crossed the line in first and second places. A splendid omen for the immediate future – and one that proved correct. On June 18, 2000, the Le Mans 24-hour race ended with a one-two-three victory for Audi. In front of more than 200,000 spectators, the three Audi R8 entries, driven by Biela/Kristensen/Pirro (the winners), Aiello/McNish/Ortelli (second place) and Abt/Alboreto/Capello (third place) captured this coveted trophy for Audi. After its triumphs in the World Rally Championship and in touring car racing, Audi had now written a fresh chapter in motor sport history.

Faster and more economical with FSI direct injection

There was no question but that Audi would enter the various European and American long-distance races in the 2001 season. But this meant exploring new technical territory: the turbocharged eight-cylinder engines were converted to direct fuel injection (FSI). The fuel-injected versions not only ran magnificently, with even more abundant torque at all engine speeds, but also proved to be even more economical. With a full tank, they were able to complete an additional lap of the Le Mans circuit with ease, while their rivals were refuelling in the pits. In Sebring, the fuel-injected R8's first race of the season, the Audis took the first four places, but this triumph was overshadowed by the death of Michele Alboreto

while testing the car for Le Mans on the Euro Speedway circuit in Germany's Lausitz region. At a speed of 211 miles an hour the R8's left rear tire burst, the car veered to one side and overturned as the airflow reached the underside of the body. Alboreto died immediately.

For this year's Le Mans race, which was mostly run in heavy rain, Joest Racing entered only two cars for Audi. Both completed the course and took first and second places. Third was a fixed-roof car, a Bentley – derived from the coupé-style Audi R8C that had disappeared from the scene a year before.

The R8 had undergone only slight modifications for the 2002 season, the most immediately obvious one being the new rear wing. After the 24 hours had elapsed in Le Mans, the sensation was complete: running with polished precision, the Audi cars had once again defeated all their rivals and taken the first three places! After this outstanding achievement, Audi decided not to enter any more works cars for Le Mans, but to support the private teams that took the previous season's R8s to the starting grid. There were three of these privately entered R8s in the 2003 race, and they were rather disappointed to have secured only a third and a fourth place. The explanation for this was simple: the event was largely dominated by the factory-entered Bentleys. After a one-two

victory on the Sarthe circuit, the VW Group decided not to enter its car, which was derived from the R8, in any further races. Bentley vanished from the long-distance motor racing scene as suddenly as it had materialized three years before.

In 2004 there were four privately entered Audi R8s in the race, two entered by Audi Sport UK, one by the Japanese Goh team and one by Champion Racing. The outcome: once again Audi took the first three places. This time the Japanese drivers were on the highest step of the winners' podium. Runner-up was Audi Sport UK, third place went to Champion Racing. The English team's second Audi slid off the track and suffered such extensive damage that it took easily an hour to repair. The team then set off determinedly to make good the lost time, to such good effect that the car took the checkered flag in fifth place.

Then came the 2005 season, the last time the R8 was to be seen on the Le Mans circuit. Three private teams with factory support went to the starting grid. Their cars were distinctly hampered by a change in the rules that obliged Audi to carry additional ballast and use air intake restrictors of smaller size. Now with only 520 hp on tap, these throttled R8s had a top speed of no more than 193 mph. Yet despite this handicap, they won the race and took third and fourth places as well.

01 Laguna Seca, 2000: Allan McNish leads Emanuele Pirro across the line
02 The Le Mans winning car of 2002
03 Mosport Park: Stefan Johansson took second place
04 Spa 2005, with the French Oreca team's R8

01

02

M. Rockenfeller
M.Werner

03

The winning car was driven across the finishing line by Tom Kristensen, who had remained at the wheel for three and a half hours in order not to endanger the team's lead by a change of drivers. It was Kristensen's seventh Le Mans victory.

The diesel racer – the twelve-cylinder R10 TDI
Until 2006 nobody had seriously tried for overall victory with a diesel-engined car in a major sports car race. Audi, the pioneer of TDI technology, decided to attempt this feat, and entered its R10 TDI, a completely new development, for Le Mans. With the air intake restrictors and boost pressure laid down by the rules, the first version of the twelve-cylinder TDI delivered more than 650 hp on the test rig, and a peak torque of 1,100 Nm. The aluminum-block engine developed its maximum power at speeds between 4,500 and 5,500 revolutions per minute – not very different from those reached by a production TDI. The R10 won the very first race for which it was entered, in Sebring.

Audi entered two cars for Le Mans. The first qualifying session, on wet roads, went badly, but after the second session, when the roads were dry, the two cars were in the first row of the starting grid. In the actual race on June 18, Audi's diesel-

296

04

01

Company chronicle

1985	Audi NSU Auto Union AG changes its name to AUDI AG and moved its headquarters to Ingolstadt, where they have remained since then
1988	Production of the Audi 100 C3 starts at the Chinese company FAW in Changchun
1993	Establishment of the subsidiary company Audi Motor Hungaria Kft. in Győr, Hungary
1995	A change in corporate identity: from now on, the "Four Rings" are the principal feature in the company's image
1997	The Audi do Brasil subsidiary is established in Curitiba. From 1999 until the fall of 2006 it built the Audi A3 for the South American market
1998	Takeover of the Italian sports car manufacturer Automobili Lamborghini S.p.A.
1998	Purchase of the English company Cosworth Technology Ltd.

03, 04

powered cars took first and third places – another new chapter in motor sport history.

For the first time since 2002, Audi had three cars on the starting grid for the 2007 Le Mans race. The rules required the R10's fuel tank to be made ten percent smaller, to compensate for the cars' greater economy compared with gasoline-engined rivals. The engineers in Ingolstadt, in cooperation with the Bosch company, had revised the electronics with the aim of optimizing both fuel consumption and response to the accelerator pedal. Only one of the three Audi cars was able to complete the course during this anniversary event, the 75th Le Mans 24-hour race – but it won! The R10 crossed the line ten laps ahead of a new rival, the Peugeot, which was also powered by a diesel engine. Audi also set the fastest lap time of 3 minutes, 27.176 seconds. Competitors' cars were able to match its top speed: the open Audi and the Peugeot Coupé were both timed at 211 mph.

In 2008, Audi decided for the first time to enter cars for the Le Mans race series, a revival of various classic European 1,000-kilometer (621-mile) events. The rules for the Le Mans 24-hour race apply unrestrictedly in this series too, and the winner qualifies automatically for that event in the following year. The program for the 2008 season consisted of races in Barcelona, Monza, Spa-Francorchamps, on the Nürburgring and in Silverstone.

After 381 laps and with a lead of just 4 minutes, 31 seconds after 24 hours, Audi was victorious for the eighth time in Le Mans, banishing Peugeot to places two and three. The two other Audi cars came in fourth and sixth. Tom Kristensen, the later winner, caused a degree of panic two hours before the end of the race by spinning the R10 on a sheet of water near Arnage. Somehow he kept control of the car and was able to continue. On this occasion Kristensen shared the driving stints with Rinaldo "Dindo" Capello and Alan McNish.

01 Flying change: Allan McNish (left) hands the car over to Rinaldo Capello
02 Sebring, 2006 – the traditional opening of the racing season
03 Impressions from Le Mans
04 In Sebring (2009) the brand-new Audi R15 TDI won first time out
05 Heading for the rising sun – and another win!

05

01

02

05

06

Audi – an overview

03

04

07

08

09

10

01 Audi 100 (C3) Avant, 1986
02 Audi 100 (C3) quattro sport, 1989
03 Audi 80 (B3) sedan, 1986
04 Audi 90 (B3) quattro 20V, 1989
05 Audi Coupé (B3) quattro 20V, 1988
06 Audi 200 (C3) quattro 20V sedan and Avant, 1989
07 Audi V8 (D1) sedan, 1988
08 Audi V8 L 4.2 (D1), 1993
09 Audi Coupé (B3) 2.6E quattro, 1992
10 Audi 100 (C4) Avant, 1994
11 Audi 100 (C4) quattro 2.8E, 1990

01

02

05

06

09

10

302

Audi – an overview

03

04

07

08

11

12

01

02

05

06

09

304

Audi – an overview

03

04

07

08

10

11

01 Audi S8 (D2) sedan, 1999
02 Audi S4 (B5) sedan, 1997
03 Audi A6 (C5) sedan, 1998
04 Audi A6 (C5) Avant quattro, 1998
05 Audi TT (8N) Coupé quattro, 1998
06 Audi A3 (8L) five-door sedan, 2001
07 Audi S3 (8L) facelift, 2002
08 Audi RS 4 (B5) Avant, 2001
09 Audi TT (8N) Roadster quattro, 2001
10 Audi A2 sedan, 2002
11 Audi allroad quattro (C5), 2000

Into the 21st century

Future perspectives

The concept of the new millennium evidently appealed to the general public, despite a degree of panic caused by allegations that computers would crash all over the world. In actual fact, there was no wholesale collapse of electronic data processing systems, and before long it was evident that electronics, in the guise of the Internet, were about to cause a fundamental change in global information exchange principles.

As a first sign that Europe was coming together, Germany introduced the euro as an accounting currency in January 1999. It took over as Germany's official currency in January 2002; the same change was made then or has since been made by 14 other EU member nations.

People

Dr. Franz-Josef Paefgen was appointed the Volkswagen Group's General Representative for Motor Sport and Research, and also Chairman of the subsidiary company Bentley Motors Ltd. His position as Chairman of the AUDI AG Board of Management was taken over on March 1, 2002, by Dr. Martin Winterkorn. From January 2003 onwards Winterkorn also became responsible at Board level for the Technical Development area. During his period of office, the foundations were laid for major extension and modernization of the Audi model program.

At the end of 2006 Dr. Winterkorn succeeded Bernd Pischetsrieder as Chairman of the

01

01 Prof. Dr. rer. nat. Martin
Winterkorn, Chairman of the
Supervisory Board of AUDI AG
02 Rupert Stadler, Chairman of
the Board of Management of
AUDI AG since January 1, 2007

Volkswagen AG Board of Management in Wolfsburg. His place at Audi was taken on January 1,
2007, by Rupert Stadler, previously the member
of the AUDI AG Board of Management with
responsibility for Finance and Organization.

From May 1994 until the end of 2005, Xaver
Meier was Chairman of the Ingolstadt plant Works
Council and the General Works Council. He was
succeeded by Peter Mosch on January 1, 2006.

02

307

01 With its high waistline, the
Audi A4 (B6) initiates a new
design idiom at Audi
02 Audi A4 (B6) Avant
03 The Audi A8 (D3) after a model
facelift in 2005

01, 02

03

04

New-model news

Between June 2000 and August 2001 the first Audi A4 model line reached full flower. Developed by quattro GmbH in conjunction with Cosworth, the RS 4 Avant's extensively modified six-cylinder twin-turbocharger engine, with five valves per cylinder, developed 280 kW (380 hp). Acceleration from 0 to 62 mph in only 4.8 seconds was a figure that could stand comparison with many a pedigree sports car.

A new A4 began to reach the showrooms in November 2000. Its styling differed from Audi's previous formal idiom: a high waistline and large-area side panels presaged a new Audi school of design. The Avant version followed in August 2001, and immediately began to notch up the same sales successes as the previous model. The third member of the new B6 series was the new Audi Cabriolet, premiered at the IAA Frankfurt Motor Show in September 2001. For the first time, an open Audi was now available with all-wheel drive; a diesel version was to be expected as well, and Audi's most powerful open car to date was introduced at the 2004 Geneva Motor Show: the S4 Cabriolet. Its eight-cylinder engine, with five valves per cylinder, developed 253 kW (344 hp)

and was capable of whisking this attractive open car up to its governed top speed of 155 mph in no time at all.

Based on the Audi A6, an emphatically sporty model appeared in the spring of 2002: the RS 6, capable of outperforming even the powerful S models. The eight-cylinder engine fitted to both the RS 6 sedan and the RS 6 Avant had twin turbo-chargers and the impressive power output of 331 kW (450 hp). When series production of this model line ceased, the previous RS 6 models were replaced by the RS 6 plus Avant. Fine tuning and water-cooled turbochargers boosted power output still further, to 353 kW (480 hp).

In September 2002 it was time for the media to be introduced to the second-generation Audi A8 (internal designation D3). Its world premiere followed shortly after at the "Mondial de l'Auto-mobile" in Paris. In 2004 the top model in this line, the 12-cylinder Audi A8 L 6.0 long-wheelbase sedan, was given the single-frame radiator grill, a styling feature that became characteristic of the entire Audi model program in the two model years that followed.

05, 06

04 Upward-extending head restraints – one of the Audi A4 (B6) Cabriolet's safety features
05 Audi A4 (B6) Cabriolet 2.4
06 Rippling muscles – the Audi S4 (B6) Cabriolet with V8 engine
07 Aerodynamic measures applied to the floor pan of the Audi A8 (D3) quattro
08 Princely space for rear-seat occupants of the A8 L (D3)
09 Audi A8 L (D3) – the long-wheelbase version

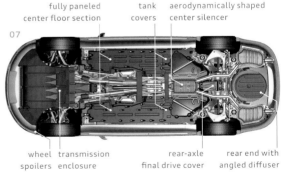

07

fully paneled center floor section | tank covers | aerodynamically shaped center silencer

wheel spoilers | transmission enclosure | rear-axle final drive cover | rear end with angled diffuser

08, 09

sheet metal
sections
castings

02

03

01 Space frame and panels for the Audi A8 (D3)

02 A modest ceremony to celebrate production of the 250,000th Audi with aluminum body

03 A detail of the Audi S8 (D3), production of which started in October 2005

04 Powered by a 10-cylinder FSI engine: the Audi S8 (D3)

05 Final inspection in the Audi A3 assembly area

06 The charm of a beautiful back! The Audi A3 Sportback, 2004

07 Audi A3, 2003 model: the last one without the single-frame radiator grill

08 Audi A3 Cabriolet – with a classic soft top

09 The open A3 cuts a fine figure from just any angle

In May 2003 Audi celebrated production of the 250,000th aluminum car body. By that time 117,000 Audi A8 and 133,000 Audi A2 cars had been built using the space frame principle patented by Audi.

At the Tokyo Motor Show in October 2005, the sportiest version of the A8 model line made its debut. The Audi S8 obtains its power from a V10 engine with direct gasoline injection; with a displacement of 5.2 liters, it develops 450 hp. The latest generation of quattro driveline is fitted: it features an asymmetric-dynamic torque distribution principle. In normal circumstances 40 percent of the torque goes to the front wheels and 60 percent to the rear, but this mild rear-wheel bias can change in response to unusual road conditions. Up to 85 percent of the power input can then be directed to the rear wheels, or alternatively a maximum of 65 percent to the front wheels. The S8 sprints from 0 to 62 mph in 5.1 seconds, and has an electronically governed top speed of 155 mph. Its power to weight ratio is impressive: each horsepower has to propel only 9.5 pounds of the car's weight – a figure normally associated only with sports cars.

310

05

06

At the Geneva Motor Show in the spring of 2003, Audi unveiled the second-generation A3. Initially available only as a three-door model, this "premium athlete in the compact class" was joined in September 2004 by the five-door Audi A3 Sport-back. It was also the first Audi A3 to have the single-frame radiator grill shown to the public previously on the A8. This appeared on the three-door A3 only in 2005, when it was given a facelift. New diesel engines with a particulate filter, four valves per cylinder and piezo injector technology

were also introduced at this time. A version with optimized fuel consumption appeared in 2007: this was the Audi A3 1.9 TDIe, which achieved consumption figures of 52.27 miles per gallon of diesel oil. For the powerful Audi S3, the first turbocharged gasoline engine with direct fuel injection was introduced in August 2006. The youngest member of the A3 model line was presented in January 2008 in Le Castellet: the Audi A3 Cabriolet. It was launched with a choice of two gasoline and two diesel engines, all with

07, 08

04

09

01 The sixth series (C6) of a successful model – the 2004 Audi A6 sedan

02 Avant not only stands for beautiful station wagons, but also for ample load-carrying space

03 RS 6 Avant – with a 426 kW (580 hp) engine, the most powerful offspring of the Audi family

04 Interior of the Audi RS 6

05 Design sketch for the interior of the Audi A6 (C6)

03, 04

four cylinders. All four engines have direct fuel injection and are turbocharged.

After a successful career, the Audi A6 from the C5 model line was succeeded in February 2004 by the C6-series A6 sedan – and promptly voted Car of the Year by readers of the German automobile club magazine *ADAC Motorwelt*. The A6 Avant station wagon version followed in March 2005, and the S version of the A6 was introduced in March 2006. Always the most sporty model in the line, it was now powered by a ten-cylinder engine. The A6 received a comprehensive facelift in August 2008, accompanied by major design improvements under the skin. Of the nine engines offered to the customer, seven were extensively modified. A new three-liter gasoline engine combining direct fuel injection with supercharging develops 213 kW (290 hp).

In January 2008 Audi announced the RS 6 Avant, followed in September 2008 at the Paris Motor Show by the Audi RS 6 sedan. Both these models have performance that would be impressive even from a powerful sports car. The ten-cylinder engine, with twin turbochargers and direct injection, has an output of 426 kW (580 hp) and a maximum torque of 650 Nm. It propels the RS 6 up to 62 mph from a standing start in 4.5 seconds. On request, Audi is prepared to raise the car's electronically governed top speed from 155 to 174 mph.

The C6 model line also serves as a basis for the second-generation Audi allroad quattro. This has a self-locking center differential that distributes engine torque in variable proportions to the front and rear axles. Electronically controlled air suspension is another feature that adds significantly to the car's capabilities. Generous ground clearance of up to 7.28 inches makes the Audi A6 allroad

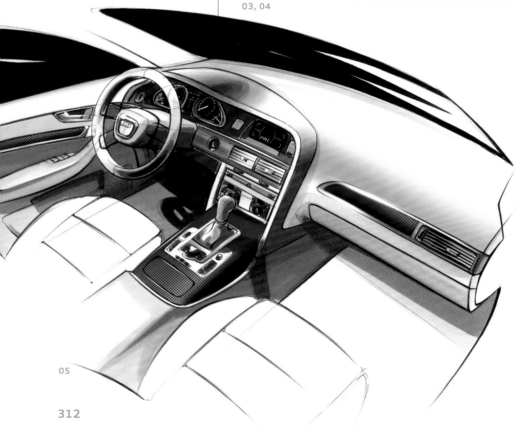

05

312

06

07

08

06 The Audi A6 allroad quattro is based on the Audi A6 Avant (C6)
07 Sketch of the Audi allroad concept first seen at the 2005 Detroit Motor Show
08 The air suspension layout for the Audi allroad quattro (C6)
09 Audi A4 (B7) Avant, built from 2004 to 2007
10 Detail of an Audi A4 (B7) light unit

quattro an even more effective means of transport when driven off the beaten track.

The next highlight in the changing model cycle fell due in the fall of 2004, when the Audi A4 was revised. This was not regarded internally merely as a facelift, but given the status of a new model line and designated B7. It also received the new single-frame radiator grill as an immediate means of identifying the new-generation B-series model. The previous model's body was not changed, but there was now a choice of no fewer than ten engines, four of them completely new developments.

09, 10

01 Audi RS 4 (B7) Cabriolet, 2006 – a high-revving concept in a seductive package

02 The Audi RS 4's V8 engine, with four valves per cylinder, delivers 309 kW (420 hp) from a displacement of 4.2 liters

03 The 2005 Audi RS 4 (B7) sedan reaches 62 mph in 4.8 seconds

The RS 4 was introduced at the top end of the eight-cylinder S model line in the summer of 2005. It was available for the first time as a sedan, Avant or Cabriolet. A 309 kW (420 hp) eight-cylinder engine using FSI technology was used to propel this most powerful version of the Audi A4 until production of the sedan and Avant models ceased in the fall of 2008. Only the Cabriolet, assembled by the Karmann company at its factory in Rheine, remained available.

Technical progress in the first decade of the new millennium has seen such innovations as diesel engines with common-rail injection, gasoline engines with direct fuel injection, diesels with soot-particle filters, a tendency for powerful gasoline engines to be downsized, variable valve lift, weight-saving suspension, electronically adjustable shock absorbers, air suspension, bodies entirely made of aluminum or of mixed aluminum and steel, and modular longitudinal and transverse platforms.

02

03

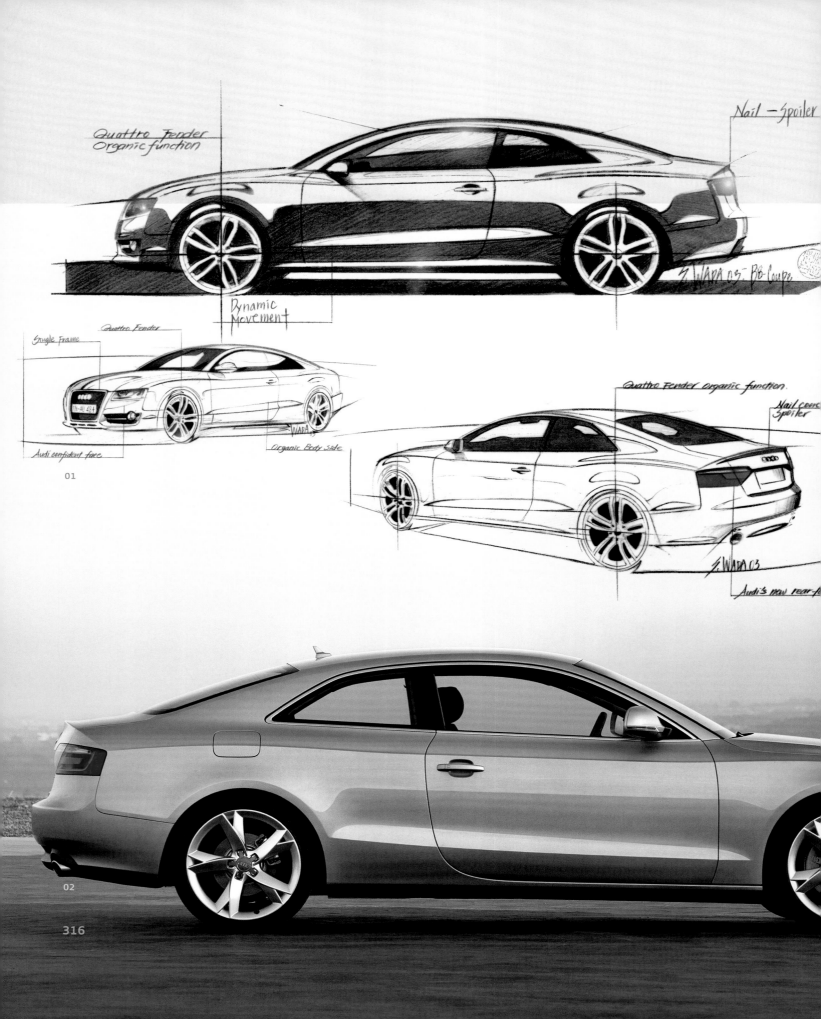

Quattro Fender
Organic function

Nail-Spoiler

S. WADA 03. B8-Coupe

Dynamic Movement

Single Frame

Quattro Fender

Audi confident face

Organic Body Side

WADA

Quattro Fender organic function.

Nail cone Spoiler

S. WADA 03

Audi's new rear-

01

02

05

03

04

A new generation of V-engines with four valves per cylinder has been largely standardized in design for production-technology reasons. All the V6 and V8 units, both diesels and gasoline engines, have standardized cylinder spacing and can therefore be machined on the same production line. Audi was the first manufacturer to install the diesel engine successfully in convertibles, just as it was the Ingolstadt-based company's achievement to popularise the diesel engine in large luxury models and in the sporty coupé market segment.

This was the period in which car design was greatly influenced by Walter de'Silva, who joined the company in March 2002. The single-frame radiator grill was his brainchild, as was the sporty, elegant design of the current model lines and above all the Audi A5 Coupé, which he himself regards as his masterpiece. This iconic design re-introduced Audi in the spring of 2007 to the four-seat coupé segment of the market, from which it had been absent for more than ten years.
The "Nuvolari" concept study of 2003 anticipated certain stylistic elements of the A5 and was much admired by the public.

01 Sketches for the Audi A5
02 The 2007 Audi A5 – a luxurious grand touring coupé with four seats and a large trunk
03 A dream in red – the interior of the 2007 Audi S5
04 The Audi S5 (B8) was launched at the same time as the A5 in 2007
05 Four exhaust tailpipes add emphasis to the S5's brawny rear end

01

02

03

04

05

06

01 The Audi Pikes Peak design study was the first car seen with LED lighting technology at the Detroit Show (2003)

02 The Q7 electronics are board-mounted for testing during the development phase

03 Hydropulsers mercilessly reveal any weak points in the body structure

04 Measured results from the road simulator are continuously evaluated

05 Tests in the climate chamber simulate arctic cold, humid tropical atmospheres and hot climates

06 Test-driving the Audi Q7 in the desert (summer 2005)

07 Test results are recorded and evaluated both during and after the test runs

318

At the Detroit Motor Show in January 2003, the Pikes Peak quattro study caused a sensation. A crossover model aimed at the American market, it combined the dynamism and comfort of a sports sedan with the capabilities of an off-road vehicle, thanks to variable-height air suspension and quattro driveline technology. By March 2006 the Audi Q7, derived from this concept study, had already reached dealers' showrooms. It makes use of the platform originally developed for the VW Touareg and Porsche Cayenne, but without their specific off-road technical features. The Q7 was introduced with a choice of eight-cylinder gasoline engine or six-cylinder diesel. These were soon joined by a newly developed 3.6-liter direct-injection gasoline engine and the 4.2-liter V8 TDI already familiar from the Audi A8. The culmination of this model line, however, is the version with 12-cylinder TDI engine, deliveries of which commenced late in 2008. With a displacement of six liters, a power output of 368 kW (500 hp) and a maximum torque of 1,000 Nm, the Q7 V12 TDI quattro is currently the most powerful

08

09, 10

07

08 Audi Q7: the brand's first SUV reached the market in the fall of 2005
09 Opening the bonnet of the Q7 V12 TDI reveals a master-piece of engine technology
10 Q7 V12 TDI, 2008 – 368 kW (500 hp) and 1,000 Nm of torque guarantee driving pleasure only a sports car could equal

V 10

Paul Ho

IN·R 805

01

diesel-engined passenger car built anywhere in the world.

At the IAA Frankfurt Motor Show in September 2003 another near-series design study, the Audi Le Mans, was exhibited. It was described as "combining the know-how from many racing triumphs with Audi's forward-looking design and technical competence." Whereas this study was propelled by a five-liter, ten-cylinder engine with twin turbochargers and direct fuel injection, the production car, designated the Audi R8, appeared with a slightly more modest power unit. The R8 had its public debut at the Paris Motor Show in the fall of 2006. Under the engine cover was a powerful eight-cylinder naturally aspirated engine with direct injection. Its output of 309 kW (420 hp) was certainly enough to guarantee vigorous forward progress, with 62 miles an hour reached from a standstill in 4.6 seconds and a top speed of 187 mph. In December 2008 the Audi R8 5.2 FSI joined the programme, needing a mere 3.9 seconds to reach 62 mph from a standing start, rocketing to twice this figure in 12 seconds and capable of attaining a top speed of 198 mph. It is powered by a ten-cylinder naturally aspirated engine. Both these cars are built according to the ASF principle; they are true supercars models and attract a corresponding amount of attention wherever they appear.

01 The Audi R8 mid-engined, all-wheel-drive sports car was introduced in January 2007
02 Carbon-fiber mirror housing for the Audi R8 5.2 FSI, 2009
03 Detail of the instrument panel in the Audi R8
04 Rear view of the Audi R8 5.2 FSI – its 10 cylinders promise monumental progress
05 Karl Lagerfeld photographs the R8 for his picture series "Kaleidoscopic Vision of a Car"

01

A successor for the Audi TT, that design icon that had been in production since 1998, was launched in the fall of 2006. This 2 + 2-seater was styled in a manner not dissimilar to the preceding model, but with a greater subjective impression of length. The new car was indeed both longer and wider. Coupé and Roadster versions were introduced at the same time.

The new TT's body used the Audi Space Frame (ASF) principle and a combination of steel and aluminum, the first time that these different materials had been combined in this way. 69 percent of the body is in aluminum, with the steel elements making up the remaining 31 percent mostly concentrated at the rear of the car. This achieves a more balanced axle-load distribution.

In April 2008 Audi announced the Audi TTS and also a diesel version of the TT, available in either body style. Cars with these engines are only available with the quattro driveline. The two-liter, four-cylinder engine in the TTS has a power output of 200 kW (272 hp) and accelerates the Coupé up to 62 mph in 5.2 seconds. Top speed is

governed electronically. A six-speed transmission and the Audi magnetic ride shock absorber system are standard features. The two-liter TDI engine, with four valves per cylinder, develops 125 kW (170 hp) and can deliver a maximum torque of 350 Nm. Its common-rail fuel supply and piezo injectors make it a refined unit with very moderate fuel consumption: although all-wheel drive is standard, the Coupé achieves fuel efficiency of 44 miles per gallon.

At the 2009 Geneva Motor Show, the TT RS was added to this model range. It is the most powerful version available, with a 2.5-liter five-cylinder engine developing 250 kW (340 hp). This engine, available in either the Coupé or Roadster, is turbocharged and has direct gasoline injection. The five-cylinder turbo revives a long tradition. Even the legendary Audi quattro dating from 1980 was powered by a 2.1-liter five-cylinder turbocharged engine rated at 147 kW (200 hp). With an unladen weight of 3,197 pounds, the TT RS can claim a power-to-weight ratio of 9.48 pounds per horsepower. On request, its electronically governed top speed can be raised to 174 mph.

02, 03

04

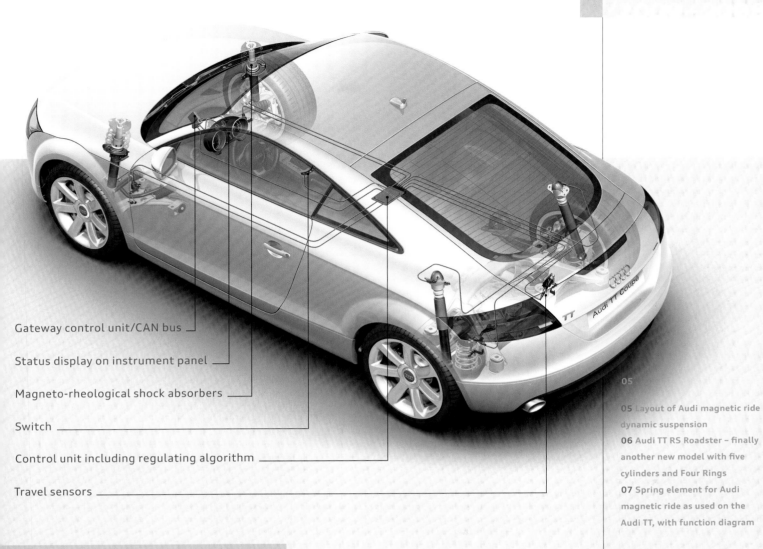

Gateway control unit/CAN bus

Status display on instrument panel

Magneto-rheological shock absorbers

Switch

Control unit including regulating algorithm

Travel sensors

05

05 Layout of Audi magnetic ride dynamic suspension
06 Audi TT RS Roadster – finally another new model with five cylinders and Four Rings
07 Spring element for Audi magnetic ride as used on the Audi TT, with function diagram

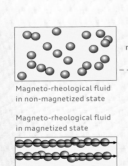

Magneto-rheological fluid in non-magnetized state

Magneto-rheological fluid in magnetized state

Magnetic field

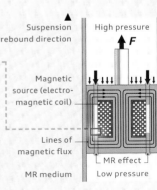

Suspension rebound direction

High pressure

F

Magnetic source (electro-magnetic coil)

Lines of magnetic flux

MR medium

MR effect

Low pressure

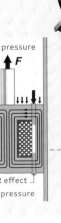

01 The generations compared:
Audi A4 (B8) (right) and Audi 80
(B2) quattro

01

04

324

The new B8-series Audi A4 sedan was announced in September 2007, with the first cars reaching their owners in December. The Avant version appeared in the media in February 2008 and had its public debut at the Geneva Motor Show a month later. The latest model generation takes it cue optically from the Audi A5. Compared with the previous model, the A4 is both longer and wider. Striking visual features in addition to the single-frame radiator grill are the new headlights with LED daytime running lights. Turn indicator repeaters are integrated into the outside mirrors.

The Audi A4 is based technically on the new modular longitudinal platform, introduced for the first time on the Audi A5. It will be used for all Volkswagen Group models with a longitudinally installed engine. For this platform, the engineers have reversed the positions of the clutch and transmission and have thus been able to move the front axle assembly forward by 6.06 inches. The steering box is located centrally at the lowest point on the subframe, for a spontaneous response to steering wheel movements. The new model line is available with a choice of five gasoline engines and four diesels. On the latest gasoline engines, the camshaft is chain-driven instead of the previous toothed belt drive.

The Audi A4 allroad quattro, based on the latest Audi A4, was exhibited at the Geneva Motor Show in March 2009. With its permanent all-wheel drive and raised suspension, it is truly the "Audi to take you everywhere."

Visual differences from the other models in this range are the flared wheel arches, boldly angled body sills and 17-inch wheels as standard equipment. The technical specification is otherwise the same as for the Audi A4 Avant quattro.

05

02 Rear view of 2007 Audi A4 (B8)
03 LED daytime running lights are the hallmark of the new Audi A4

06

07

04 Audi has the look it wants –
the single-frame radiator grill on
the Audi A4 (B8), 2008
05 An Avant for rough country –
the Audi A4 (B8) allroad quattro
goes on sale in 2009
06 Ample space for an adventure
holiday
07 Contrasts: A4 (B8) allroad
quattro in a hostile setting

02

01

03

326

05

The Audi Q5 compact SUV was first shown to the public at the Auto China Beijing in April 2008, and reached the market in November. It is built in Ingolstadt, but production in China as well is planned later. Like the Audi A4 B8 and Audi A5, the Q5 is built on the new modular longitudinal platform (MLP), which has been designed to accept engines mounted along rather than across the vehicle's centerline. The Q5 entered production in October 2008 with an initial choice of one gasoline engine and two diesels.

04

01 Daytime running lights and details of the current Audi design idiom on the Q5
02 Rear view of the Audi Q5

03 Flared wheel arches and wheels with reduced dish depth add strength to the visual impression
04 The Q5 is also to be built in China, at the Changchun factory
05 Thinking on paper – ideas for the Audi Q5
06 Internals of the DSG transmission with two clutches and a hollow shaft

06

Clutch 1
Clutch 2

Input shaft 2
Input shaft 1

Drive to rear-axle differential
Drive to front-axle differential

Center differential

4th gear
6th gear
2nd gear
Reverse

5th gear
7th gear
3rd gear
1st gear

01 A combination of materials gives the Audi A5 Cabriolet its extremely rigid body

02 Summer, sun, sport – advertising arouses desire!

03 New in the S5 Cabriolet: a supercharged six-cylinder engine

04 The top S5 Cabriolet has LED rear lights

05 Interior of the Audi S5 Cabriolet

06 Audi has remained loyal to the soft top for the A5 Cabriolet

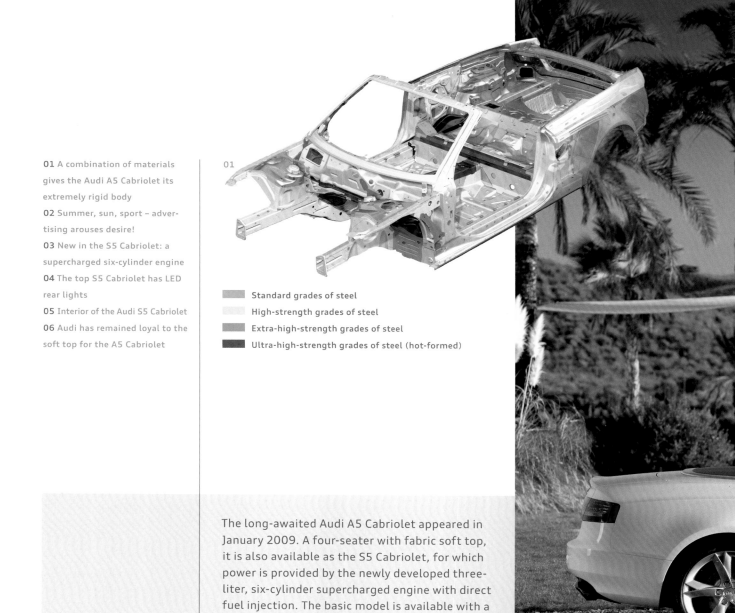

01

- Standard grades of steel
- High-strength grades of steel
- Extra-high-strength grades of steel
- Ultra-high-strength grades of steel (hot-formed)

The long-awaited Audi A5 Cabriolet appeared in January 2009. A four-seater with fabric soft top, it is also available as the S5 Cabriolet, for which power is provided by the newly developed three-liter, six-cylinder supercharged engine with direct fuel injection. The basic model is available with a choice of three gasoline engines and two diesels. With the more powerful engines, the quattro all-wheel driveline is an alternative to front-wheel drive.

02

03

04, 05

Company chronicle

2007 Assembly of the Audi A6, and of
the Audi A4 from 2008 onwards, began
at the Indian factory in Aurangabad; the
Brussels factory was integrated into the
Audi production alliance

06

01

02

05

06

09

10

330

Audi – an overview

03

04

01 Audi A4 (B6) sedan, 2000
02 Audi A4 (B6) Avant, 2001
03 Audi A8 (D3) sedan, 2002
04 Audi A3 (8P) sedan, 2003
05 Audi A6 (C6) Avant and sedan, 2004
06 Audi A3 (8PA) Sportback, (first car with single-frame grill), 2004
07 Audi A4 (B7) sedan, 2004
08 Audi A4 (B7) Avant 3.2 FSI quattro, 2003
09 Audi allroad quattro (C6) with appropriate target group, 2006
10 Audi Q7, 2006
11 Audi TT Coupé, 2006
12 Audi R8 5.2 FSI, 2008

07

08

11

12

01

02

05

06

09

10

332

Audi – an overview

03

04

07

08

11

Attractive styling for ca

Since 1965, when the Audi brand was revived, seven people in succession have shaped the motor vehicles produced by the company with the four-ring emblem.

Rupert Neuner was Head of the Auto Union GmbH Styling Department from 1965 to 1970. He moved from Mercedes to Auto Union in 1963, at the same time as Ludwig Kraus. During his time with the company the first Audi, based on the DKW F 102, was introduced. The C1-series Audi 100 sedans and coupés entered production, and formed the basis for the B1-series Audi 80, which appeared later.

From 1970 until his death in 1973, Georg Bertram was Head of the Styling Department at Audi NSU Auto Union AG. He had been employed by DKW

01

01 Design changes with modeling clay to a prototype Audi 100 (C1) body
02 Motor-show presentation of the facelifted Audi 100 Coupé S, 1973

02

03

04

th the four-ring emblem

before the war, worked from 1949 to 1965 in the Auto Union Body Development department in Ingolstadt, then left the company for a time before returning as the successor to Rupert Neuner in 1970. The Audi 80 B1 and Audi 50 were introduced while the department was under his management.

Between 1976 and 1993, Hartmut Warkuss was Head of Design at AUDI AG. He joined the company in 1968 and, as Chief Designer, exerted a strong influence on the design of Audi models in the 1980s and 1990s. A sensation in the early 1980s was undoubtedly the Audi quattro, with its angular body styling and the boldly flared wheel arches that other European carmakers such as Opel, Volkswagen and Lancia were to adopt subsequently. In addition to the strictly geometrical design of these earlier models – though Warkuss himself

described the Audi Coupé and Audi quattro as "cute" – the C3-series Audi 100, the aerodynamic world champion among passenger cars, and also the Avus quattro and quattro Spyder showcars were milestones in Audi design and evidence of the sheer versatility of their designer.

Between January and December 1994 an American, J. Caroll Mays, was Chief Designer in Ingolstadt. He had worked for Audi already between 1980 and 1986, with one short break, and was closely involved in the Audi 80 B3's body styling. In 1989 he moved to Volkswagen's design studio in California, where he worked on the Audi Avus quattro. In January 1994 he succeeded Hartmut Warkuss, who had moved to Wolfsburg as Head of Design and Strategy for all the Volkswagen Group's brands.

03 Audi quattro in the facelifted version – according to Hartmut Warkuss, a "cute" car
04 Finishing work on the full-scale model of the Audi 100 (C3) in 1978; Hartmut Warkuss is on the right of the picture
05 Airflow-optimized design on the Audi 100 (C3), with characteristic smooth surfaces
06, 07 Comparing wheel designs on the Audi 200 (C3); none of these reached series production!
08 The Audi Avus quattro, highlight of the 1991 Tokyo Motor Show
09 Interior of the Audi Avus quattro

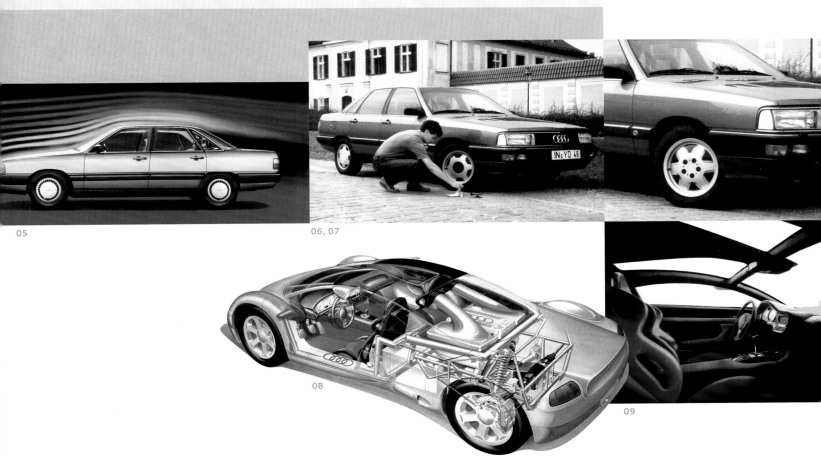

05   06, 07   08   09

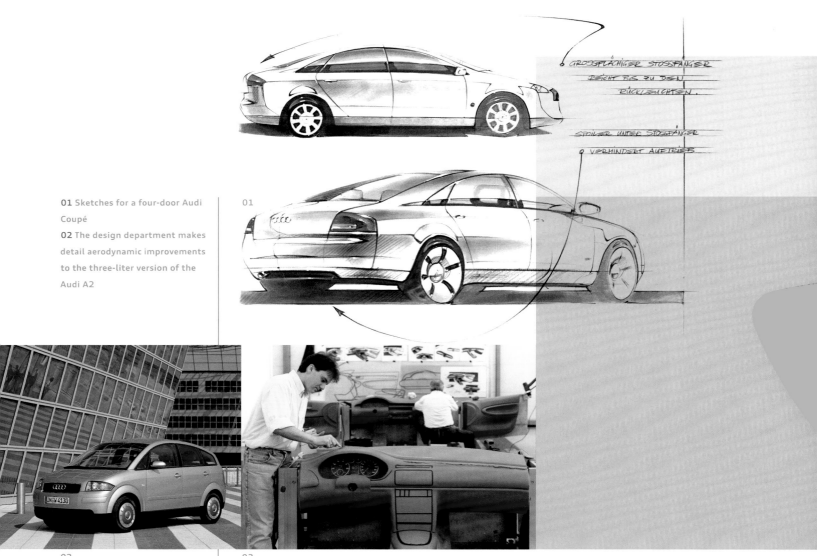

01 Sketches for a four-door Audi
Coupé

02 The design department makes
detail aerodynamic improvements
to the three-liter version of the
Audi A2

01

02

03

03 In an early phase of development, a modeler shapes the first
proportional model for the Audi
A6 (C5) in clay

04 Stefan Sielaff with the Audi
Cross Cabriolet quattro

05 Walter de'Silva

06 An Audi A1 Sportback concept
study at the 2008 Paris Motor
Show

07 Design sketch for the Audi A1
quattro project, 2007

08 Wolfgang Josef Egger

09 A glimpse of Audi's future
formal idiom: the Audi Sportback
concept, unveiled at the 2009
North American International
Automobile Show in Detroit

From November 1, 1994, until the end of 2001
Peter Schreyer held the position of Head of Design
at AUDI AG. He had first worked in Ingolstadt in
1980, but moved in 1991 to the Design Center of
Volkswagen of America in California, where he
contributed greatly to the Audi quattro Spyder
concept study.

During his period with the company, the Audi
brand was repositioned higher up the market in
relation to its competitors. During the last ten
years of the 20th century the Audi A8, the Audi
A3, the Audi A2 as a premium compact car, two
Audi A4 model generations with their derivatives
and the C5-series Audi A6 all reached the market.
Many of these cars were awarded prestigious
design prizes several in succession in many cases.
In January 2002 Peter Schreyer moved to Wolfsburg as Volkswagen's Chief Designer.

Gerd Pfefferle was appointed AUDI AG's Head of
Design in March 2002. He had joined Auto Union
GmbH in 1966, initially as a modeler in the
design department. From 1977 onwards he was
Main Group Leader for Interior Equipment Design,
but transferred to the Exterior Design area in
1980. In 1989 he was appointed head of this
department, but moved to Volkswagen in 1997
as Head of Exterior Design. He returned to Ingolstadt in March 2002 as Head of Design. When he
retired in 2006, Stefan Sielaff became Head of
Audi Design.

It was also in March 2002 that Walter de'Silva
took over responsibility for design in the Audi
Brand Group, which at that time included the
Lamborghini and Seat brands. De'Silva had worked
earlier for the Alfa Romeo Design Center in Milan,

04

05

A1
Sportback concept

06

07

08

as well as being Head of the Fiat Design Center.
In January 1990 he moved to Seat S.A. as Head
of the Design Centre there.

Since May 2007 Wolfgang Josef Egger has been
Head of Design for the Audi Group. Like his
predecessor, he had previously worked for Alfa
Romeo, where the Alfa Competizione sports car
was among his designs. His move to Audi was the
second occasion on which he had followed in the
footsteps of Walter de'Silva, who had moved to
Wolfsburg in February 2007 as Chief Designer for
the entire Volkswagen Group. During the de'Silva
period, Audi's design underwent a fundamental
change that had enabled the company, as a
premium manufacturer, to close the gap separating it from its rivals BMW and Mercedes and,
with its latest models, to overtake them.

09

The past meets the future – the Audi Front Roadster first appeared at a motor show in 1935; in 2009 the spotlight on the Audi stand at the Detroit Motor Show was on the concept study for the future Audi A7

Global player

When production of the Audi A3 ceased at the factory in Curitiba, Brazil, in September 2006, no fewer than 57,093 Audi A3 cars had been built there for the South American market.

Production of Audi models for the Indian market began in 2007 at the Aurangabad factory in the Indian state of Maharashtra. The Audi A6 executive sedan has been assembled there since November 2007 and was joined in the fall of 2008 by the Audi A4, a second successful model. Both of them arrive as completely knocked down (CKD) sets of parts from Germany; assembling the cars in India reduces import duty by more than half.
With its decision to start car production on the Indian sub-continent, AUDI AG has continued its international growth policy and made a long-term investment in one of the world's most promising car markets.

The Audi family also celebrated a new arrival in 2007. The factory in Brussels, which employs 2,200 people, was integrated into the Audi production alliance as part of a restructuring process. In the year in which it was taken over from Volkswagen AG it had a production capacity of 84,000 vehicles. Within the turntable concept, which makes it possible to produce high-volume models at two locations, the Audi A3 Sportback is now being built in both Ingolstadt and Brussels. The factory there is also being considered for production of the forthcoming Audi A1 model.

The contracts with the Karmann company for production of the Audi Cabriolet, which began in 1997 with the final, facelifted B3-series Audi Cabriolet, were allowed to lapse in 2007. The new Audi A5 Cabriolet is being built by Audi itself at the Ingolstadt factory. Assembly of the open-top Audi A4 at Karmann's factory in Rheine continued until the end of production midway through 2009.

Audi Hungaria Motor Kft. in Győr, Hungary, celebrated an important anniversary in the spring of 2008. Since production began in 1993, more than 16 million engines have left this factory, which is one of the largest engine manufacturing facilities in the world.
Car production in Győr had something to celebrate as well. More than 400,000 cars have left the assembly lines since the factory opened in 1998. On this site, which measures more than 17.22

03

01

02

04

million square feet in area, up to 7,000 engines and 300 complete vehicles are built every day. As well as cars from the TT model line, the factory cooperates with AUDI AG in Ingolstadt on production of the A3 Cabriolet.

For more than 20 years AUDI AG has cooperated most successfully in China with the China FAW Group Corporation (FAW), the country's oldest-established automobile manufacturer. To celebrate the anniversary in June 2008, the foundation stone for a new assembly building was laid. It will increase output and help to satisfy growing demand for the A6 L and A4 models.

Since the end of 2008 the A4 L, a long-wheelbase version, has been built there exclusively for the Chinese market, and will be joined in 2010 by the Audi Q5. Following Germany, China is the Audi brand's most important sales market, selling more than 100,000 cars annually.

05, 06

07

Promoting culture, art and sport

01 Herbert von Karajan (2nd from left) was an enthusiastic Audi owner since the 1980s, and one of the first enthusiastic drivers of an Audi quattro

02 Audi has been main sponsor of the Salzburg Festival since 1995. This reception was held in the M 32 restaurant in Salzburg on "Audi Night"

AUDI AG has been the main sponsor of the Salzburg Festival since 1995. Year after year, for five weeks in summer, theater enthusiasts and music-lovers are attracted to the city closely associated with Mozart, and the surrounding Salzkammergut area. For three years now, Audi has extended its commitment by holding an "Audi Night," which is visited by prominent people from business, culture and society.

Audi has also been supporting, as the main sponsor since 2007, the Salzburg Easter Festival initiated by the famous conductor Herbert von Karajan. A unique feature of this event is that the Berlin Philharmonic Orchestra plays here and here only for opera performances.

In addition to its international cultural sponsoring, Audi is an active supporter of events in the region surrounding its home base in Ingolstadt. 2009 is the twentieth year in which the successful series of "Summer Concerts between Danube and Altmühl," organized jointly by Audi and the Bayerischer Rundfunk broadcasting corporation, will have been held. At this, its own festival, AUDI AG has the function of event organizer rather than sponsor. Since 1990, world-famous artists have captivated the audiences in and around Ingolstadt. The list of stars that have appeared at these events reads like a "Who's Who" of classical music. Since their inauguration, the Audi Summer Concerts have been attended by

01

02

03

03, 04 The Salzburg Festival gave a guest performance of Edward Grieg's *Peer Gynt* at the 2008 Audi Summer Concerts

05 Since 2004 the annual "Shooting Star Festival" has been held on the piazza of the Audi Forum Ingolstadt. At this weekend event, AUDI AG joins forces with Bayern 3 radio to present rock and pop stars and newcomers

06 At the Audi Youth Choir Academy, young singers rehearse major musical compositions under professional guidance

04

05, 06

07

08

2000–2009

more than a quarter of a million music lovers. It is also more than a quarter of a century since Audi began to support the Ingolstadt Jazz Days as a main sponsor. For several weeks while this festival is on, the city is transformed into a jazz metropolis. International stars from the jazz scene come together with talented local performers. At the Audi Forum Ingolstadt, the company regularly hosts memorable concerts during the Jazz Days.

A partnership that has lasted many years between Audi and the Museum for Concrete Art in Ingolstadt led in 2007 to the establishment of a Foundation for Concrete Art and Design. Audi is a founding member of this body, which has no equivalent anywhere in Germany, and has set itself the task of safeguarding the estates of leading artists and designers, cataloging them and making them accessible to the public.

07 Chinese pianist Lang Lang at the 2008 Audi Summer Concerts. He has been an Audi cultural ambassador since 2006
08 Martin Grubinger and his ensemble at a highlight concert held at the Audi Forum during the 2008 Ingolstadt Jazz Days

01

Sport promotion

In addition to its commitment to art and culture, Audi has for many years supported sports events and promoted up-and-coming sportsmen and women.

The company has a long tradition of supporting golf and equestrian sport. The Audi quattro Cup is among the largest amateur golf tournament series in the world. Audi also supports selected professional tournaments and, by awarding the Audi quattro Cup and the Audi Ladies' Cup, has created two prestigious new competition events. Audi also sponsors the HVB Ladies' German Open and the Business Golf Cup organized by the *Süddeutsche Zeitung* newspaper.

On the equestrian sports scene, Audi supports important international tournaments in Germany and the Audi Championship events. The Audi Cup for young horses has the aim of preparing highly talented young jumpers for the highest levels of this sport, and therefore of maintaining the high standard of performance and public appeal of equestrian events in Europe.

Audi has been general sponsor of the German Ski Federation since 1994, and also supports that organization's work in encouraging young competitors, the aim being to maintain the country's existing record of success at Olympic Games, in

world championships and in World Cup events. The Ingolstadt company is also title sponsor of the FIS Ski World Cup.

From land to water: AUDI AG is title sponsor of the international Audi MedCup, the most important yacht racing series in the Mediterranean. Unlike most other regattas, the Audi MedCup is an opportunity to experience pure racing on the water, with the boats competing against each other in real time, not merely against the clock.

In soccer too, Audi takes an international approach. The company supports the German record championship holder, World Cup, Champions League and UEFA Cup winner as well as the home club of five national heroes of the 2006 World Cup: FC Bayern Munich.
The partnership between FC Bayern Munich and AUDI AG began on July 1, 2002. A new international commitment is that between Real Madrid and the Audi brand, both of whom can look back on more than a hundred years of club or company history. Audi is also the official car supplier to what is probably the best-known soccer club of all, Manchester United. As the club's first carmaking partner, Audi supplies about 20 cars as personal transport for leading officials and players. And the players at FC Barcelona, the most successful soccer team in Europe, drive Audi too!

02, 03

04

01 As an outstanding promoter of sport, AUDI AG also supports equestrian events. At the 2007 Audi Polo Challenge in Ascot, Prince William is riding the white horse

02 The sign of the Four Rings – Michelle Wie at the Ladies' German Open in May 2008

03 Double Olympic champion Benjamin Raich (Austria) at the skiing world championship held in Val d'Isère, France, in February 2009

04 Audi in yacht racing – the 2008 Audi MedCup, one of six regattas held off Majorca

345

Appendix

Who's who?

Cars have made the Audi brand well known all over the world – but those cars would never have taken to the road without people to develop, build and sell them.

The spotlight is seldom on the people who work in the various departments of AUDI AG, but nonetheless they often achieve great things. They are the motor that keeps the four rings turning smoothly.

Works Council Chairmen

NSU Motorenwerke AG		
Michael Haug		1945 – 1952
Karl Walz		1952 – 1969

Auto Union GmbH		
Fritz Kuntschik	Ingolstadt factory	1949 – 1951
Fritz Böhm	Ingolstadt factory	1951 – 1969
	General Works Council	1961 – 1962
J. Fischer	Düsseldorf factory	1950 – 1953
Fritz Schiffer	Düsseldorf factory	1953 – 1957
	General Works Council	1957 – 1961
Paul Jabs	Düsseldorf factory *	1957 – 1962

Audi NSU Auto Union AG, AUDI AG		
Fritz Böhm	Ingolstadt factory	Aug. 21, 1969 – Dec. 31, 1985
	General Works Council	May 30, 1972 – May 5, 1987
Erhard Kuballa	Ingolstadt factory	Jan. 1, 1986 – July 19, 1993
	General Works Council	May 5, 1987 – Aug. 18, 1993
Adolf Hochrein	Ingolstadt factory	July 19, 1993 – Apr. 30, 1994
	General Works Council	Aug. 18, 1993 – Apr. 30, 1994
Xaver Meier	Ingolstadt factory and General Works Council	May 1, 1994 – Dec. 31, 2005
Peter Mosch	Ingolstadt factory and General Works Council	since 01.01.2006
Karl Walz	Neckarsulm factory	Aug. 21, 1969 – Oct. 31, 1977
Heinz Christ	Neckarsulm factory	Nov. 1, 1977 – Apr. 30, 1987
Theo Schirmer	Neckarsulm factory	May 1, 1987 – June 30, 2000
Norbert Rank	Neckarsulm factory	since July 1, 2000

Chairmen of the Boards of Management of earlier companies

NSU		
Christian Schmidt		1873 – 1884
Gottlob Banzhaf		1884 – 1910
Dr. Georg Schwarz		1910 – 1927
Dr. Otto Merkens		1927 – 1928
Ferrucio Valobra		1929 – 1931
Fritz Gehr		1931 – 1933
Fritz von Falkenhayn		1933 – 1945
August Böhringer		1945 – 1946
Walter E. Niegtsch		1946 – 1951
Board Committee:	Dr. Gerd Stieler von Heydekampf	1951 – 1952
	Viktor Frankenberger	1951 – 1952
	Walter Wertheim	1951 – 1952
	Philipp Wesp	1951 – 1952
Dr. Gerd Stieler von Heydekampf		1953 – 1969

Chairmen of the Boards of Management of earlier companies

Audi		DKW (Zschopauer Motorenwerke)	
Dr. August Horch	1909 – 1920	Dr. Jörgen Skafte Rasmussen	1907 – 1932
Hermann Lange	1920 – 1922		
Ernst Baus	1922 – 1926		
Fritz Fikentscher	1926 – 1928		
Heinrich Schuh	1928 – 1932		

Horch		Wanderer (until 1932) **	
Dr. August Horch	1899 – 1909	Johann Baptist Winklhofer	1885 – 1902
Jakob Holler	1909 – 1920	Adolf Jaenicke	1885 – 1897
Dr. Arthur Loewenstein	1920 – 1932	Georg Daut	1902 – 1929
		Herrmann Klee	1929 – 1932

Auto Union AG (1932 – 1948)		Auto Union GmbH (1949 – 1969)	
Dr. Richard Bruhn	1932 – 1945	Dr. Richard Bruhn	1949 – 1956
Dr. Hanns Schüler	1945 – 1948	Dr. Werner Henze	1956 – 1965
		Dr. Rudolf Leiding	1965 – 1968
		Willhelm R. Neuwald	1968 – 1969

Chairmen of the Boards of Management of Audi NSU Auto Union AG (Sept. 1, 1969 – Dec. 31, 1984) and AUDI AG (from Jan. 1, 1985)

Dr. Gerd Stieler von Heydekampf		Sept. 1, 1969 – Mar. 31, 1971
Dr. Rudolf Leiding		Apr. 1, 1971 – Oct. 18, 1971
Dr. Gerhard Prinz		Jan. 12, 1972 – June 30, 1973
Dr. Werner P. Schmidt		Dec. 1, 1973 – July 31, 1975
Gottlieb M. Strobl		Aug. 1, 1975 – Dec. 31, 1978
Dr. Wolfgang R. Habbel		Jan. 1, 1979 – Dec. 31, 1987
Dr. Ferdinand Piëch		Jan. 1, 1988 – Dec. 31, 1992
Franz-Josef Kortüm		Jan. 1, 1993 – Feb. 4, 1994
Dr. Herbert Demel	Board Spokesman	Feb. 4, 1994 – Mar. 21, 1995
	Board Chairman	Mar. 22, 1995 – June 30, 1997
Dr. Franz-Josef Paefgen	Board Spokesman	July 1, 1997 – Mar. 17, 1998
	Board Chairman	Mar. 18, 1998 – Feb. 28, 2002
Dr. Martin Winterkorn		Mar. 1, 2002 – Dec. 31, 2006
Rupert Stadler		since Jan. 1, 2007

Board of Management, AUDI AG

Rupert Stadler	Chairman
Ulf Berkenhagen	Purchasing
Michael Dick	Technical Development
Frank Dreves	Production
Peter Schwarzenbauer	Marketing and Sales
Axel Strotbek	Finance and Organization
Dr. Werner Widuckel	Human Resources

Status: May 2009

* The Düsseldorf factory was taken over by Daimler-Benz AG in 1962

** In 1932, only the car division was included in Auto Union; Wanderer Werke AG continued to operate as an independent company manufacturing machine tools, office machinery, bicycles and small motorcycles

Personal data

Dr. August Horch

August Hermann Lange

Johann Baptist Winklhofer

August Horch

1868	Born on October 12 in Winningen (Mosel); apprentice farrier and journeyman; studied at the Technical College in Mittweida; factory engineer at various engine construction companies
1896	Joined the Benz company in Mannheim; Head of Motor Vehicle Construction until 1899
1899	Opened his own workshop in Cologne
1902	Moved to Reichenbach in the Vogtland region of Germany
1904	A. Horch Motorwagenwerke AG established in Zwickau
1909	After a dispute, established Audi Werke in Zwickau
1912–14	Motor sport triumphs for Audi cars in the world's most severe events
1920	Moved to Berlin and acted as an expert and specialist assessor in automotive technical matters
1922	Awarded honorary doctorate by Braunschweig College of Advanced Technology on February 20
1932	Member of the Supervisory Board of Auto Union AG, Chemnitz
1944	Forced to leave Berlin due to bombing raids; moved to Langenhessen, Saxony
1945	Fled to Upper Franconia at the end of the war, and settled after a time in Münchberg
1949–50	Participated in re-establishment of Auto Union in Ingolstadt
1951	Died in Münchberg on February 3; buried in Winningen

August Horch must be considered as one of the pioneering automotive engineers. As early as the turn of the century, he had a hand in solving the problems associated with the early years of the motor car, and made many a contribution of great significance in day-to-day car-industry practice. He was for example the first engineer to use aluminum for engine crankshafts; he introduced shaft drive and adopted high-strength steels for transmission components. Horch's activities as an engineer were aimed at improving the basic invention, namely the automobile, to such an extent that it could be regarded to be of genuine usability.

After 1909, Horch severed his connection with the company bearing his name. After leaving the 'Horch Werke' which he had established, his products henceforward bore the brand name 'Audi.'

In 2000, in recognition of his outstanding services to the development of the motor vehicle, August Horch was granted a place in the Automotive Technology Hall of Fame in Detroit; in 2003 he was similarly honored by the European Hall of Fame in Geneva.

August Hermann Lange

1867	Born on November 7, 1867, in Strehla (near Torgau); son of August Lange, an estate owner, and his wife Amalie, née Kopsch
1874–84	Attended school in Leipzig
1884	On April 1, began a three-year apprenticeship as a lathe operator at Maschinenfabrik Bleichert & Co. in Leipzig; remained with this company after training until November 2, 1888
1892–94	Studied engineering at the Technical College in Mittweida
1894–95	Employed by Motorenfabrik Grob & Co. in Leipzig as a designer
1895	From November 1, designer at the Leipziger Dampfmaschinen- and Motorenfabrik
1897	From January 1, designer at Rheinische Gasmotorenfabrik Benz & Co. in Mannheim; later Head of the Engine Testing Department
1904	From April 1, Factory Manager and independent designer at Eisengiesserei and Motorenfabrik Osers & Bauer in Vienna, an iron foundry and engine manufacturer; from September 1, Technical Director of Horchwerke AG in Zwickau (appointed Senior Engineer in 1905)
1909	From July, Technical Director and later Factory Director at Audi
1915	Member of the Board of Management
1922	Died on February 19 in Zwickau and is buried in the main cemetery there

Johann Baptist Winklhofer

1859	Born on June 23 in Munich, son of a brewer
1875	Apprenticed to the Royal Laboratory in Munich, then employed as a lathe operator
1880	Moved to the Josef Hofer mechanical engineering company in Ingolstadt, remaining there until 1883
1883	Travelling salesman for 'penny-farthing' bicycles made by the English Rudge company; this brought him into contact with Jaenicke, who was later to be his business partner
1885	Established a bicycle repair workshop with Jaenicke in Chemnitz; this was converted to a joint stock company in 1896
1897	From October 1, sole Director of Wanderer Fahrradwerke AG
1902	On October 4, resigned as Chairman of the Board of Management and joined the Supervisory Board, remaining a member until 1929
1911	Granted the title of Councilor of Commerce
1916	Established a company in Munich to make munitions initially, later drive chains; these became known under the brand name IWIS
1949	Died on March 28 in Landsberg am Lech

348

Jörgen Skafte Rasmussen

1878   Born on July 30 in Nakskov (Denmark); after leaving school, apprenticed to a farrier in Copenhagen

1898–   Studied engineering in Mittweida, completing
1900   his studies in Zwickau

1901–02 Employed as an engineer at Rheinische Maschinenfabrik, a mechanical engineering company in Düsseldorf

1902   Established Rasmussen & Ernst OHG in Chemnitz

1907   Opened a factory for pipe fittings in Zschopau

1917   Moved from Chemnitz to Zschopau

1916   Experimental work on a steam-driven car led to the product name 'DKW'

1921   Company name changed to Zschopauer Motorenwerke; production of DKW motorcycles starts; in the 1920s, Zschopauer Motorenwerke was built up into an industrial group, with strong financial support from the State Bank of Saxony; the main activity remained the production of DKW engines and motorcycles

1924   Takeover of Slaby-Beringer, a manufacturer of small cars in Berlin; the Berlin location is extended later into a full-scale car factory

1926   A factory in Scharfenstein is acquired from Moll-Werke; Rasmussen was one of the first businessmen to manufacture domestic and commercial electric refrigerators here; (the name was changed in 1931 to Deutsche Kühl- and Kraftmaschinengesellschaft mbH, Scharfenstein)

1928   Car production started at the DKW factory in Spandau; takeover of Audiwerke AG in Zwickau

1931   Rasmussen contributed greatly to the idea and concept that led to formation of Auto Union by merging various car and motorcycle manufacturers in Saxony (Audi, DKW, Horch, Wanderer); his plan, however, envisaged the reprivatization of these companies later

1932–34 Member of the Auto Union AG Board of Management for Technical Matters

1935   Ineradicable differences of opinion regarding management of Auto Union led to his leaving the company and to subsequent legal proceedings awarding him a sum of money in compensation

1937   Moved to Sacrow, near Berlin

1938   Honorary doctorate of engineering granted by the Dresden College of Advanced Technology on Rasmussen's 60th birthday, to commemorate his services to public motorization; he also cooperated at this time on introduction of the Imbert wood-gas equipment, which was initially manufactured by Framo

1945   Fled to Flensburg at the end of the war

1948   Returned to Denmark; together with the Danish Industrial Syndicate (DISA) initiated and financed the design of cars and motorcycles: three models were built and sold under the DISA brand name

1964   Died on August 12 in Copenhagen

Dr. Jörgen Skafte Rasmussen

Paul Daimler

1869   Born on September 13

1897   After leaving school and studying engineering at the Stuttgart College of Advanced Technology, became a designer at Daimler-Motoren-Gesellschaft

1902–05 Managing Director of the Austrian Daimler-Motoren-Gesellschaft in Vienna

1907–22 Member of the Board of Management and Chief Designer of Daimler-Motoren-Gesellschaft in Stuttgart; responsible for the design of the Mercedes racing cars that scored a legendary one-two-three victory in the 1914 French Grand Prix

1915   Appointed Government Building Counselor; during this period, earned much respect for his development work on aircraft-engine superchargers; after the war, continued this work on road vehicles

1922   Left Daimler in Untertürkheim after severe differences of opinion with the Board of Management; on July 1, joined Argus-Motoren-Gesellschaft mbH in Berlin-Reinickendorf as Chief Designer; negotiated a contract as engine development consultant for the Horchwerke (of which Argus was the majority shareholder)

1926   In December, the Horch Type 303 with straight-eight engine, which he had designed, was exhibited at the Berlin Motor Show; this engine established the Zwickau-based company's reputation as the leading manufacturer of eight-cylinder engines in the German motor-vehicle industry

1929   Continued to hold numerous honorary positions after his retirement

1945   Died in Berlin on December 15

Paul Daimler

Heinrich Schuh

1886   Born on February 28 in Edingen (Baden), a farmer's son

1901–09 Apprenticeship as a metalworker, journeyman's years

1910–11 Truck designer at Benz in Gaggenau

Heinrich Schuh

349

Klaus Detlof von Oertzen

Hugo Ruppe

Dr. Carl Hahn

1911–18 Zeppelin airship engineer for Deutsche Luftschifffahrts AG (DELAG); manager of Zeppelin airship factory in Potsdam

1919–20 Factory Manager for Maybach Motorenbau engine company in Potsdam

1920 Appointed Audi Plant Director in Zwickau

1923 Study trip to the United States financed by Audi

1926 From April 1, Technical Director of Audiwerke AG, and also successor to Erich Horn as Chief Designer

1927 Introduction of his R 19/100 hp design, Audi's first eight-cylinder engine; increasing involvement in production technology; a reference acknowledges his exceptional practical experience in motor-vehicle and machine-tool construction, test equipment and precision volume production: *"He has complete command of toolmaking and fixture construction. Several thousand fixtures have been designed and constructed according to his plans and have proved outstandingly successful in practice."*

1931 Assuring reliable production of the DKW Front; joint responsibility for achieving the breakthrough to the volume production of small cars with front-wheel drive at the Audi factories in Zwickau.
Schuh's management during the Third Reich was notable for it expertise and humane treatment of the workforce

1945 Denounced in October, arrested by the Red Army and taken to the camp in Mühlberg

1950 Died at an unknown location in Russia

Klaus Detlof von Oertzen

1894 Born on April 13 in Inowroclaw (Hohensalza), Poznan Province; after leaving school, signed up as an officer cadet with the Imperial Flying Squad; obliged to retire from military service after being severely wounded in 1916

1919–24 Began a commercial career at the Harburg-Vienna tire company (later Phoenix-Harburg)

1925–28 Manager of the Phoenix office in Dresden, Sales Manager for Central Germany

1928 From September, Member of the Board of Management of Wanderer Werke AG in Chemnitz-Schönau, with responsibility for Marketing and Sales

1931–32 Made a major contribution to the establishment of Auto Union AG, and is regarded as the "father of the four-ring emblem"

1932–35 Full member of the Auto Union AG Board of Management with responsibility for Sales

1935–39 Export General Manager for Auto Union in South Africa, Asia and Australia

1940–46 Interned in India during the war

1946–48 Managing Director of China Diesel Motors Corporation in Shanghai, a company within the General Motors Group

1949 Moved to Johannesburg (South Africa), acted as independent liaison officer for VW and Büssing

1950 Appointed Head of VW Exports for Africa, Australia and Asia

1963 Retired from business life on December 31

1991 Died on July 25 in Lausanne (Switzerland)

Hugo Ruppe

1879 Born on August 15 in Apolda; after apprenticeship as a mechanic, studied engineering at the Technical College in Ilmenau

1904 Designed and built the Apoldania motorcycle, with four-stroke engine

1907 Established his own car factory in Markranstädt, near Leipzig

1910 Company reorganized as Markranstädter Automobilfabrik (MAF) GmbH

1912–14 Experimental work on two-stroke engines and flywheel ignition magnetos

1914–18 Military service

1918 Moved to Zschopau, where he offered his two-stroke engine to Rasmussen

1921 Severed contact with Rasmussen and moved to Berlin; founded Berliner Kleinmotoren Fabrik (Bekamo), a factory for small engines, there

1925 Established Ruppe Motor GmbH in Berlin to build auxiliary engines for bicycles

1929 Moved to Rumburg, Czechoslovakia, and founded the Kaehler & Ruppe company to build lightweight motorcycles; in the early 1930s, after working for Framo in Frankenberg (a company within the Rasmussen Group) for a short time, moved to Festenberg, Silesia and built up a mechanical engineering business there

1945 Fled to Zschopau at the end of the war and attempted in vain to build up production of small stand-by generators

1949 Died on January 23 in Gornau (near Zschopau) immediately after the death of his wife; he was destitute and almost completely forgotten

Carl Hahn

1894 Born on March 4, 1894, in Nove Hrady (Gratzen, Bohemia); after World War I, studied agronomy at the University of Natural Resources in Vienna; granted a doctorate in 1922

1922	On April 20, joined Zschopauer Motorenwerke J.S. Rasmussen in Zschopau, Saxony; Hahn became Rasmussen's loyal assistant and built up an effective Sales and Marketing organization
1932	Appointed to the Board of Management of the newly established Auto Union AG in Chemnitz, with responsibility for Sales
1945	Escaped to the West and became a founding member of the Central Depot for Auto Union spare parts in Ingolstadt
1949	When Auto Union GmbH was founded in Ingolstadt on 3 September, Carl Hahn was elected Deputy General Manager of the new company
1957	Retired from the company for health reasons on June 30
1961	Died on June 5 in Le Zoute (Belgium)

Richard Bruhn

1886	Born on June 25 in Cismar, Eastern Holstein; after commercial training, learned the electrical technician's trade
1907	Commercial employee at AEG, Bremen and Berlin
1910	Commercial Manager of AEG's London office
1914–18	Studied economics at Kiel University; military service as officer of the reserve; studies recommenced, concluding with doctorate in political science
1921	Director of Neufeld & Kuhnke in Kiel
1927	On the staff of Prof. Junkers in Dessau; Member of the Board of Management, Pöge Elektrizitätswerke, Chemnitz; Member of the Supervisory Board of Zschopauer Motorenwerke AG (Member of the Board of Management from 1930)
1932	Chairman of the Auto Union AG Board of Management
1949	Chairman of the Auto Union GmbH Board of Management, Ingolstadt
1952	Honorary engineering doctorate from Aachen University to commemorate his promotion of motor vehicle construction in Germany and the revival of Auto Union
1956	Retired from the Board of Management on November 6, and was elected to the Auto Union GmbH Supervisory Board
1958	Retired from active business life on May 6
1964	Died on July 8 in Düsseldorf

William Werner

1893	Born on November 7 in New York
1907	Returned to Germany with his parents, who came from Oederan, Saxony

1912	After apprenticeship as a mechanic, joined the mechanical workshop of the Berlin branch of the American company Multigraph GmbH
1914–18	Attended evening school and passed the mechanical engineer's examination; as an American citizen, he was exempt from military service
1920–24	Production engineer for leading German tool suppliers such as Bergmann-Borsig, Berliner AG vorm. Freund and Schuchardt & Schütte
1924	Factory Director at the Ludwig Loewe machine tool company
1925	Technical Director at Schiess AG in Düsseldorf
1926	Study tour of the American automobile industry; worked for the Chrysler Corporation in Detroit
1926	Joined Horchwerke AG, in Zwickau/Berlin
1927	Technical Director of Horchwerke AG
1929	From May 24, full Member of the Horchwerke AG Board of Management
1934	Technical Director of Auto Union AG, Chemnitz
1942	Honorary doctorate from Dresden College of Advanced Technology for his services to the modernization and rationalization of production in the German motor-vehicle industry
1945	Fled to Bad Homburg at the end of the war
1948	Equipped and managed a factory for the production of motorcycles and mopeds for the Plivier company in Rotterdam
1956	Joined the Auto Union GmbH Board of Management with responsibility for Technology; based initially in Düsseldorf, from 1961 in Ingolstadt
1962	Left Auto Union, went into retirement
1970	Died on June 20 in Sempach (Switzerland)

Robert Eberan-Eberhorst

1902	Born on April 4 in Vienna; trainee positions after leaving school and studying
1922	Worked for Puch in Graz, Austria
1924	Worked for Elite in Brand-Erbisdorf, Saxony
1927–28	Self-employed driving instructor in Vienna
1928–33	Assistant at the Motor Transport Institute of Dresden College of Advanced Technology; his tasks included investigating mass balance phenomena and the balancing of rotating bodies, vibration on motor-vehicle chassis and bodies, carburetors and brakes
1933	On June 1, joined Auto Union AG, Chemnitz, as a test engineer
1937	On July 1, appointed Head of the Testing Department of the Auto Union Racing Department in Zwickau; designed the Auto Union 12-cylinder, 3-liter racing engine/the Type D racing car

Dr. Richard Bruhn

Dr. William Werner

Prof. Robert Eberan-Eberhorst

351

Dr. Georg Schwarz

Fritz von Falkenhayn

Albert Roder

1940   Doctorate on the charging of forced-aspiration
        engines, based on an Auto Union test report
        "Gas exchange processes in high-speed racing
        engines"
1941   From September 1, full professor at Dresden
        College of Advanced Technology, Chair of
        Motor Transport and Lightweight Engines; at
        the same time, Director of the College's
        Motor Transport Institute
1947   Worked for Porsche in Gmünd (Austria);
        cooperated there on development of the
        Cisitalia racing car
1949   Chief Engineer at ERA in England
1950   Chief Engineer at Aston Martin in England
1953–56 General Manager of Technical Development
        at Auto Union GmbH
1956   Appointed Head of the Mechanical Engineering
        Department of the Batelle Institute, Frankfurt/
        Main; successor to Prof. Wunibald Kamm
1960   Appointed by Vienna Technical University as
        Director of the Institute for Internal
        Combustion Engines and Motor Transport
1965   Emeritus status
1982   Died on March 14 in Vienna

Georg Schwarz
1862   Born on December 20 in Bolheim a. d. Brenz
1879   Employed on the construction of large engines
1901–04 Joined Daimler Motoren-Gesellschaft in
        Cannstatt and Untertürkheim; worked closely
        with Wilhelm Maybach on technical matters
1904–12 Technical Director of the vehicle manufacturer
        Fahrzeugwerke Eisenach
1912–27 Technical Director of NSU Werke
1924   Awarded honorary engineering doctorate by
        the Stuttgart College of Advanced Technology
1925   Designer of the successful supercharged NSU
        racing car
1929   Died on August 5 in Heilbronn

Fritz von Falkenhayn
1890   Born on September 27 in Oldenburg
1896–   Attended school in Tsingtau (China); advanced
1900   school-leaving certificate at the Lyceum in Metz
1910   Career soldier
1914   Appointed Air Force Captain in January
1914–18 Head of section on the staff of the
        commanding Air Force General
1919–21 Commercial work in the motor-vehicle industry
1921–23 Manager of the Daimler Motoren-Gesellschaft's
        first branch in New York
1923   Head of an American export company
1924–25 Head of Sales of the K. Klein automobile
        dealership

1926   Commercial Director of Mannesmann
        Automobil-Gesellschaft in Remscheid
1927–28 Spokesman for Mannesmann Brothers in
        Spain and Morocco
1930   From January, Head of Sales and Deputy
        Member of the Board of Management of NSU
        Vereinigte Fahrzeugwerke AG
1933   Full Board Membership in May
1937–45 Chairman of the Board of Management
1948–58 General Manager of the major Opel dealer
        Auto-Staiger GmbH
1953–61 On the Supervisory Board of NSU Werke AG
1959   Retired to Ronco, Ascona
1973   Died in Italy on March 3

Albert Roder
1896   Born on January 20 in Nuremberg
1910   Apprenticeship as a mechanic
1912   Built his own 25 cc two-stroke engine
1914   Granted the first of more than 100 patents
        and registered designs
1916–18 Military service
1919   Mechanical equipment designer
1920   With the mechanic Karl Zirkel, founded the
        Ziro-Motoren GmbH company in Forchheim;
        it built five motorcycles per week
1923   Company went into liquidation; Roder joined
        forces with another partner from Erlangen,
        and founded Erlanger Motoren AG (ERMAG);
        its first products were motorcycles with
        two-stroke engines
1924   ERMAG motorcycle with 250 cc, 12 hp single-
        cylinder four-stroke OHV engine
1928   Zirkel and he left the company; Zirkel opened
        a driving school in Fürth, Roder joined the
        Zündapp company
1930   Richard Küchen became Zündapp's Chief
        Designer; Roder's task was to prepare his
        creative draft designs for production
1936   Moved to NSU as deputy under the English
        Chief Designer Walter William Moore; Roder
        also worked on the supercharged racing
        motorcycles and those with vertical shaft
        and bevel pinion valve gear
1939   Moved to the Victoria company as Chief
        Designer
1947   Chief Designer at NSU
1949   Developed the Fox motorcycle
1951   Developed the Lux motorcycle
1952   Developed the Max motorcycle and the
        associated racing designs
1958   Developed the NSU Prima motor scooter
1961   Retirement
1970   Died on September 3 in Neckarsulm

Gerd Stieler von Heydekampf

1905	Born in Berlin on January 5
1925	Studied mechanical engineering at the Braunschweig College of Advanced Technology
1929	Doctorate in engineering, Braunschweig College of Advanced Technology
1930	Worked for Babcock and Baldwin Automotive in the United States
1933	Buyer for Adam Opel AG, Rüsselsheim
1936	Purchasing Director at Opel
1938	Director of the Opel truck factory in Brandenburg (Havel)
1942	Managing Director of Henschel & Sohn GmbH in Kassel
1945	Deputy Chairman of the Henschel Group
1948	Regional Field Sales Manager, NSU Werke AG, Neckarsulm
1950	Member of the NSU Board of Management
1953	Chairman of the Board of Management
1957	Oversaw conversion from motorcycle to car factory
1956	Development of the Wankel engine
1967	NSU Ro 80 voted "Car of the Year 1967"
1969	Takeover by Volkswagenwerk AG and merger with Auto Union GmbH, Ingolstadt, to form Audi NSU Auto Union AG with headquarters in Neckarsulm
1969	Chairman of the Audi NSU Auto Union AG Board of Management
1971–78	Moved to the Supervisory Board
1983	Died in Heilbronn on January 25

Ewald Praxl

1911	Born on July 5 in Postelberg (Czechoslovakia)
1937	Attended the German Advanced Technical College in Prague and obtained a degree in mechanical engineering
1939	Joined NSU as designer in the off-road vehicle department
1949	Deputy to Chief Designer Albert Roder
1951	Head of Testing and Racing Department; also undertook production-vehicle development work
1951	Eight world speed records
1952–54	NSU racing department wins four world championships under his management
1954	Racing department shut down
1956	Under his management, NSU captures world speed records in all classes
1962	Head of Development Department
1971	Head of Rotary-Piston/Wankel Research
1974	Head of Division
1976	Retirement; his task area is taken over by Richard van Basshuysen
1988	Died on December 27 in Neckarsulm

Praxl made a decisive contribution to the company's international motor sport successes.

His life's work includes such highlights as development of the NSU Prinz, Ro 80 and K 70 cars for production, development of the half-track motorcycle and research work on the Wankel engine.

Ludwig Kraus

1911	Born on December 26 in Hettenhausen, Pfaffenhofen
1931	Higher school-leaving certificate at the upper secondary school in Ingolstadt
1933–37	Studied mechanical engineering in Munich, Stuttgart and Hanover
1937	Joined Daimler-Benz AG on September 1 as designer for airship and high-speed boat engines
1939–40	Military service
1941	Return to the Daimler-Benz engine design department
1951	Head of Design, Racing Cars
1954	Honorary title of Senior Engineer
1956	Head of Design, Fluid Flow Machines
1958	Head of Advance Passenger Car Development
1963	From October 1, Director of Development at Auto Union GmbH in Ingolstadt
1965	Member of the Board of Management, Auto Union GmbH
1969	From September 1, Member of the Board of Management, Audi NSU Auto Union AG, with responsibility for Development
1973	Retired on December 31
1974	Honorary engineering doctorate from Hanover Technical University, for services to car construction
1976–85	Member of the Supervisory Board, Audi NSU Auto Union AG
1997	Died on September 19 in Munich

Werner Henze

1910	Born on December 19 in Leopoldshall, Anhalt
1928	Studied business management at Cologne and Bonn Universities; doctorate in political sciences from Breslau University; Head of Main Accounts Department at the vehicle and engine manufacturer Fahrzeug- and Motorenwerke FAMO, Breslau
1939–45	Labor service, military service, active service and imprisonment
1950	Karl Schmidt GmbH, Neckarsulm; VDM Central Office, Frankfurt
1956	From October 15, Chairman of the Board of Management, Auto Union GmbH, Ingolstadt
1965	Retirement on March 31
1999	Died on February 4 in Baden-Baden

Dr. Gerd Stieler von Heydekampf

Ewald Praxl

Dr. Ludwig Kraus

Dr. Werner Henze

Dr. Rudolf Leiding

Dr. Gerhard Prinz

Dr. Werner P. Schmidt

Gottlieb M. Strobl

Rudolf Leiding

1914	Born on September 4 in Busch, Altmark
1928–32	Four-year apprenticeship as motor-vehicle mechanic
1932–35	Attended Magdeburg School of Mechanical Engineering
1935–45	Labor service, military service, active service
1945	From August 1, Factory Engineer at VW
1949	Head of Customer Service
1958	Factory Director, VW's Kassel factory
1964	Director of Volkswagen AG
1965	From July 29, Chairman of the Board of Management, Auto Union GmbH, Ingolstadt
1968	From July 1, Chairman of the Board of Management, Volkswagen do Brasil
1971	From April 1, Chairman of the Board of Management, Audi NSU Auto Union AG
1971	From October 1, Chairman of the Board of Management, Volkswagen AG
1975	Retirement
1976	Honorary engineering doctorate from Berlin Technical University for the promotion of efficient production methods in the car industry
2003	Died on September 3 in Baunatal

Gerhard Prinz

1929	Born on April 5 in Solingen
1949–58	Higher school-leaving certificate, studied economics and legal sciences, gained doctorate in law
1958–60	Assistant to General Manager, German Iron and Steel Business Association, Düsseldorf
1962–67	Senior executive, Brown, Boveri & Cie.
1964	Authorized signatory
1967	Senior executive, Volkswagenwerk AG, Wolfsburg
1969	Member of the Board of Management
1972	From January 12, Chairman of the Board of Management, Audi NSU Auto Union AG, Ingolstadt
1973	June 30: Retired from Audi NSU Auto Union AG
1983	Died in Stuttgart on October 29

Werner P. Schmidt

1932	Born on July 5 in Borken, Westphalia; higher school-leaving certificate, studied economics and business management, gained a doctorate in political science at Cologne University
1956	Ford Werke AG, Cologne; Sales (field service in Germany and the United States); Head of Passenger Car Marketing; Head of Domestic Sales
1967	Head of Exports, Volkswagenwerk AG
1971	From April, Chairman of the Board of Management, Volkswagen do Brasil

1973	From July 1, Spokesman of the Board of Management, Audi NSU Auto Union AG, Ingolstadt
1973–75	Chairman of the Board of Management, Audi NSU Auto Union AG, Ingolstadt
1975	With effect from August 1, Member of the Volkswagenwerk AG Board of Management with responsibility for the Sales Division

Gottlieb M. Strobl

1916	Born on October 14 in Munich
1936	High school-leaving certificate in Munich
1936	Trainee at Mitteldeutsche Motorenwerke, Taucha, a subsidiary of Auto Union AG
1939–45	Military service
1946–48	Commercial employee at Koenen & Regel, Ratingen
1948–50	Commercial employee at Hoffmann-Werke, Lintorf
1950	Deputy Chief Buyer, Auto Union GmbH, Düsseldorf factory
1961	Deputy Division Manager
1962	Division Manager, Material Procurement, Auto Union GmbH, Ingolstadt
1971	Appointed to the Board of Management, Audi NSU Auto Union AG, with responsibility for Purchasing and Materials Management
1973	Moved to the Volkswagenwerk AG Board of Management with the same task area
1975	On August 1, appointed Chairman of the Board of Management, Audi NSU Auto Union AG, Ingolstadt; retained his seat on the VW Board of Management in VW in Wolfsburg for the new Audi NSU division
1979	Retired on January 1
1979–87	Member of the Supervisory Board, Audi NSU Auto Union AG
2004	Died on March 12 in Ingolstadt

Wolfgang R. Habbel

1924	Born on March 25 in Dillenburg
1942–46	Higher school-leaving certificate in Koblenz; military service, prisoner of war
1946–50	Studied law in Bonn and Cologne
1951–57	Management assistant, provisional Head of Exports, Auto Union GmbH Ingolstadt/ Düsseldorf
1957	Doctorate in legal sciences, Cologne University
1957–67	Human Resources Manager, Ford Werke, Cologne
1967–69	European Coordinator for Labor Law and Social Matters, Ford Europe, Warley, England
1970–71	Partner and General Manager for Human Resources, C.H. Boehringer Sohn Ingelheim

1971	On October 18: appointed to the Audi NSU Auto Union Board of Management with responsibility for Human Resources
1979–87	Chairman of the Audi NSU Auto Union AG (from January 1, 1985, AUDI AG) Board of Management
1988	Retired on January 1
1988–93	Member of the AUDI AG Supervisory Board

Ferdinand Piëch

1937	Born on April 17 in Vienna, son of Dr. jur. Anton Piëch, a lawyer, and his wife Louise, née Porsche
1962	Degree from the Swiss Federal Institute of Technology in Zurich
1963	Test engine specialist, Dr.-Ing. h. c. F. Porsche KG, Stuttgart-Zuffenhausen
1966	Head of Test Department, Porsche KG
1968	Head of Technical Development, Porsche KG
1971	Technical General Manager, Porsche KG
1972	Main Division Manager for Special Tasks, Technical Development, Audi NSU Auto Union AG
1973	Head of Division General Test Departments
1974	Head of Technical Development
1975	Appointed to the Audi NSU Auto Union AG Board of Management with responsibility for the Technical Development Division
1984	Granted an honorary doctorate – Dr. tech. h. c. – in technical sciences by Vienna Technical University in recognition of his services to automobile construction
1988	On January 1 appointed Chairman of the AUDI AG Board of Management
1993	Appointed Chairman of the Volkswagen AG Board of Management
From 2002	Chairman of the Volkswagen AG Supervisory Board

Franz-Josef Kortüm

1950	Born on August 18 in Billerbeck
1974	Studied business management, graduate in business studies
1976	Junior salesman, Daimler-Benz AG, Bielefeld
1977–79	General management, Kortüm Kfz- und Reifenhandel, Billerbeck
1979–84	Commercial vehicle sales, Daimler-Benz AG, Berlin; Assistant to Head of Sales; Deputy Head of Sales
1984	Junior sales organization group, England; Assistant to Domestic Sales Director
1985–89	Branch Manager, Saarbrücken
1989	Domestic Commercial Vehicle Sales, Daimler-Benz AG, Stuttgart; Member of the Executive Board
1991	Branch Manager, Authorities and Diplomatic Service Sales, Bonn branch

| 1992 | Member of the AUDI AG Board of Management, Ingolstadt, Marketing and Sales Division |
| 1993–94 | Chairman of the AUDI AG Board of Management, Ingolstadt |

Herbert Demel

1953	Born on October 18 in Vienna
1971	Studied mechanical engineering at Vienna Technical University
1978	Technical and scientific assistant at the Institute for Internal Combustion Engines and Motor Vehicle Construction, Vienna
1981	Doctorate in engineering
1984	ABS Application Coordination, Robert Bosch GmbH, Stuttgart
1985	Head of ABS/ASR Applications
1988	Main Departmental Head, ABS/ASR Applications and Quality Assurance
1989	Responsibility for the Transmission Control Systems Development Department
1990	Head of Mechanical Assemblies Development, AUDI AG, Ingolstadt
1993	From March 1, Member of the AUDI AG Board of Management, Technical Development Division
1994	From February 4, Spokesman for the Board of Management; additional responsibility for the Technical Development and Marketing/Sales Divisions
1995–97	Chairman of the AUDI AG Board of Management

Franz-Josef Paefgen

1946	Born on May 10 in Büttgen, Neuss
1967	Studied mechanical engineering and business management at Karlsruhe and Aachen Technical Universities; obtained doctorate in engineering sciences
1976	Graduate trainee, Ford Werke AG; worked in the Engine Development and Quality Assurance areas
1980	Audi NSU Auto Union AG, Neckarsulm factory: responsibility for Interior Equipment and Electrics Design areas
1987	Head of Equipment and Air Conditioning Development; Head of Technical Development, AUDI AG, Ingolstadt
1991	Head of Product Planning and Project Management
1994	Acting Head of Technical Development
1995	From March: Member of the AUDI AG Board of Management, Technical Development Division
1997	From January 1, Deputy Chairman of the AUDI AG Board of Management, appointed Board Spokesman
1998–02	Chairman of the AUDI AG Board of Management

Dr. Wolfgang R. Habbel

Dr. Ferdinand Piëch

Franz-Josef Kortüm

Dr. Herbert Demel

Dr. Franz-Josef Paefgen

Dr. Martin Winterkorn

Rupert Stadler

Martin Winterkorn

1947	Born on May 24 in Leonberg
1966	Studied metallurgy and metal physics at Stuttgart University
1973–77	Post-graduate studies, Max Planck Institute for Metals Research
1977	Doctorate in natural sciences – Dr. rer. nat.; Robert Bosch GmbH
1981	Assistant to the Member of the Board for Quality Assurance, Audi NSU Auto Union AG
1988	Division Head for Central Group Quality Assurance
1990	Head of Quality Assurance
1993	Head of Group Quality Assurance, Volkswagen AG
1994	From March: General Manager with Power of Attorney, Volkswagen AG
1995	From June: additionally responsible for Product Management
1996	Member of the Brand Board of Management, Technical Development, Volkswagen AG
2000	From July: Member of the Group Board of Management for Research and Development
2002	From March 1: Chairman of the AUDI AG Board of Management; Head of the Audi Brand Group
2003	In addition, from January 1, Head of the Technical Development Division
2007	Since January 1: Chairman of the Volkswagen AG Board of Management

Rupert Stadler

1963	Born on March 17 in Titting; Studied business management at Augsburg University of Applied Sciences, specializing in corporate planning/controlling, finance, banking and investment; Received degree in business management; joined Philips Kommunikation Industrie AG, Nuremberg
1990	AUDI AG, Ingolstadt; Controlling, Sales and Marketing areas
1994	VW/Audi España SA, Barcelona: General Commercial Manager; Controlling, Accounts and Human Resources, Organization
1997	Volkswagen AG, Wolfsburg; Head of General Secretariat of Chairman of the Board
2002	In addition, from January 1: Head of Group Product Planning
2003	January 1: Member of the AUDI AG Board of Management, Ingolstadt; from April 1, responsibility for Finance and Organisation Division (until August 31, 2007)
2007	January 1: Chairman of the AUDI AG Board of Management, Ingolstadt

Type summary

The main Horch models, 1901–1945

Designation Type	No. of cylinders/ layout	Bore x stroke in inches	Displacement in cc	Output in hp	Period of manufacture	Notes
Model 1	2			4 – 5	1901	
Model 2	2 inline		2500	10 – 12	1902 – 1904	
Model 3	4 inline	3.35 x 4.13	2383	18 – 22	1903 – 1905	
Model 4	4 inline	3.35 x 3.94	2270	14 – 17	1903 – 1905	
also for Sport	4 inline	3.35 x 4.72	2725	22 – 25	1903 – 1905	
Model 5	4 inline	4.53 x 5.51	5810	35 – 40	1903 – 1905	
Z	4 inline	3.31 x 4.72	2660	11/22	1906 – 1909	
ZD	4 inline	4.53 x 5.51	5810	23/40	1906 – 1910	
6 cylinder	6 inline	4.53 x 5.51	8725	31/60	1907 – 1908	
S	4 inline	4.53 x 6.10	6440	25/55	1908 – 1922	
K	4 inline	3.27 x 4.72	2600	10/25	1910 – 1911	
H	4 inline	3.94 x 5.31	4240	17/42	1910 – 1919	
C	4 inline	2.93 x 4.72	2090	8/24	1911 – 1922	
N	4 inline	3.15 x 5.12	2600	10/30	1911 – 1921	
P	4 inline	3.94 x 5.91	4710	18/50	1914 – 1922	
10 M 200	4 inline	3.15 x 5.12	2600	10/35	1922 – 1924	
10 M 201	4 inline	3.15 x 5.12	2600	10/50	1924 – 1926	
303	8 inline	2.56 x 4.65	3132	12/60	1927	2 camshafts
305	8 inline	2.66 x 4.65	3378	13/65	1927 – 1928	
350	8 inline	2.87 x 4.65	3950	16/80	1928 – 1930	
400	8 inline	2.87 x 4.65	3950	16/80	1930 – 1931	
420	8 inline	3.43 x 3.74	4517	18/90	1931 – 1932	1 camshaft
500	8 inline	3.43 x 4.09	4944	20/100	1930 – 1932	
670	V12	3.15 x 3.94	6021	120	1932 – 1934	
750	8 inline	3.43 x 3.74	4517	90	1932 – 1934	
830	V8	2.95 x 3.35	3004	62	1933 – 1934	
830 B/BK	V8	3.07 x 3.35	3250	70/75	1934 – 1936	
830 BL	V8	3.07 x 3.62	3517	75	1935 – 1940	From 1937: 82 hp From 1938: 92 hp
850	8 inline	3.43 x 4.09	4944	100	1935 – 1938	From 1937: 120 hp
853	8 inline	3.43 x 4.09	4944	100	1935 – 1939	From 1937: 120 hp
855	8 inline	3.43 x 4.09	4944	120	1938 – 1939	Special roadster
930 V	V8	3.07 x 3.94	3823	92	1937 – 1940	
951	8 inline	3.43 x 4.09	4944	120	1937 – 1940	

The main Audi models, 1910–1945

Designation Type	No. of cylinders/ layout	Bore x stroke in inches	Displacement in cc	Output in hp	Period of manufacture	Notes
A	4 inline	3.15 x 5.12	2600	10/22	1910 – 1912	
B	4 inline	3.15 x 5.12	2600	11/28	1911 – 1917	
C	4 inline	3.54 x 5.51	3560	14/35	1911 – 1925	
Ct	4 inline	3.54 x 5.51	3560	14/35	1912 – 1928	Truck
D	4 inline	3.94 x 5.91	4710	18/45	1911 – 1920	
E	4 inline	4.33 x 5.91	5700	22/50	1911 – 1924	
G	4 inline	2.95 x 4.65	2071	8/22	1914 – 1926	
K	4 inline	3.54 x 5.51	3560	14/50	1921 – 1926	First LHD production car
M	6 inline	3.54 x 4.80	4655	18/70	1924 – 1928	
R	8 inline	3.15 x 4.80	4900	19/100	1927 – 1929	"Imperator"
S	8 inline	3.25 x 4.76	5130	19/100	1929 – 1932	Rickenbacker engine
T	6 inline	3.25 x 4.76	3838	15/75	1930 – 1932	Rickenbacker en.
P	4 inline	2.48 x 3.54	1122	5/30	1931	Peugeot engine
Front UW	6 inline	2.76 x 3.35	1949	40	1933 – 1934	Front-wheel drive
Front 225	6 inline	2.80 x 3.74	2255	50 (55)	1934 – 1938	Front-wheel drive
920	6 inline	3.43 x 3.62	3281	75	1939 – 1940	

The main Wanderer motorcycle models, 1902–1929

Designation Type	No. of cylinders/ layout	Displacement in cc	Output in hp	Period of manufacture	Notes
1.5 hp	1	217	1.5	1902 – 1903	Bicycle frame
1.5 hp	1	228	1.5	1903	Reinforced frame
2 hp	1	249	2	1903 – 1904	Motorcycle frame
2.5 hp	1	308	2.5	1904 – 1905	
3 hp	1	454	3	1905 – 1907	
4 hp	V-twin	538	4	1905 – 1907	
5 hp	V-twin	706	5	1905 – 1909	
2.5 hp	1	327	2.5	1906 – 1909	
1.5 hp	1	198	1.5	1908 – 1910	
3 hp	V-twin	408	3	1910 – 1914	Rear cylinder vertical
1.5 hp	1	204	1.5	1910 – 1914	
2 hp	1	252	3	1914 – 1919	New side-valve engine
4 hp	V-twin	504	6	1914 – 1919	New side-valve engine
2.5 hp	1 vertical	327	6	1919 – 1920	
2.5 hp	1 vertical	346	6	1920 – 1925	
4.5 hp Type 616	V-twin	616	10	1919 – 1924	
5.4 hp Type 708	V-twin	708	14	1924 – 1927	4 valves per cylinder
1.5 hp	1 horizontal	196	4.5	1924 – 1926	4 valves per cylinder
1.4 hp	1 horizontal	184	4	1926 – 1928	
5.7 hp Type 750	V-twin	748	17	1927 – 1929	
1.5 hp Type 200	1 horizontal	196	4.5	1928 – 1930	
K 500	1 vertical	499	16	1928 – 1930	Shaft drive

The main Wanderer car models, 1913–1945

Designation Type	No. of cylinders/ layout	Bore x stroke in inches	Displacement in cc	Output in hp	Period of manufacture	Notes
W 3, 5/12 hp	4 inline	2.44 x 3.74	1147	12	1913 – 1914	
W 3/II, 5/15 hp	4 inline	2.52 x 3.74	1222	15	1914 – 1919	
W 3/III, 5/15 hp	4 inline	2.52 x 3.94	1280	15	1919 – 1921	
W 6, 6/18 hp	4 inline	2.64 x 4.33	1551	18	1920 – 1924	
W 8, 5/15 hp	4 inline	2.54 x 3.94	1307	15	1921 – 1925	
W 8, 5/20 hp	4 inline	2.54 x 3.94	1307	20	1925 – 1927	
W 9, 6/24 hp	4 inline	2.64 x 4.33	1551	24	1924 – 1926	
W 10/I, 6/30 hp	4 inline	2.64 x 4.33	1551	30	1926 – 1927	
W 10/II, 8/40 hp	4 inline	2.83 x 4.72	1953	40	1927 – 1928	
W 10/III, 6/30 hp	4 inline	2.83 x 3.78	1563	30	1927 – 1929	
W 10/IV, 6/30 hp	4 inline	2.83 x 3.78	1563	30	1930 – 1932	
W 11, 10/50 hp	6 inline	2.83 x 4.09	2540	50	1928 – 1932	
W 15	6 inline	2.56 x 3.35	1692	35	1932 – 1933	
W 17	6 inline	2.76 x 3.35	1963	40	1932 – 1933	
W 21	6 inline	2.56 x 3.35	1692	35	1933 – 1935	
W 22	6 inline	2.76 x 3.35	1963	40	1933 – 1935	
W 235	6 inline	2.56 x 3.35	1692	35	1935 – 1936	
W 240	6 inline	2.76 x 3.35	1963	40	1935 – 1936	
W 250	6 inline	2.80 x 3.74	2255	50	1935 – 1936	
W 35	6 inline	2.56 x 3.35	1692	35	1936	
W 40	6 inline	2.76 x 3.35	1963	40	1936 – 1938	
W 50	6 inline	2.80 x 3.74	2255	50/55	1936 – 1938	
W 51	6 inline	2.80 x 3.74	2255	50/55	1936 – 1937	
W 52	6 inline	2.95 x 3.94	2632	62	1937 – 1938	
W 23	6 inline	2.95 x 3.94	2632	62	1937 – 1942	
W 24	4 inline	2.95 x 3.94	1767	42	1937 – 1941	
W 25 K	6 inline	2.76 x 3.35	1963	85	1936 – 1938	Supercharged
W 26	6 inline	2.95 x 3.94	2632	62	1937 – 1941	

The main DKW motorcycle models, 1919–1945

Designation Type	No. of cylinders/ layout	Displacement in cc	Output in hp	Period of manufacture	Notes
Auxiliary engine	1 horizontal	118	1	1919 – 1923	On bicycle luggage rack
Golem, reclined seat	1	118	1	1921 – 1922	
Golem, reclined seat	1	143	1.5	1922 – 1925	
Reich Rally model	1	148	2.25	1922 – 1924	
ZL	1	148	2.25	1923 – 1924	
ZM	1	170	3	1924 – 1925	Also with 181 and 206 cc engine
SM	1	170	3	1924 – 1925	Welded frame-tank unit
E 206	1	206	4	1925 – 1928	Also with 125 and 175 cc engine
E 200	1	198	4	1928	
E 300	1	293	8	1928 – 1929	
Z 500	2 transverse	494	12	1927 – 1928	Air-cooled engine
ZSW 500	2 transverse	494	14	1928 – 1929	Water-cooled engine
Super Sport 500	2 transverse	494	18	1929 – 1933	Water-cooled engine
Luxus 200	1	198	4	1929 – 1932	Pressed-steel frame
Luxus 300	1	293	8	1929 – 1930	
Luxus 500	2 transverse	494	14	1929 – 1930	Air-cooled engine
Sport 500	2 transverse	494	18	1931 – 1932	Water-cooled engine
People's Bike	1	198	4	1929 – 1930	No transmission
ZIS	1	198	4	1929 – 1931	With 2-speed transmission
Block 350	1	345	11	1931 – 1932	Schnürle scavenging
Block 200	1	192	6	1931 – 1933	Schnürle scavenging
KM 175	1	175	4	1930 – 1933	Tubular frame
SB 200	1	192	7	1933 – 1938	
SB 350	1	345	11	1934 – 1938	
SB 500	2	494	15	1934 – 1939	
RT 100, 2,5 hp	1	98	2.5	1934 – 1936	
KM 200	1	198	6	1934 – 1936	
KS 200	1	198	7	1936 – 1940	
RT 100, 3 hp	1	98	3	1936 – 1940	
Sport 250	1	247	9	1936 – 1938	Sports model in SB line
NZ 250	1	247	9	1938 – 1941	
NZ 350	1	346	11.5	1938 – 1945	
NZ 500	2	489	18.5	1939 – 1942	First model with rear suspension
RT 125	1	123	4.75	1939 – 1944	

The main DKW car models, 1928–1945

Designation Type	No. of cylinders/ layout	Bore x stroke in inches	Displacement in cc	Output in hp	Period of manufacture	Notes
P 15	2 inline	2.91 x 2.68	584	15	1928 – 1930	Rear-wheel drive
PS 600	2 inline	2.91 x 2.68	584	18	1929 – 1932	Rear-wheel drive
4 = 8, V 800	V4	2.36 x 2.58	780	22	1930 – 1931	Rear-wheel drive
4 = 8, V 1000	V4	2.68 x 2.70	980	25	1931 – 1932	Rear-wheel drive
Sonderklasse 432	V4	2.68 x 2.70	988	26	1932 – 1933	Rear-wheel drive
Sonderklasse 1001	V4	2.68 x 2.70	988	26	1933 – 1935	Rear-wheel drive
Schwebeklasse	V4	2.68 x 2.70	988	26	1934	Rear-wheel drive
		2.68 x 2.70	988	30	1935	Rear-wheel drive
		2.76 x 2.70	1047	32	1935 – 1937	Rear-wheel drive
Sonderklasse '37	V4	2.76 x 2.70	1054	32	1937 – 1940	Rear-wheel drive

The main DKW car models, 1928–1945

Designation Type	No. of cylinders/ layout	Bore x stroke in inches	Displacement in cc	Output in hp	Period of manufacture	Notes
Front FA 500 (F1)	2 inl., transverse	2.68 x 2.68	494	15	1931 – 1932	Front-wheel drive
Front FA 600 (F1)	2 inl., transverse	2.91 x 2.68	584	18	1931 – 1932	Front-wheel drive
F 2 Meisterklasse	2 inl., transverse	2.91 x 2.68	580	18	1932	Front-wheel drive
F 2 Meisterklasse 601	2 inl., transverse	2.91 x 2.68	580	18	1933	Front-wheel drive
F 2 Meisterklasse 701	2 inl., transverse	2.99 x 2.99	684	20	1933 – 1934	Front-wheel drive
F 2 Reichsklasse	2 inl., transverse	2.91 x 2.68	580	18	1933 – 1935	Front-wheel drive
F 4 Meisterklasse	2 inl., transverse	2.99 x 2.99	684	20	1934 – 1935	Front-wheel drive
F 5 Reichsklasse	2 inl., transverse	2.91 x 2.68	580	18	1935 – 1937	Front-wheel drive
Meisterklasse		2.99 x 2.99	684	20	1935 – 1937	Front-wheel drive
Front-Luxus		2.99 x 2.99	684	20	1935 – 1938	Front-wheel drive
F 7 Reichsklasse	2 inl., transverse	2.91 x 2.68	580	18	1937 – 1939	Front-wheel drive
Meisterklasse		2.99 x 2.99	684	20	1937 – 1939	Front-wheel drive
Front-Luxus		2.99 x 2.99	684	20	1938 – 1939	Front-wheel drive
F 8 Reichsklasse	2 inl., transverse	2.91 x 2.68	580	18	1939 – 1942	Front-wheel drive
Meisterklasse		2.99 x 2.99	684	20	1939 – 1942	Front-wheel drive
Front-Luxus		2.99 x 2.99	684	20	1939 – 1942	Front-wheel drive
F 9 Prototype	3 inline	2.76 x 3.07	900	28	1939 – 1943	Front-wheel drive

The main DKW motorcycle models, 1949–1958

Designation Type	No. of cylinders/ layout	Bore x stroke in inches	Displacement in cc	Output in hp	Period of manufacture	Notes
RT 125 W	1	2.05 x 2.28	123	4.75	1949 – 1952	"W" = "West"
RT 125/2	1	2.05 x 2.28	123	5.7	1952 – 1954	On request, Jurisch rear susp.
RT 125/2H	1	2.05 x 2.28	123	5.7	1954 – 1957	Rear suspension standard
RT 175	1	2.44 x 2.28	174	9.6	1954 – 1955	Plunger-type rear suspension
RT 175 S	1	2.44 x 2.28	174	9,6	1955 – 1956	Swinging arm rear suspension
RT 175 VS	1	2.44 x 2.28	174	9.6	1956 – 1958	Swinging arm fr. and r. suspension
RT 200	1	2.44 x 2.52	191	8.5	1951 – 1952	
RT 200 H	1	2.44 x 2.52	191	8.5	1952 – 1953	Plunger-type rear suspension
RT 200/2	1	2.60 x 2.28	197	11	1954 – 1955	Plunger-type rear suspension
RT 200 S	1	2.60 x 2.28	197	11	1955 – 1956	Swinging arm rear suspension
RT 200 VS	1	2.60 x 2.28	197	11	1956 – 1958	Swinging arm fr. and r. suspension
RT 250 H	1	2.76 x 2.52	244	11.5	1952 – 1953	Plunger-type rear suspension
RT 250/1	1	2.76 x 2.52	244	11.5	1953	4-speed transmiss.
RT 250/2	1	2.76 x 2.52	244	14.1	1953 – 1955	New engine
RT 250 S	1	2.76 x 2.52	244	15	1956	Swinging arm rear suspension
RT 250 VS	1	2.76 x 2.52	244	15	1956 – 1957	Swinging arm fr. and r. suspension
RT 350 S	2	2.44 x 2.28	348	18.5	1955 – 1956	Swinging arm rear suspension
Hobby	1	1.77 x 1.85	74	3	1954 – 1957	Stepless V-belt transmission
Hummel	1	1.57 x 1.54	49	1.35	1956 – 1958	Three-speed transmission

The main Auto Union/DKW car types, 1949–1968

Designation Type	No. of cylinders/ layout	Bore x stroke in inches	Displacement in cc	Output in hp	Period of manufacture	Notes
Rapid delivery vans						
F 89 L	2 inline	2.99 x 2.99	684	20	1949 – 1954	Transverse engine; from 1952: 22 hp
F 800 Type 30	2 inline	3.07 x 3.27	792	30	1954 – 1955	Longitudinal engine
F 800/3 Type 3 = 6	3 inline	2.80 x 2.99	896	32	1955 – 1962	
F 1000 L Imosa	3 inline	2.91 x 2.99	980	40	1963 – 1968	Built in Spain
Off-road vehicles						
F 91/4, 900	3 inline	2.80 x 2.99	896	40	1956 – 1959	M (multipurpose) vehicle
F 91/6, 900	3 inline	2.80 x 2.99	896	40	1958 – 1959	6 seats
F 91/4, 1000	3 inline	2.91 x 2.99	980	44	1958 – 1968	M vehicle; from 1962: Munga
F 91/6, 1000	3 inline	2.91 x 2.99	980	44	1959 – 1968	6 seats
F 91/8, 1000	3 inline	2.91 x 2.99	980	44	1962 – 1968	8 seats
Passenger cars						
F 10	2 inline	2.99 x 2.99	684	20	1950	Interim model with Baur body
F 89 P "Meisterklasse"	2 inline	2.99 x 2.99	684	23	1950 – 1954	Transverse engine
F 91 "Sonderklasse"	3 inline	2.80 x 2.99	896	34	1953 – 1955	DKW 3 = 6; station wagon until 1956
F 93/94 "Sonderklasse"	3 inline	2.80 x 2.99	896	38	1955 – 1959	Large 3 = 6; from 1957: 40 hp
3 = 6 Monza	3 inline	2.80 x 2.99	896	40	1956 – 1959	From 1958: also with 1,000 cc engine
Auto Union 1000	3 inline	2.91 x 2.99	980	44	1957 – 1962	From 7/1959: 2-door sedan with wraparound windshield
Auto Union 1000 S	3 inline	2.91 x 2.99	980	50	1959 – 1963	2-door sedan and coupé with wraparound windshield
Auto Union 1000 Sp	3 inline	2.91 x 2.99	980	55	1958 – 1965	2-seater sports car
F 11 Junior	3 inline	2.68 x 2.68	741	34	1959 – 1962	First passenger car from Ingolstadt
F 11 Junior de Luxe	3 inline	2.78 x 2.68	796	34	1961 – 1963	
F 11/64	3 inline	2.78 x 2.68	796	34	1963 – 1965	Body as for F 12
F 12	3 inline	2.93 x 2.68	889	40	1963 – 1965	1965 model: 45 hp
F 12 Roadster	3 inline	2.93 x 2.68	889	45	1964	
F 102	3 inline	3.19 x 2.99	1175	60	1964 – 1966	

The main NSU motorcycle models, 1901–1969

Designation Type	No. of cylinders/ layout	Bore x stroke in inches	Displacement in cc	Output in hp	Period of manufacture	Notes
Neckarsulm 1.75 hp	1	2.60 x 2.76	240	1.75	1902 – 1903	
Neckarsulm 2.5 hp	1	2.95 x 2.95	329	2.5	1903 – 1905	
Neckarsulm 1.25 hp	1	2.44 x 2.76	211	1.5	1907 – 1908	
Neckarsulm 4 hp	1	2.52 x 2.95	578	4	1907 – 1910	
Neckarsulm 2.5 hp	2	2.05 x 2.91	331	2.5	1905 – 1910	
Neckarsulm 6 hp	2	2.95 x 3.54	793	8	1909 – 1910	
NSU 2.5 hp	1	2.87 x 3.07	326	2.5	1913 – 1915	
NSU 3.5 hp	2	2.48 x 3.15	495	3.5	1913 – 1921	
NSU 6.5 hp	2	2.95 x 3.70	830	6.5	1913 – 1921	
NSU 4 hp	2	2.48 x 3.15	495	4	1920 – 1925	
NSU 8 hp	2	3.15 x 3.90	995	12	1924 – 1927	
NSU 251 R	1	2.48 x 3.15	248	6	1924 – 1928	
NSU 502 T	2	3.15 x 3.90	498	10	1924 – 1927	
NSU 251 T/S	1	2.36 x 3.15	249	6	1928 – 1931	
NSU 501 S	1	3.15 x 3.90	497	20	1928 – 1930	
NSU 201 R/T	1	2.22 x 3.15	199	4.5	1928 – 1930	
NSU 301 T	1	2.60 x 3.46	298	7	1929 – 1930	
NSU 351 TS	1	2.80 x 3.46	346	8	1930 – 1932	
NSU 175 Z/ZD	1	2.32 x 2.52	174	4.5	1930 – 1933	
NSU 201 Z	1	2.48 x 2.52	198	5	1930 – 1932	
NSU 251 Z	1	2.76 x 2.52	244	5.5	1930 – 1933	
NSU 501 SS	1	3.15 x 3.90	494	30	1930 – 1935	
NSU 601 SS	1	3.44 x 3.90	592	38	1930 – 1935	
NSU 501 TS	1	3.15 x 3.90	494	12.5	1930 – 1936	
NSU 601 TS	1	3.44 x 3.90	592	16	1930 – 1939	
NSU Motosulm	1	1.77 x 1.57	63	1.25	1931 – 1935	
NSU 251 OSL	1	2.52 x 2.95	242	10.5	1933 – 1952	
NSU 201 OSL	1	2.28 x 2.95	198	8.5	1933 – 1939	
NSU 201 ZDB Pony	1	2.48 x 2.52	198	6.5	1934 – 1940	
NSU 351 OSL	1	2.80 x 3.46	346	18	1932 – 1940	
NSU 501 OSL	1	3.15 x 3.90	494	22	1935 – 1939	
NSU Quick	1	1.93 x 2.05	98	3	1936 – 1953	
NSU 351 OT	1	2.95 x 2.95	331	12.5	1936 – 1939	
NSU 601 OSL	1	3.35 x 3.90	562	24	1937 – 1940	
NSU 125 ZDB	1	2.05 x 2.28	123	4.5	1941 – 1951	
NSU Fox 4 Takt	1	1.97 x 1.97	98	5.2	1949 – 1954	
NSU Fox 2 Takt	1	2.05 x 2.28	123	5.4	1951 – 1954	
NSU Lambretta	1	2.05 x 2.28	123	4.5	1950 – 1956	
NSU Lux/Super Lux	1	2.44 x 2.60	198	8.6	1951 – 1956	
NSU Konsul I	1	2.95 x 3.11	349	18	1951 – 1953	
NSU Konsul II	1	3.15 x 3.90	498	22	1951 – 1954	
NSU Max/Super Max	1	2.72 x 2.60	247	17	1952 – 1963	
NSU Quickly	1	1.57 x 1.54	49	1.4	1953 – 1966	
NSU Super Fox	1	2.05 x 2.28	123	8.8	1955 – 1957	
NSU Prima	1	2.24 x 2.28	146	6.2	1956 – 1960	
NSU Maxi	1	2.44 x 2.28	174	12.5	1957 – 1964	

The main NSU car models, 1905–1969

Designation Type	No. of cylinders/ layout	Bore x stroke in inches	Displacement in cc	Output in hp	Period of manufacture	Notes
Sulmobil	1	3.23 x 3.39	451	3.5	1905 – 1906	
6/10 hp	4	2.68 x 3.54	1420	12	1906 – 1907	
8/15 hp	4	2.99 x 3.94	1750	15	1907 – 1910	
10/20 hp	4	3.35 x 4.53	2608	20	1907 – 1910	
6/12 hp	4	2.76 x 3.94	1540	12	1907 – 1908	
6/18 hp	4	2.95 x 3.46	1550	18	1911 – 1914	
5/10 hp	4	2.36 x 3.94	1132	10	1909 – 1911	
10/30 hp	4	3.35 x 4.53	2608	30	1911 – 1916	
13/35 hp	4	3.82 x 4.53	3397	35	1911 – 1914	
8/24 hp	4	3.15 x 4.09	2110	24	1912 – 1925	
5/15 hp	4	2.76 x 3.07	1232	15	1914 – 1918	
2.5-tonne	4	3.58 x 5.12	3380	54	1914 – 1926	
14/40 hp	4	3.70 x 5.12	3606	54	1921 – 1925	
5/25 hp	4	2.68 x 3.54	1307	25	1924 – 1928	
6/30 hp	6	2.39 x 3.90	1567	30	1928	
7/34 hp	6	2.44 x 3.90	1781	34	1928 – 1931	
Prinz I/II/III	2	2.95 x 2.60	583	20/30	1958 – 1962	
Sport-Prinz	2	2.95 x 2.60	583	30	1959 – 1967	
Prinz 4	2	2.95 x 2.60	598	30	1961 – 1973	
Wankel Spider	Rotary piston	0.04 x 19.57	497	50	1964 – 1967	
Prinz 1000	4	2.72 x 2.62	996	43	1964 – 1972	
Prinz 1000 TT	4	2.83 x 2.62	1085	55	1965 – 1967	
Typ 110/S/SC	4	2.95 x 2.62	1085	53	1965 – 1967	
NSU TTS	4	2.72 x 2.62	996	70	1967 – 1971	
NSU TT	4	2.95 x 2.62	1177	65	1967 – 1972	
NSU 1200 C	4	2.95 x 2.62	1177	55	1967 – 1973	
NSU RO 80	Rotary piston	0.08 x 19.57	995	115	1967 – 1977	

Audi models, 1965–2009, with selected engine sizes

Designation Type/model line	No. of cylinders/ layout	Bore x stroke in inches	Displacement in cc	Output in kW/hp	Period of manufacture	Quantity (complete model line)
Audi F 103					**1965 – 1972**	**416,852**
Audi 72	4 inline	3.15 x 3.32	1696	53/72	1965 – 1968	
Audi 80 Variant	4 inline	3.15 x 3.32	1696	59/80	1966 – 1969	
Audi Super 90	4 inline	3.21 x 3.32	1760	66/90	1966 – 1971	
Audi 60	4 inline	3.15 x 2.93	1496	40/55	1968 – 1972	
AB platform					**1974 – 1978**	**180,828**
Audi 50 LS	4 inline	2.74 x 2.83	1093	37/50	1974 – 1978	
Audi 50 GL	4 inline	2.74 x 2.83	1093	44/60	1974 – 1976	
Audi A2					**2000 – 2005**	**176,293**
A2 1.2 TDI	3 inline	3.01 x 3.40	1191	45/61	2000 – 2005	
A2 1.6 FSI	4 inline	3.01 x 3.42	1598	81/110	2002 – 2005	
A2 1.4 TDI	3 inline	3.13 x 3.76	1422	66/90	2001 – 2005	
Audi A3					**1996 – 2003**	**787,095**
A3 1.6	4 inline	3.19 x 3.05	1595	74/101	1996 – 2003	
A3 1.8 T quattro	4 inline	3.19 x 3.40	1781	132/180	1998 – 2003	
A3 1.9 TDI	4 inline	3.13 x 3.76	1896	81/110	1997 – 2003	
Audi A3					**From 2003**	
A3 1.6 FSI	4 inline	3.01 x 3.42	1595	85/115	2003 – 2008	
A3 2.0 TDI quattro	4 inline	3.19 x 3.76	1968	125/170	2006 –	
A3 1.4 TFSI	4 inline	3.01 x 2.98	1390	92/125	2007 –	

Audi models, 1965–2009, with selected engine sizes

Designation Type/model line	No. of cylinders/ layout	Bore x stroke in inches	Displacement in cc	Output in kW/hp	Period of manufacture	Quantity (complete model line)
Audi A3 Sportback					**From 2004**	
A3 Sportback 1.6 FSI	4 inline	3.01 x 3.42	1595	85/115	2004–2008	
A3 Sportback 2.0 TFSI	4 inline	3.25 x 3.65	1984	147/200	2004–	
A3 Sportback 3.2 quattro	V6	3.31 x 3.78	3189	184/250	2004–	
Audi A3 Cabriolet					**From 2008**	
A3 Cabriolet 1.8 TFSI	4 inline	3.25 x 3.31	1798	118/160	2008–	
A3 Cabriolet 2.0 TDI	4 inline	3.19 x 3.76	1968	103/140	2008–	
B platform						
Audi 80 B1					**1972–1978**	**932,403**
Audi 80 L	4 inline	2.91 x 2.89	1297	40/55	1972–1978	
Audi 80 GLS	4 inline	3.01 x 3.15	1470	62/85	1972–1975	
Audi 80 GT	4 inline	3.13 x 3.15	1588	74/100	1973–1975	
Audi 80 B2					**1978–1986**	**1,351,773**
Audi 80 LS	4 inline	3.13 x 3.15	1588	55/75	1978–1981	
Audi 80 CL	4 inline	3.13 x 3.15	1588	55/75	1981–1984	
Audi 80 GTE	4 inline	3.19 x 3.40	1781	82/112	1982–1986	
Audi 80 quattro	5 inline	3.13 x 3.40	2144	100/136	1982–1984	
Audi 80 quattro C	5 inline	3.19 x 3.05	1994	85/115	1983–1984	
Audi Coupé B2					**1981–1987**	**166,222**
Audi Coupé GL	4 inline	3.19 x 3.40	1781	55/75	1981–1982	
Audi Coupé quattro	5 inline	3.19 x 3.40	2226	88/120	1985–1987	
Audi Coupé GT	4 inline	3.19 x 3.40	1781	82/112	1986–1987	
Audi quattro					**1980–1991**	**11,452**
Audi quattro	5 inline	3.13 x 3.40	2144	147/200	1980–1989	
Audi quattro 20V	5 inline	3.19 x 3.40	2226	162/220	1989–1991	
Audi quattro sport	5 inline	3.12 x 3.40	2133	225/306	1984–1986	**214**
Audi 90 B2					**1984–1986**	**66,101**
Audi 90 2.2 E quattro	5 inline	3.19 x 3.40	2226	100/136	1984–1986	
Audi 90 TD	4 inline	3.01 x 3.40	1588	51/70	1985–1986	
Audi 80 B3					**1986–1991**	**1,287,799**
Audi 80 1.8 S	4 inline	3.19 x 3.40	1781	66/90	1986–1991	
Audi 80 Diesel	4 inline	3.01 x 3.40	1588	40/54	1986–1989	
Audi 80	4 inline	3.19 x 3.05	1595	51/70	1989–1991	
Audi 90 B3					**1987–1991**	**141,145**
Audi 90 2.3 E	5 inline	3.25 x 3.40	2309	98/133	1987–1991	
Audi 90 quattro 20V	5 inline	3.25 x 3.40	2309	125/170	1988–1991	
Audi Coupé B3					**1988–1995**	**68,367**
Audi Coupé 2.2 E	5 inline	3.19 x 3.40	2226	98/133	1988–1994	
Audi Coupé 2.0	4 inline	3.25 x 3.40	1984	85/115	1990–1995	
Audi Coupé 2.6 E	V6	3.25 x 3.19	2598	110/150	1992–1995	
Audi Cabriolet B3					**1991–2000**	**71,510**
Audi Cabriolet 2.3 E	5 inline	3.25 x 3.40	2309	98/133	1991–1994	
Audi Cabriolet 2.8 E	V6	3.25 x 3.40	2771	128/174	1992–2000	
Audi Cabriolet 1.9 TDI	4 inline	3.13 x 3.76	1896	66/90	1995–2000	
Audi Cabriolet 1.8	4 inline	3.19 x 3.40	1781	92/125	1997–2000	
Audi 80 B4					**1991–1995**	**789,335**
Audi 80	4 inline	3.25 x 3.65	1984	66/90	1991–1994	
Audi 80 Avant 2.6 E	V6	3.25 x 3.19	2598	110/150	1991–1994	
Audi 80 Avant 1.9 TDI	4 inline	3.13 x 3.76	1896	66/90	1991–1995	
Audi 80 16V sport edition	4 inline	3.25 x 3.65	1984	103/140	1993–1994	

Audi models, 1965–2009, with selected engine sizes

Designation Type/model line	No. of cylinders/ layout	Bore x stroke in inches	Displacement in cc	Output in kW/hp	Period of manufacture	Quantity (complete model line)
Audi A4 B5					**1994–2001**	**1,620,010**
A4 1.6	4 inline	3.19 x 3.05	1595	75/101	1994–2000	
A4 1.8 T	4 inline	3.19 x 3.40	1781	110/150	1994–2000	
A4 2.8 Avant	V6	3.25 x 3.40	2771	142/193	1995–2001	
A4 Avant 1.9 TDI	4 inline	3.13 x 3.76	1896	81/110	1995–1999	
A4 2.4 quattro	V6	3.19 x 3.05	2393	121/165	1997–2000	
A4 Avant 2.5 TDI	V6	3.08 x 3.40	2496	110/150	1997–2001	
Audi A4 B6					**2000–2004**	**1,074,278**
A4 Avant 3.0	V6	3.25 x 3.65	2976	162/220	2000–2004	
A4 2.5 TDI quattro	V6	3.08 x 3.40	2496	132/180	2000–2004	
A4 1.8 T	4 inline	3.19 x 3.40	1781	140/190	2002–2004	
Audi Cabriolet B6					**2002–2006**	**104,798**
A4 Cabriolet 1.8 T	4 inline	3.19 x 3.40	1871	120/163	2002–2006	
A4 Cabriolet 2.5 TDI	V6	3.08 x 3.40	2496	120/163	2002–2005	
Audi A4 B7					**2004–2007**	**1,000,338**
A4 2.0	4 inline	3.25 x 3.65	1984	96/130	2004–2007	
A4 3.0 TDI quattro	V6	3.27 x 3.60	2967	150/204	2004–2005	
A4 Avant 2.7 TDI	V6	3.27 x 3.27	2698	132/180	2005–2007	
Audi Cabriolet B7					**2006–2009**	
A4 Cabriolet 2.0 TFSI	4 inline	3.25 x 3.65	1984	147/200	2006–2009	
A4 Cabriolet 3.2 FSI	V6	3.33 x 3.65	3123	188/255	2006–2009	
A4 Cabriolet 2.0 TDI	4 inline	3.19 x 3.76	1968	103/140	2006–2009	
Audi A4 B8					**From 2007**	
A4 2.0 TDI	4 inline	3.19 x 3.76	1968	105/143	2007–	
A4 3.0 TDI quattro	V6	3.27 x 3.60	2967	176/240	2007–	
A4 Avant 2.0 TFSI	4 inline	3.25 x 3.65	1984	155/211	2008–	
Audi A5 B8					**From 2007**	
A5 3.2 FSI	V6	3.33 x 3.65	2976	195/265	2007–	
A5 2.7 TDI	V6	3.27 x 3.27	2698	140/190	2007–	
A5 Cabriolet 2.0 TFSI	4 inline	3.25 x 3.65	1984	132/180	2009–	
C platform						
Audi 100 C1					**1968–1976**	**796,787**
Audi 100	4 inline	3.21 x 3.32	1760	59/80	1968–1971	
Audi 100 S	4 inline	3.21 x 3.32	1760	66/90	1968–1971	
Audi 100 GL	4 inline	3.31 x 3.32	1871	82/112	1971–1976	
Audi 100 Coupé S	4 inline	3.21 x 3.32	1871	85/115	1970–1971	} 30,676
Audi 100 Coupé S	4 inline	3.21 x 3.32	1871	82/112	1971–1976	
Audi 100 C2					**1976–1982**	**Sedan 801,489** **Avant 49,688**
Audi 100 L	4 inline	3.13 x 3.15	1588	63/85	1976–1982	
Audi 100 5E	5 inline	3.13 x 3.40	2144	100/136	1977–1982	
Audi 100 Avant L	4 inline	3.13 x 3.15	1588	63/85	1977–1980	
Audi 100 CD 5E	5 inline	3.13 x 3.40	2144	100/136	1978–1981	
Audi 100 5D	5 inline	3.01 x 3.40	1986	51/70	1978–1982	
Audi 100 Avant L 5D	5 inline	3.01 x 3.40	1986	51/70	1978–1981	
Audi 200 C2					**1980–1982**	**32,938**
Audi 200 5E	5 inline	3.13 x 3.40	2144	100/136	1980–1982	
Audi 200 5T	5 inline	3.13 x 3.40	2144	125/170	1980–1982	
Audi 100 C3					**1982–1991**	**1,151,709**
Audi 100 CC	5 inline	3.13 x 3.40	2144	100/136	1982–1984	
Audi 100 Avant turbo	5 inline	3.19 x 3.40	2226	121/165	1986–1991	
Audi 100 TDI	5 inline	3.19 x 3.76	2460	88/120	1989–1991	
Audi 200 C3					**1983–1991**	**93,559**
Audi 200 turbo	5 inline	3.13 x 3.40	2144	134/182	1983–1988	
Audi 200 quattro 20V	5 inline	3.19 x 3.40	2226	162/220	1988–1991	

Audi models, 1965–2009, with selected engine sizes

Designation Type/model line	No. of cylinders/ layout	Bore x stroke in inches	Displacement in cc	Output in kW/hp	Period of manufacture	Quantity (complete model line)
Audi 100 C4					**1990 – 1994**	**429,739**
Audi 100 2.3 E	5 inline	3.25 x 3.40	2309	98/133	1990 – 1994	
Audi 100 Avant 2.0 E	4 inline	3.25 x 3.65	1984	85/115	1991 – 1994	
Audi 100 Avant quattro 2.8 E	V6	3.25 x 3.40	2771	128/174	1991 – 1994	
Audi A6 C4					**1994 – 1997**	**290,834**
A6 Avant 1.9 TDI	4 inline	3.13 x 3.76	1896	66/90	1994 – 1997	
A6 2.5 TDI	5 inline	3.19 x 3.76	2460	103/140	1994 – 1997	
A6 1.8	4 inline	3.19 x 3.40	1781	92/125	1995 – 1997	
Audi A6 C5					**1997 – 2005**	**1,010,518**
A6 Avant 1.8 T	4 inline	3.19 x 3.40	1781	110/150	1997 – 2005	
A6 2.4 quattro	V6	3.19 x 3.05	2393	125/170	2001 – 2004	
A6 1.9 TDI	4 inline	3.13 x 3.76	1896	96/130	2001 – 2004	
allroad quattro 2.7	V6	3.19 x 3.40	2671	184/250	2003 – 2005	
Audi A6 C6					**From 2004**	
A6 2.4 quattro	V6	3.19 x 3.05	2393	130/177	2004 – 2008	
A6 Avant 3.2 FSI	V6	3.33 x 3.65	3123	188/255	2005 – 2008	
A6 2.0 TDIe	4 inline	3.19 x 3.76	1968	100/136	2008 –	
allroad quattro 2.7 TDI	V6	3.27 x 3.27	2698	132/180	2006 –	
D platform						
Audi V8 D1					**1988 – 1994**	**21,565**
V8	V8	3.19 x 3.40	3562	184/250	1988 – 1994	
V8 L 4.2	V8	3.33 x 3.66	4172	206/280	1991 – 1994	
Audi A8 D2					**1994 – 2002**	**104,630**
A8 2.8	V6	3.25 x 3.40	2771	128/174	1994 – 1996	
A8 4.2	V8	3.33 x 3.66	4172	220/300	1994 – 1998	
A8 3.7 quattro	V8	3.33 x 3.24	3697	191/260	1999 – 2002	
A8 3.3 TDI	V8	3.08 x 3.40	3328	165/225	2000 – 2002	
A8 6.0 long-wheelbase	W12	2.52 x 3.55	5998	309/420	2001 – 2002	
Audi A8 D3					**From 2002**	
A8 4.2 quattro	V8	3.33 x 3.66	4172	246/335	2002 – 2006	
A8 4.0 TDI quattro	V8	3.19 x 3.76	3936	202/275	2003 – 2005	
A8 3.2 FSI quattro	V6	3.33 x 3.65	3123	191/260	2005 –	
S models						
Audi S2 B4					**1990 – 1995**	**9488**
S2 Coupé	5 inline	3.19 x 3.40	2226	162/220	1990 – 1992	
S2 Avant	5 inline	3.19 x 3.40	2226	169/230	1992 – 1995	
Audi S4 C4					**1991 – 1994**	**15,928**
S4 Avant	5 inline	3.19 x 3.40	2226	169/230	1991 – 1994	
S4 4.2	V8	3.33 x 3.66	4172	206/280	1992 – 1994	
Audi S6 C4					**1994 – 1997**	**9725**
S6	5 inline	3.19 x 3.40	2226	169/230	1994 – 1997	
S6 4.2 Avant	V8	3.33 x 3.66	4172	213/290	1994 – 1997	
Audi S6 Plus C4	**V8**	**3.33 x 3.66**	**4172**	**240/326**	**1996 – 1997**	**952**
Audi S6 C5	**V8**	**3.33 x 3.66**	**4172**	**250/340**	**1999 – 2004**	**10,652**
Audi S6 C6	**V10**	**3.33 x 3.65**	**5204**	**320/435**	**From 2006**	
Audi S3					**1999 – 2003**	**32,021**
S3	4 inline	3.19 x 3.40	1781	154/210	1999 – 2001	
S3	4 inline	3.19 x 3.40	1781	165/225	2001 – 2003	
Audi S3					**From 2006**	
S3 2.0 TFSI quattro	4 inline	3.25 x 3.65	1984	195/265	2006 –	
S3 Sportback 2.0 TFSI quattro	4 inline	3.25 x 3.65	1984	195/265	2008 –	

Audi models, 1965 – 2009, with selected engine sizes

Designation Type/model line	No. of cylinders/ layout	Bore x stroke in inches	Displacement in cc	Output in kW/hp	Period of manufacture	Quantity (complete model line)
Audi S4 B5	**V6**	**3.19 x 3.40**	**2671**	**195/265**	**1997 – 2001**	**14,095**
Audi S4 B6					**2002 – 2006**	**21,669**
S4 B6 Avant	V8	3.33 x 3.65	4163	253/344	2002 – 2004	6591
S4 B6 Cabriolet	V8	3.33 x 3.65	4163	253/344	2003 – 2006	5331
Audi S4 B7					**2004 – 2008**	**13,580**
S4 B7 sedan	V8	3.33 x 3.65	4163	253/344	2004 – 2008	6726
S4 B7 Cabriolet	V8	3.33 x 3.65	4163	253/344	2006 – 2008	2134
Audi S4 B8	**V6**	**3.33 x 3.50**	**2995**	**245/333**	**From 2009**	
Audi S5 B8					**From 2007**	
S5 B8	V8	3.33 x 3.65	4163	260/354	2007 –	
S5 B8 Cabriolet	V6	3.33 x 3.50	2995	245/333	2009	
Audi S8 D2					**1996 – 2002**	**12,267**
S8	V8	3.33 x 3.66	4172	250/340	1996 – 1998	
S8	V8	3.33 x 3.66	4172	265/360	1999 – 2002	
Audi S8 D3	**V10**	**3.33 x 3.65**	**5204**	**313/450**	**From 2006**	

Sports cars						
Audi TT					**1998 – 2006**	**265,346**
TT Coupé 1.8 T	4 inline	3.19 x 3.40	1781	132/180	1998 – 2006	
TT 1.8 T Roadster	4 inline	3.19 x 3.40	1781	110/150	2001 – 2005	
TT 3.2 quattro Coupé	V6	3.31 x 3.78	3189	184/250	2003 – 2006	
TT quattro sport	4 inline	3.19 x 3.40	1781	176/240	2005 – 2006	
Audi TT					**From 2006**	
TT Roadster 1.8 TFSI	4 inline	3.25 x 3.31	1798	118/160	2007 –	
TT 2.0 TFSI quattro	4 inline	3.25 x 3.65	1984	147/200	2006 –	
TT Roadster TDI	4 inline	3.19 x 3.76	1968	125/170	2008 –	
TTS Coupé	4 inline	3.25 x 3.65	1984	200/272	2008 –	
Audi R8					**From 2007**	
R8 4.2 FSI	V8	3.33 x 3.65	4163	309/420	2007 –	
R8 5.2 FSI	V10	3.33 x 3.65	5204	386/525	2008 –	

SUV						
Audi Q5					**From 2008**	
Q5 2.0 TFSI	4 inline	3.25 x 3.65	1984	155/211	2008 –	
Q5 3.0 TDI	V6	3.27 x 3.60	2967	176/240	2008 –	
Audi Q7					**From 2005**	
Q7 4.2 FSI quattro	V8	3.33 x 3.65	4163	257/350	2005 –	
Q7 3.6 FSI quattro	V6	3.50 x 3.80	3597	206/280	2006 –	
Q7 V12 TDI quattro	V12	3.27 x 3.60	5934	368/500	2008 –	

RS models						
Audi RS 2 B4	**5 inline**	**3.19 x 3.40**	**2226**	**232/315**	**1994 – 1995**	**2908**
Audi RS 4 B5	**V6**	**3.19 x 3.40**	**2671**	**280/380**	**2000 – 2001**	**6046**
Audi RS 4 B7					**2005 – 2008**	**14,344**
RS 4 B7 sedan	V8	3.33 x 3.65	4163	309/420	2005 – 2008	7653
RS 4 B7 Cabriolet	V8	3.33 x 3.65	4163	309/420	2006 – 2008	1194
Audi RS 6 C5					**2002 – 2004**	**7562**
RS 6 C5 Avant	V8	3.33 x 3.66	4172	331/450	2002 – 2004	4815
RS 6 Plus C5	V8	3.33 x 3.66	4172	335/480	2004	564
Audi RS 6 C6	**V10**	**3.33 x 3.50**	**4991**	**426/580**	**From 2008**	

Publisher
Auto Union GmbH
85045 Ingolstadt

Commissioned by
AUDI AG
Audi Tradition
85045 Ingolstadt
www.audi.com

Archives and sources
J.S. Rasmussen Archives, Hammersbach
Volkswagen AG Archives, Wolfsburg
Authors' archives
August Horch Museum, Zwickau
Picture archive, Preussischer Kulturbesitz, Berlin
Federal German Archives, Koblenz
Deutsches Museum, Munich
Günter Doveren, Lugau
dpa, Munich
Woldemar Lange, Waldkirchen
Library of the Free State of Saxony/German Fotothek, Dresden
Archives of the Free State of Saxony, Chemnitz
Wilhelm Speder, Essen
stock.xchng
Süddeutscher Verlag publishing house, Munich
ullstein bild, Berlin
AUDI AG Corporate Archives, Ingolstadt/Neckarsulm
Wolff & Tritschler, Offenburg
Zbyněk Zikmund, Prague

Texts
Thomas Erdmann
Ralf Friese
Prof. Dr. Peter Kirchberg
Ralph Plagmann

English translation
Colin Brazier, Munich
Audi Akademie, Ingolstadt

Design
ö_konzept Zwickau
Matthias Kaluza, Sven Rahnefeld

Printing
Kunst- und Werbedruck, Bad Oeynhausen

Delius Klasing Verlag
Siekerwall 21, 33602 Bielefeld
Tel. +49 / 521 / 559-0 Fax +49/ 521 / 559-115
info@delius-klasing.de
www.delius-klasing.de

1st edition
ISBN 978-3-7688-2674-7

© AUDI AG
May 2009

1945
Zentraldepot für Auto Union Ersatzteile Ingolstadt GmbH

1949
Auto Union GmbH, Ingolstadt

AUDI NSU

1969
Audi NSU Auto Union AG, Neckarsulm

Audi
Truth in Engineering

1985 AUDI AG, Ingolstadt